Kittler Now

Theory Now

Series Editor: Ryan Bishop

Kittler Now

Current Perspectives in Kittler Studies

Edited by
Stephen Sale and Laura Salisbury

polity

First published in 2015 by Polity Press

Polity Press
65 Bridge Street
Cambridge CB2 1UR, UK

Polity Press
350 Main Street
Malden, MA 02148, USA

ISBN-13: 978-0-7456-5300-6
ISBN-13: 978-0-7456-5301-3 (pb)

A catalogue record for this book is available from the British Library.

Typeset in 11/13 Bembo by
Servis Filmsetting Limited, Stockport, Cheshire
Printed and bound in the United Kingdom by T.J. International Ltd, Padstow, Cornwall

The publisher has used its best endeavours to ensure that the URLs for external websites referred to in this book are correct and active at the time of going to press. However, the publisher has no responsibility for the websites and can make no guarantee that a site will remain live or that the content is or will remain appropriate.

Every effort has been made to trace all copyright holders, but if any have been inadvertently overlooked the publisher will be pleased to include any necessary credits in any subsequent reprint or edition.

For further information on Polity, visit our website: www.politybooks.com

Contents

Acknowledgements

This volume was conceived following the conference 'Media Matters: Friedrich Kittler and Technoculture' held at Tate Modern, London, in 2008. That event was supported both financially and intellectually by Birkbeck, University of London, and the London Consortium, and the editors are profoundly grateful to all those who helped to bring some of the most radical aspects of German *Medienwissenschaft* to London. We would also like to thank the contributors to this volume for their belief in the project, their good humour and their patience. The support and dedication of the editors of Polity Press have similarly been invaluable.

We are grateful for permission to reproduce the lyrics from Pink Floyd's 'Brain Damage' to Warner Chappell Music Ltd ('Brain Damage' Words and Music by Roger Waters © Roger Waters Music Overseas Ltd (NS). All rights administered by Warner Chappell Music. Australia Pty Ltd.) and to Hampshire House Publishing Corp. ('Brain Damage'. Words and Music by Roger Waters. TRO–©–Copyright 1973 (Renewed). Hampshire House Publishing Corp., New York, New York. International Copyright Secured. Made in U.S.A. All Rights Reserved Including Public Performance for Profit. Used by permission. 'Deathless Aphrodite of the spangled mind', 'Here to me from Krete to this holy temple' from *If Not, Winter: Fragments of Sappho*, by Anne Carson, copyright © 2002 by Anne Carson, are used by permission of Alfred A. Knopf, a division of Random House, Inc., and Little, Brown Book Group Limited. An extract from 'Oh England My Lionheart' is reproduced by permission of EMI Music Publishing. A version of the chapter 'If the Cinema Is an Ontology, the Computer Is an Ethic' by Alexander R. Galloway was first published in his book *The Interface Effect* (Cambridge: Polity, 2012).

The editors would like to thank Paul Feigelfeld, in particular, for his assistance in bringing the volume to completion. Not only did he undertake meticulous translations for the volume, he also liaised carefully and sensitively with the late Friedrich Kittler, who was committed to the dissemination of his ideas and to the success of this volume to the last. Without Friedrich Kittler's generosity and dedication to his intellectual project beyond any reasonable expectations, *Kittler Now* simply would not have happened. We would also like to extend our thanks to Susanne Holl, Kittler's widow, whose cooperation with this project has been sincerely appreciated.

Finally, we would like to thank Roger Luckhurst for his intellectual and practical guidance, and Fiona Robertson for her unstinting support throughout the gestation of the project.

Contributors

Caroline Bassett is Professor of Media and Communications and Director of the Centre for Material Digital Culture at the University of Sussex. She is author of *The Arc and the Machine* (Manchester University Press, 2007). She has recently been writing on expertise and digital media, and on silence as a response to digital media in *First Monday*. She is currently completing a monograph on anti-computing for Manchester University Press.

Katherine Biers is an Associate Professor in the Department of English and Comparative Literature at Columbia University. She is the author of *Virtual Modernism: Writing and Technology in the Progressive Era* (University of Minnesota Press, 2013). Her articles and reviews have appeared in *Representations, Textual Practice* and several edited collections.

Steven Connor is Grace 2 Professor of English in the University of Cambridge and fellow of Peterhouse, Cambridge. He has published books on Dickens, Beckett, Joyce and postmodernism, as well as on topics such as ventriloquism, skin, flies, air and sport. His most recent books are *Beyond Words: Sobbing, Humming and Other Vocalizations* (Reaktion, 2014) and *Beckett, Modernism and* *the Material Imagination* (Cambridge University Press, 2014). His website at www.stevenconnor.com includes lectures, broadcasts, unpublished work and work in progress.

Paul Feigelfeld worked for Friedrich Kittler from 2004 to 2011 and is the editor of Kittler's source code and software for the upcoming *Collected Works*. Feigelfeld worked as a teacher and researcher at Humboldt University's Institute for Media Theories from 2010 to 2013, and since 2013 has coordinated the Digital Cultures Research Lab at Leuphana University Lüneburg.

Alexander R. Galloway is a writer and computer programmer working on issues in philosophy, technology and theories of mediation. Professor of Media, Culture, and Communication at New York University, he is the author of several books on digital media and critical theory, most recently *The Interface Effect* (Polity, 2012).

Mark B. N. Hansen is Professor of Literature and Arts of the Moving Image at Duke University. His books include *Embodying Technesis: Technology Beyond Writing* (University of Michigan Press, 2000), *New Philosophy for New Media* (MIT Press, 2004), *Bodies in Code: Interfaces with New Media* (Routledge, 2006) and the forthcoming *Feed-Forward* (University of Chicago Press).

Friedrich A. Kittler (1943–2011) was a literary scholar and media historian. In the course of a long and distinguished career, Kittler pioneered a new technologically inflected approach to the humanities. He was Professor of Aesthetics and History of Media at the Humboldt University, Berlin, and held visiting professorships at Columbia University, Yale, Stanford, Berkeley and other institutions. His works include *Discourse Networks 1800/1900* (Stanford University Press, 1990), *Gramophone, Film, Typewriter* (Stanford University Press, 1999) and *Musik und Mathematik* (Wilhelm Fink, 2006; 2009).

Anthony Moore is Professor of Art and Media Sciences at the Academy of Media Arts Cologne (KHM), where he works on the theory and history of sound. Initially Professor for Musik, Klang, Geräusch and founder of the Music Department, from 2000 to 2004 he was the elected Rector of the Academy in Cologne. He is the founder of the symposia 'per->SON' and festival series 'Nocturnes'.

Gill Partington is Associate Research Fellow at Birkbeck, University of London. She works on media, fictionality, histories of reading and the material text. Her recent work includes articles on textual erasure and a chapter on the work of Tom McCarthy. She has also co-edited two volumes with Adam Smyth: *Missing Texts*, a 2013 special edition of *Critical Quarterly*, and *Book Destruction in the West* (Palgrave, 2014).

John Durham Peters is A. Craig Baird Professor in the Department of Communication Studies at the University of Iowa. He is the author of *Speaking into the Air* (University of Chicago Press, 1999), *Courting the Abyss* (University of Chicago Press, 2005) and a forthcoming book, *The Marvelous Clouds*.

Stephen Sale is a PhD candidate at the London Consortium. His research focuses on the relationship between technology and culture, with a particular interest in German media theory. He has published articles in several journals including *Theory, Culture & Society* and *Journal of War and Culture Studies*.

Laura Salisbury is a Senior Lecturer in Medicine and English Literature at the University of Exeter. She is the author of *Samuel Beckett: Laughing Matters, Comic Timing* (Edinburgh University Press, 2012) and the co-editor of *Neurology and Modernity: A Cultural History of Nervous Systems, 1800–1950* (Palgrave, 2010). She is currently writing a study of the relationship between modernism, modernity and neurological theories of language, entitled *Aphasic Modernism: A Revolution of the Word*.

Geoffrey Winthrop-Young completed an MA at the University of Freiburg and a PhD at the University of British Columbia, Vancouver, where he is now Professor of German in the

Department of Central, Eastern and Northern European Studies. He is the author of *Kittler and the Media* (Polity, 2010). His main areas of research are theories of media and cultural techniques and issues related to the emergence of the posthumanities in Germany and North America.

Editors' Introduction

Stephen Sale and Laura Salisbury

Aristotle, T. S. Eliot, Hermann von Helmholtz, Friedrich Hölderlin, The Jimi Hendrix Experience, Pink Floyd, Sappho: only Friedrich Kittler could pull off such an insouciantly provocative, learned yet eye-popping, run of bibliographic entries in a piece of academic writing. To read Kittler in any sustained way is, however, to come to expect to find such strange attractions; it is to begin to understand the ways in which Goethe brushes up against literacy manuals, Alan Turing is calculating alongside Mallarmé and Lacan, and Syd Barrett makes music with the Greek gods. Kittler the literary critic, Kittler the historian, Kittler the Heideggerian, Kittler the computer programmer, Kittler the Hellenophile: this was a writer for whom the 'Two Cultures' divide between the arts and sciences, or the split between high and popular cultures, never even seemed like barriers to overcome. From this description, it is possible to imagine Kittler as a poster-boy for the extraordinary creative possibilities of interdisciplinary research and writing beloved of the contemporary neo-liberal university system, but he was and remains a paradoxically resistant figure, a provocatively conservative outsider, who defies the usual interdisciplinary frames and whom even devotees find hard to digest in any wholesale way.

Kittler's academic career began at Freiburg in the 1960s and, following stints at Basel and Bochum in the 1980s, he established an institutional home at the Humboldt University for what came to be known as the 'Berlin School' of media studies or, in its international variant, 'German media theory'. Kittler always claimed to be more concerned with history than theory, though, and it is his radical programme to bring questions concerning the history of media technologies to the centre of intellectual endeavour that has attracted interest from literary studies, media studies, film studies and the digital humanities. For at the most basic, most disruptive level, what Kittler's concentration on mediality offers is an alternative frame of reference for the humanities – one that rejects the standard governing concepts of understanding, subjectivity and representation in favour of the 'materiality of communication'.[1] It is this profound challenge to our research models that has ensured that, despite his death in 2011, Kittler's influence shows no sign of diminishing.

Although Kittler's work may be becoming increasingly accessible and influential, it remains relatively uncolonized by introductory guides and primers. This is at least partly because his texts are characterized by mastery of a truly dizzying range of material that sits alongside complex and unorthodox political positions. Kittler is also capable of throwing out breezily devastating apercus, such as the now notorious opening pronouncement from his best-known work, *Gramophone, Film, Typewriter*, that '[m]edia determine our situation' (xxxix), that seem simple, but that nevertheless suggest fundamental alterations to our disciplinary frameworks. For Kittler was a technological determinist who argued that although technical media are decisive in shaping cultural production, they have been largely ignored by the humanities, which continues in its solipsistic interpretation of the content of communications. Kittler, however, celebrates those concrete technologies that, unbeknownst to us 'end-users', provide the very conditions of possibility for our thoughts. Following the material, technical forms of media rather than the texts they produce, Kittler's work ranges across traditional disciplinary boundaries, deftly melding French poststructuralism (particularly Foucault and Lacan) with McLuhan and the Toronto School, while always following a path set down by his beloved Germans: Heidegger, Hegel and Nietzsche. There are also some

British influences, but they are not the usual suspects: we hear about Alan Turing and Pink Floyd rather than Raymond Williams. The result is assertively eccentric work that is determinedly lively, sometimes baffling, but always distinctive.

Kittler's singular approach makes itself felt across an oeuvre that includes several major monographs and some influential collections.[2] *Discourse Networks 1800/1900* and *Gramophone, Film, Typewriter* have been translated into multiple languages; several essays on diverse topics are collected in *Draculas Vermächtnis: Technische Schriften* and the English volume *Literature, Media, Information Systems*; a lecture course from 1999 was published in translation in 2010 as *Optical Media*; and his multi-volume project *Musik und Mathematik*, though truncated by his death, has seen two of its volumes published in German. Several of Kittler's essays have appeared in special editions of journals, including *Cultural Politics, Grey Room* and *Theory, Culture & Society*, alongside valuable exegeses, interviews and critical engagements with his work. Journals such as *Thesis Eleven* have also devoted editions to expanding the readership for Kittler's work and German media theory in general. In terms of secondary literature, Geoffrey Winthrop-Young deserves special mention for his role in bringing Kittler to a wider audience and acting as respected commentator for both Anglo- and Germano-phone audiences. His *Kittler and the Media* is an excellent, wide-ranging introduction to the work. The introduction to this volume, though by no means exhaustive, works to complement these existing resources by outlining the contours of Kittler's thought to an Anglophone audience. It takes a broadly chronological approach in order to contextualize the chapters that follow, covering the discourse analytical work from the 1980s and the radical interdisciplinarity that gradually emerged from it, Kittler's later investigations into the martial origins of media technologies and the politics of 'command and control', and his final turn to cultural technique in ancient Greece.

Discursive Regimes

Kittler was a literary scholar in Freiburg's German department when he produced his *Habilitation* thesis, *Aufschreibesysteme 1800/1900*, published in 1985 and translated into English in 1990 as *Discourse Networks 1800/1900*. Composed in two parts, each with an introit and three chapters, *Discourse Networks* structurally mirrors Foucault's *The Order of Things* and, following its diachronic model of historical rupture, offers an account of the discursive construction of the German Romantic subject and its dissolution with the advent of modernism. Then a leading figure in the German reception of poststructuralism, Kittler argues that traditional disciplinary approaches are unwittingly implicated in their objects of study and are therefore unable to address their own conditions of possibility. Even Foucault, whose discourse analysis had attempted to reconstruct the rules through which an epoch's discourses are organized, fell victim to this methodological blind-spot through an under-analysed reliance upon the written word. Kittler ascribes Foucault's supposed inability to grapple with historical developments post-1850 to this limitation; for it is in the latter half of the nineteenth century that the monopoly of the written word as a means of data storage came to an end with the invention of photography, cinematography and phonography. Kittler's solution is to extend Foucault's archaeological toolkit through a historical analysis of the discourse *network*. In this broadened conception, written archives stored in libraries are merely a single instance of 'the network of technologies and institutions that allow a given culture to select, store, and process relevant data' (Kittler, *Discourse Networks* 369).

In Kittler's analysis, the historically contingent figure of 'so-called Man' that Foucault famously likens to a face drawn in sand at the edge of the sea is predicated upon a particular set of discursive practices that characterize the discourse network of '1800'. The autonomous, self-determining subject is first glimpsed in Goethe with Faust's free translation of the Gospel according to Saint John, which Kittler reads as the epistemological break that inaugurated the discipline of hermeneutics – a form of reading determined by the primacy of subjective interpretation and understanding. The significance of Faust is that he stepped outside the discursive controls that regulated the transcription and circulation of texts in the 'Republic of Scholars' and instituted the production of signs as an act of individual authorship. Referring to a number of pedagogical reforms that occurred in Prussia at that time, Kittler argues that the precondition for this epistemological break was the transformation of language from an arbitrary material force into a channel for the newly discovered 'inner voice'. During this period, compulsory state education replaced the rote learning of language with maternal instruction through which pupils were encouraged to understand the putatively intrinsic 'meaning' of language. The inner voice came to stand in for a transcendental signified that preceded, underwrote and bound language to the realm of truth.

Accompanying these changes were the burgeoning literary, military and bureaucratic institutions of the modern nation state and the consolidation of the nuclear family. For the first time, the author was granted copyright protection, universities were brought under direct state control, and the voice of the 'individualized universal' was heard in Romantic poetry. At the same time, German Idealism served to legitimate the discursive regime through the theorization of an originary subjectivity that took the place of the divine as the guarantor of meaning. At the centre of Kittler's Discourse Network 1800 may be the generative source of Nature, the soul and the maternal, but its machinery was that of the Prussian state. Paradoxically, then, it turns out that Romanticism's poets and philosophers were the products of a civil servant factory, with their artistic freedom always state-sanctioned. Their inspired audience, intoxicated by gaining access to the inner voice sounding from the realm of truth, was equally the product of state intervention in the family home that implemented universal alphabetization.

But if subjects are formed by a technology of the letter they are also tied to its fate. And just as Faust's penmanship serves to introduce the discourse network of '1800', Kittler uses Nietzsche's experiences with the typewriter to usher in the discourse network of '1900'. Late in his life, the exiled and half-blind Nietzsche, sitting in front of his new writing machine, had an epiphany concerning the raw materiality of language. In the typewriter's forced separation of hand and word he was able to recognize the 'irreducible facticity' of words for the first time and see that words are not simply ciphers for ideas – 'language is no longer the translation of prelinguistic meanings' (Kittler, *Discourse Networks* 186). The inner voice had fallen silent and Nietzsche was left instead with the hum and the roar of white noise, crafting contingently meaningful accidents with words. With Nietzsche, then, the primacy of the transcendental signified of 1800 was replaced with the 'logic of the signifier'; the Romantic subject dissolved into a sea of alphabet soup, and the human subject was no longer the agent of writing.

For Kittler, the precondition for this new epistemological break was the development of alternative storage media – the phonograph and photo-/cinemato-graph – able to capture both acoustical and optical data respectively, and thus reveal writing as just one medium within a broader paradigm of information. Once again disciplinary practices played their part: maternal instruction was replaced with the idea of a language that had to be directed, controlled and formed by schooling until it became, in this case, High German. With the disappearance of the 'Mother's Mouth' as the source of discursive production, language unravelled into a tangle of nervous, sensory-motor threads and material, differential marks. As Kittler sees it, Foucault's prediction for the 'end of man' had already come to pass, in or around 1900.

Kittler has described *Discourse Networks* as 'written in black in every sense of the word' (Griffin and Hermann 286), referring both to its radical conservative agenda, influenced by Martin Heidegger, Carl Schmitt and Ernst Jünger, and to its private attacks on the German academic establishment. In this period, the world of German letters was dominated by hermeneutics, a practice which, as we have seen, Kittler sought to demote to a side-effect of eighteenth-century bureaucratic history. The critical theoretical Left in the form of the Frankfurt School fared little better, attracting scorn for its technological naivety in attempting to develop a theory of communication almost without reference to technology,[3] while Kittler's championing of poststructuralism came at a time when Habermas was defending the emancipatory potential of the Enlightenment project from the incursions of the French, and Derrida in particular. Courting enmity from both Left and Right, then, *Discourse Networks* met with hostility and the thesis was passed only reluctantly. Kittler was reportedly told, '[o]ne Foucault is enough. That is why we are against you.'[4]

Science and the Humanities

Alongside Foucauldian discourse analysis, the methodological machinery of *Discourse Networks* draws heavily upon a discipline less familiar to the humanities: information theory. Kittler suggests that hermeneutics deals in continuity and context, but as we move to Discourse Network 1900, the logic of the signifier requires a different approach: 'the relative value of signifiers [. . .] is given mathematically', Kittler writes; 'its articulation is called counting' (*Discourse Networks* 190). Here, the tools appropriate for analysing discourse networks are seen to be not those of the interpretative reader, but those of the engineer. Kittler found inspiration in the work of Claude Shannon, an engineer at Bell Labs in the United States who, in the course of optimizing the national telephone network in the 1940s, had offered a new definition of information. In Shannon's view, information can be defined mathematically as the statistical measure of uncertainty given in the selection of data from a range of options. This definition gave Kittler licence to ignore the questions of meaning that exercised practitioners of hermeneutics and instead look at the system-wide discursive regularities that determine which statements are selected as meaningful – those that become information – and those that are designated as noise. In analysing the systems themselves, he adopted Shannon's functional model of communication systems as comprising five elements: information source, transmitter, channel, receiver and destination (Shannon and Weaver). Kittler tells us that while Foucault is able to describe 'the production of discourses', he fails to account for 'the source of these discourses, of the channels or the receivers of discourse in the form of [. . .] readers or consumers' (Armitage 19), and this is what *Discourse Networks* sets out to rectify. Early readers can certainly be forgiven for not recognizing that the project is as much about generators, oscillators, amplifiers and receivers as it is about the canonical texts of German Romanticism. These themes were, however, made more explicit in the 'Afterword' published in later editions, where Kittler urged his colleagues to 'learn from an information theory that has formalised the current state of technical knowledge' (*Discourse Networks* 369).

One branch of the humanities that had embarked on a relatively early engagement with the new technological paradigm, Kittler tells us, is Lacanian psychoanalysis, which he accordingly elevates to the status of a privileged discourse. When, in *Gramophone, Film, Typewriter*, the 'technological addendum' to *Discourse Networks*, Kittler details the media differentiation that he argues is characteristic of '1900', he suggests that Lacan's famous triumvirate of registers – the symbolic, imaginary and real – are themselves a theorization, or 'historical effect', of media–technological developments. The typewriter stripped writing of its surrogate sensuality to lay bare its symbolic function – that is, encoding the sound sequences of language into discrete units – and new storage technologies were able to capture what were previously unwritable data flows. The noise of the bodily real could now be captured by sound recording, and the development of film technologies, which allowed 'memories and dreams, the dead and ghosts' (Kittler, *Gramophone* 10) to become technically represented, replaced the hallucinations that accompanied reading in '1800'.

By Kittler's account, indexical media – media that register the imprint of the real – brought the monopoly of the alphabet to an end and with it the medial configuration that supported the conception of the human as autonomous and self-determined. For as soon as optical, acoustical and textual data flows are separated, Kittler tells us, machines can begin to take over functions of the central nervous system in registering and processing the world. The result: 'man's' 'essence escapes into apparatuses' (Kittler, *Gramophone* 16). As with Marshall McLuhan, another important influence on Kittler, human capabilities start to appear as imperfect implementations of media technology. However, Kittler is emphatic in avoiding what he views as a residual anthropocentrism in McLuhan. He claims that 'McLuhan, who was originally a literary critic, understood more about perception than about electronics, and therefore he attempted to think about technology in terms of bodies instead of the other way around' (Kittler, *Optical Media* 29). Kittler, also a literary theorist but one who soldered circuit boards in his spare time, suggests that we 'forget humans, language, and sense' and 'move on to the particulars of Shannon's five elements and functions instead' (*Optical Media* 44). For Kittler, the advent of mechanical storage 'designates the turning point at which communications technologies can no longer be related back to humans. Instead, the former have formed the latter' (*Gramophone* 211). In his essay 'Global Algorithm: The History of Communication Media' Kittler describes this shift as the implementation in physical reality of Shannon's five functions: (human) communication networks gradually give way to (machinic) information systems and thus reveal the contingency of the human–technological relationship. Humanity's functional role is dwindling as the machineries become actualized and autonomous. What were mistakenly identified as uniquely human attributes are instead revealed to be the poor cousins of optimized computing processes. As Geoffrey Winthrop-Young puts it, '[w]here subjects were, there programs shall be – because programs were there in the first place' ('Silicon Sociology' 397).

War and Politics

From the mid-1980s, Kittler's technical histories became increasingly concerned with warfare as the crucible of technological change. *Gramophone, Film, Typewriter* and a constellation of associated essays[5] detail the military origins of contemporary media technologies. We are told that Thomas Edison, who was a telegrapher during the American Civil War, invented the phonograph 'in an attempt to improve the processing speed of the Morse telegraph beyond human limitations' (Kittler, *Gramophone* 190), and that it was the gun manufacturer Remington & Son that began commercial production of the typewriter in 1874 in order to make use of surplus capacity following the 'boom' of the war. Following Virilio's *War and Cinema*, Kittler also draws attention to the military's role in the development of film technology, with

Étienne-Jules Marey's indirect adoption of the revolving chambers of the machine gun for his 'chronophotographic rifle' one of the precursors of cinema. Kittler is then able to tell us that 'the history of the movie camera thus coincides with the history of automatic weapons' (*Gramophone* 124).

If the American Civil War provided the impetus for the development of the new storage media, it was the First World War that led to the production of the new transmission technologies that could connect them. To overcome the stalemate in the trenches, troops needed to be mobilized, and that required communications systems such as radio to coordinate dispersed units in the field. These transmission technologies had been perfected by the time of the Second World War, which enabled a distributed and all-consuming form of warfare: for Kittler, 'VHF tank communications and radar images, those military developments parallel to television, meant total mobilisation, motorisation and blitzkrieg from the Vistula in 1939 to Corregido in 1945' (*Gramophone* 243).

But the star of Kittler's narrative of the Second World War is the British mathematician and pioneer of computer science Alan Turing. Turing was one of the cryptographers working at Bletchley Park whose efforts in cracking the Enigma code proved decisive in determining the outcome of the war. Enigma was a modified typewriter used by the German military to encrypt messages that were then broadcast freely via radio. Turing had earlier theorized a machine that could simulate the workings of other machines and, together with his team, built Colossus – a reverse-engineered Enigma – which was capable of probabilistically determining what had been encoded by the other machine. It incorporated a simple feedback loop whereby it was able to adapt its processes according to the results of calculations. For Kittler, again drawing on Lacan, this gave computers the 'operational reflexivity' previously believed to be an exclusively human attribute. As well as storage and transmission, machines were now also capable of *processing* information. With subsequent developments in cybernetics, these conditional jumps were implemented in machines and '[c]omputers themselves became subjects' (Kittler, *Gramophone* 258) with the ability to out-perform humans. Binary coding also meant that all media can be stored and processed by a modern computer: 'the medium to end all media' (Winthrop-Young and Wutz xxx). What is occasionally referred to as Discourse Network 2000 is characterized by the digitization and consequent *de*-differentiation of acoustical, optical and textual data streams. The time of media as traditionally understood is over. In Kittler's Hegelian vision of ubiquitous computing, all knowledge will one day circulate in an endless loop.

As has become clear, war performs an important and controversial methodological role for Kittler. In his call for us to understand 'technological a prioris in a technological sense' (Kittler, *Gramophone* 117), Kittler states that the starting point for any general theory of media should be the independent histories of individual technological media, with the 'subject' (and, therefore, social relations) bracketed off from the analysis. But by arguing for the relative autonomy of the technical realm, Kittler requires a mechanism for historical change, an alternative to the standard societal dynamics of politics or economics. The one that he supplies can be described as 'strategic escalation', as rather broadly summarized here:

> [You] have, for example, the book, and the military generals in considering how they can subvert the book or the written word, come up with the telegraph, namely, the telegraph wire; and then to offset the military telegraph, they come up with the wireless radio, which Hitler builds into his tanks. In England Alan Turing or Churchill ponder a way to beat Germany's radio war, and they arrive at the computer to crack the radio signals – and the German goose is cooked, that's the end of the war. (Kittler, 'Technologies' 738)

But in using this model of 'strategic escalation', Kittler reactivates in a German context a number of inter-war conservative discourses concerning the role of technology and war that had long been tarnished by their proximity to fascism. Of course, many of the conservative revolutionary thinkers who influenced Kittler – Jünger, Schmitt and, of course, Heidegger – had already found an audience in France in the post-war period, when disillusioned Marxists adopted the anti-Enlightenment rhetoric of the German Right to articulate anxieties about the more oppressive qualities of

modernity. This, in turn, serves to explain why Kittler's early identification with a French poststructuralism, which was, in its way, a
cryptic alignment with German thinkers still felt to be implicated
with the catastrophe of the Second World War, found such a frosty
reception in Germany in the 1980s.

By pressing on the question of war and Jünger's concept of
mobilization explicitly, however, we can perhaps begin to see how
Kittler places some distance between himself and both French and
German Marxist thinkers, as he attempts to displace the industrial-
technological paradigm with a military-technological one. Like
the conservative revolutionaries of the Weimar Republic, Kittler
adopts a martial rather than an economic model of social relations
(what Foucault calls the 'Nietzsche hypothesis' (90)), but Kittler,
infused with Lacanian cybernetics and posthumanism, rejects the
existential underpinnings of Schmitt and Jünger and, in so doing,
manages to elide, though he never quite evades, their questionable political affiliations. Kittler posits, instead, a timeless model
of command and control, with technical infrastructures supporting an economy of instructions developing autonomously, with
little relation to human needs. Instead of the base units of people,
the exchange of goods and communication, Kittler substitutes
addresses, data and commands ('Global Algorithm').

Command and Control

As Kittler turned his attention to the post-war period and the
development of computing technologies, he began to ask urgent
questions about the changing nature of command structures and
their effects on humans, most notably in two influential essays,
'Protected Mode' and 'There Is No Software'.[6] With humans
increasingly taken out of the loop, previously accessible data flows
disappear 'into black holes and boxes' (Kittler, *Gramophone* xxxix);
as such, the old antechambers of governmental power are gradually
replaced by access privileges hardwired into silicon. By partition-
ing their hardware in this way, Kittler argues that companies such
as Intel and IBM are implementing a military-industrial logic that

effectively restricts access to higher-level computing functions. In cahoots with the state, these companies withhold technical capabilities that may bring national strategic advantage, and what they release to the public acts to circumscribe the experience of the 'end-user'. We are thrown the bone of entertainment, fobbed off with software applications that serve to obfuscate the core hardware functions of our machines, while reinforcing our delusions of agency. An example Kittler often gave was Microsoft Windows, which, far from opening up the contents of our computers to us, merely implements the one-way mirrors of a surveillance state. With layers of user interfaces, programs and operating systems, our interactions with computers are mediated to an ever greater extent until '[w]e simply do not know what our writing does' (Kittler, 'There Is No Software' 148). For Kittler, then, any attempt to grasp how our current situation is determined by media must look to the technical specifications of both hardware and software, for power structures are now implemented at the level of system design. In essays such as 'Protected Mode', Kittler asks us to take a political stance against the technological domination of the USA, and the surrendering of the state to an expression of the military-industrial complex that effectively makes us all subjects of Microsoft Corporation. For pockets of resistance can be found, and, characteristically, they reside within the communities engaging with the workings of technical media themselves, notably those in the Open Source/Free Software movements.

As with the 1800 and 1900 discourse networks, Kittler demonstrates how these technical developments have structural implications for the production of knowledge. He argues that the model of intellectual property inherent in the contemporary separation of an algorithmic instruction (software) from what it can do (hardware) merely serves to perpetuate the myth of humans as creators. Kittler proposes, instead, that knowledge should be seen as a collective endeavour and promotes the free circulation of ideas underpinned by the institution of the university. After all, universities have been based on an open source model since the Athenians, he tells us, and, despite their infiltration by 'monkish' (Kittler, 'Universities' 251) elements in the Middle Ages, have operated as a successful model of cultural production ever since. But moves to marketize the university, with faculties as clusters of profit centres, effectively privatize knowledge. For Kittler, however, intellectual goals should not be subordinated to short-term or commercial ends, and he viewed the leeching of Silicon Valley on educational establishments as particularly scandalous, with students encouraged to develop ideas in the university and then cash in as entrepreneurs. Even the printing press, which broke the monopoly on storage and transmission of data, left the processing of data to the academics. For Kittler, then, the most contemporary forms of digital media, far from simply being handmaidens to an upstart late capitalism, need to be thought alongside forms of knowledge circulation that emerged when Western civilization was in its infancy.

Cultural Techniques and Ancient Greece

By the turn of the millennium, *Medienwissenschaft* was a success-fully established field in German academia with a small army of students working on topics such as the history of the tape recorder or researching the archive of Claude Shannon. But rather than following other media professors in analysing the evils of social networking or the proliferation of mobile devices, Kittler chose to emphasize the historicity of mediality. And his research into the origins of symbolic systems took him back to antiquity, like his intellectual heroes Foucault, Heidegger and Nietzsche before him. He became compelled by the invention in ancient Greece circa 800 BCE of the first vowel alphabet. With the addition of vowel characters, an alphabet was able, for the first time, to record language as it was spoken and to guarantee its faithful future repro-duction. Furthermore, in a simple move, the same characters could be used for numbers as well as letters, and even to identify musical notes. Kittler saw in the Greek alphabet a near-universal notation system that points to the underlying unity of all cultural data.

Kittler championed the work of classicist Barry B. Powell, who had controversially argued that the Greek alphabet had been devel-oped for the transmission of sung Homeric poetry and not, as was widely assumed, for economic, legal or political reasons. To understand this media-historical foundation for Western culture, Kittler delved into a newly discovered entanglement of gods, sex, music and mathematics. No longer interested in charting the history of modern warfare, he began to celebrate the story of 'love in Europe', with *The Odyssey* as the ur-text for European cultural history. To this end, Kittler embarked on a magnum opus – a proposed tetralogy entitled *Musik und Mathematik* – but was able to publish only two parts of the first volume (*Aphrodite* and *Eros*) before he died. The series was an ambitious cultural-historical project to chart European notation systems from ancient Greece and Rome, through the Middle Ages, and up to the present day. For Kittler, the encoding of the Sirens' song, and the desire for knowledge that it enacts, inaugurates Western culture. He sought its traces around the shores of the Mediterranean and its echoes in European literature. In so doing, he identified a historical short circuit connecting ancient Greece to the modern Turing age (*Turingzeit*); for binary code once more grants culture a universal notation system via a universal medium: the computer. In this era of advanced technological conditions, Kittler discerned the possibility of a reclamation of the gifts of ancient Greek culture – a liberation of desire and knowledge. But, in Kittler's account, there are considerable obstacles to attaining the supposed plenitude of the Greeks in a world that is corrupted by the monotheism of Christianity, Islam and Judaism, and blighted by the technical hegemony of the United States.

Kittler's change of direction caused more than a few academic eyebrows to be raised, with many taking the view that the turn to the Greeks and the cult of Aphrodite was the ever-crazier outpourings of the ever-crazy Kittler. More sympathetic commentators, such as Claudia Breger, engaged directly with his ideas but raised concerns about his Hellenophilia. Others, such as John Durham Peters in this volume, question some of the ethical and political implications of Kittler's late turn. This work is certainly far removed from the set texts of literary or media studies courses, as it jumps eccentrically, and sometimes alarmingly, from close readings of Greek poetry to travelogue, and then to lascivious descriptions of 1960s rock concerts. Kittler's turn to the Greeks is sometimes seen as a dramatic departure from his interests; but there is much continuity, notably the linking of bodies with notation systems and their media. The question of alphabetization, so central to his later work, is of course also a key theme of *Discourse Networks* – a book that uses equations as epigraphs for each of its two main sections. Indeed, his later work could be described as unearthing the remains of Discourse Network 350 BCE.

Kittler's Influence

In his essays on the status of the university, Kittler calls for an overcoming of the contemporary science/humanities divide through a revised implementation of *Wissenschaft* as a technically inflected higher learning. For Kittler, the future of the university itself depends upon the recognition of the 'essential unity' of letters and numbers and a radical engagement with the possibilities opened up by the computer, now the common hardware of knowledge across the disciplines. In *Turingzeit* it becomes clear that the sciences are historical and the humanities are technical; science departments thus need historians, and cultural studies departments require computing and mathematical expertise – something recognized in the emerging field of digital humanities. Kittler himself embodied (t)his connection between the disciplines, being equally at ease with Philolaus and low-level assembly code. Just as he thought that literary scholars should have (at least) composed poetry, so he believed that scholars commenting on technological changes should also have hands-on experience of their objects of study. Programming was a regular feature in his seminars, as he sought to ensure that scholars wishing to analyse the 'daily data flow' that constitutes cultural production were able to understand the dominant contemporary cultural codes.

When university literature departments first began to examine the relationship between technology and texts, their resources were limited. There was Derrida and hypertext, Foucault and the archive, and then Kittler, who, in the wake of French poststructuralism, issued a disciplinary challenge to analyse the economy of the letter as our means of access to culture. For Kittler there is no

'universal grammatology', but rather an untold history of notation systems and their accompanying technologies that must be
unearthed. In literary studies, his ideas have been most influential
among scholars interested in the materiality of media in transition,
particularly in the modernist period described in the second half
of *Discourse Networks* when literature's monopoly came to an end
with media differentiation. His influence is less marked in Anglo-
American studies of Romanticism, at least in part because the first
half of *Discourse Networks* is primarily concerned with German
literary texts. For modernists, though, as gramophones, film and
typewriters have become major objects of study, Kittler's work has
become a key reference point. Literary scholars who have addressed
the typewriter's role in modernity through Kittler include Tim
Armstrong and Pamela Thurschwell, while Sam Halliday has used
the work to theorize an understanding of the relationship between
sound technologies and modernism. Kittler's analysis of the gramophone and digital signal processing has helped form the emerging
field of sound studies through the work of Douglas Kahn and
(contra Kittler) Jonathan Sterne, while film scholars such as Mary
Ann Doane, Thomas Elsaesser and Vivian Sobchack have all drawn
on Kittler's approach.

Kittler never dropped his identification as a literary critic, but
it is worth noting that his refusal of hermeneutics and determined deprioritization of the content of media in one sense sets
his approach profoundly at odds with the interpretative thrust
of much work in literary studies – work that maintains (at least)
a residual interest in the investments, engagements and ideas of
'so-called Man'. That said, in *Discourse Networks* and *Gramophone,
Film, Typewriter*, Kittler did offer literary criticism an influential
method that allowed the content and form of texts, and technologies of writing and transmission, to be understood as necessarily
and structurally implicated within one another. Indeed, Kittler's
repeated use of Nietzsche's condensed and cryptic aphorism that
'our writing tools are also working on our thoughts' (*Gramophone*
200) has been the most influential aspect of his work for literary-
critical readings of culture, precisely because it enables interpretations of the content and form of 'texts' to be linked back to the
possibilities for thought itself that are structured and enabled by

particular media channels. Even though Kittler himself resisted the broadly hermeneutic aims of many critics working in the literary critical tradition, the fact that even the most conservative readers now struggle to engage with modernist texts without acknowledging their frequently self-conscious positioning within a broader discourse network of gramophones, film cameras and typewriters is testament to Kittler's often implicit but nevertheless vital influence.

While Kittler certainly argues for the subordination of literary studies to a more broadly understood media studies, he offers a radically different vision of media studies to that conventionally practised in Anglo-American universities. Eschewing the traditional concerns of communication, ideology and representation, Kittler's arguments are marshalled against those who argue that it is the social that shapes media rather than the other way round. Kittler is not interested, for example, in the ideological effect of mass media; instead, he urges media studies to study *media* and not the content that fills their channels. He argues that by their nature media conceal themselves, and that by relying on concepts such as understanding and subjectivity we are victims of a systematic deception. He deploys the same criticism against cultural studies (both Raymond Williams and the Birmingham School get short shrift) and also against sociology. His redefinition of society as a data processing machine has indeed prompted Nicholas Gane to call for a posthuman sociology to replace traditional subject-centred approaches. Kittler can be aligned here with other neo-cybernetic discourses emanating from Germany, particularly that of Niklas Luhmann, another broadly conservative thinker who focused on the differentiation of self-referential social systems.

So, a Kittlerian media studies must lay its foundations on a material base, for information always has a material substrate, whether it is marks on paper, voltage variations on a copper wire, or the frequency of light in an optical cable. But Kittler also raises questions about the possible links between computers and 'non-programmable systems' such as humans, and this work resonates with other materialist approaches to technology such as those pursued by Rosi Braidotti, Sean Cubitt, Manuel DeLanda and Jussi Parikka. In its early theorization of digital media, Kittler's radical hardware approach is often contrasted with Lev Manovich's focus on software, a pernicious fallacy in Kittler's opinion, and interface, which he dismisses as mere 'eyewash'. His ideas also form one of the main poles in current work on media aesthetics. For Kittler's proposal that aesthetics can be reduced to perception and that sense perception is the 'dependent variable' of a 'compromise between engineers and sales people' (*Gramophone* 2) determinedly opposes the primacy of aesthetics over technology. Mark Hansen, a contributor to this volume, is a leading figure in this field.

A persistent criticism of Kittler's radical materialism is that it lacks the vocabulary to discuss media as constituted and constituting forms of power. But, in Germany, the hardcore technophilia that characterized Kittlerian media theory in the 1980s and 1990s has subsequently softened. The school of media archaeology, led by figures such as Wolfgang Ernst and Siegfried Zielinski, is pursuing a more strongly Foucault-inflected route and is gaining influence far beyond Germany.[7] More contemporary work on cultural techniques (*Kulturtechnik*) also offers a broader view of the imbrication of human cultural practices with technologies.[8] If Kittler's preference for physics over biology had expelled questions of life and practice, the concept of *Kulturtechnik* has allowed them back in.

One of the most striking aspects of Kittler's reception, however, is his strong influence outside the university. His work on the changes wrought by computing technologies found an ardent fan base outside the usual channels for media theory. Indeed, part of Kittler's early appeal was his rebellious outsider status and enthusiastic adoption of tools that were alien to fusty professors. As we have seen, Kittler was a supporter of the Open Source and Free Software movements and their challenges to the technical hegemony of Microsoft et al. 'Protected Mode' and 'There Is No Software' gave theoretical succour to the exploits of many in the hacker community, and Kittler was a frequent guest at the Chaos Computer Club, probably the largest association of hackers in Europe. Similarly, glitch and net artists, in their bids to resist the networks of control that he describes, have found inspiration in Kittler's work, while he himself found delight in the effects of phasing and the moiré patterns of the interplay of technical standards, as described in 'Computer Graphics: A Semi-Technical Introduction'.

The chapters in this volume offer new analyses of and engagements with Kittler's work from across the disciplines we have
described. The first section of the volume begins by assessing and
contextualizing Kittler's turn to the gods, to ancient Greece, to
music and to mathematics in his later work, and is bookended by
two translations of essays by Kittler. The first, 'The God of Ears', is
a relatively early piece that originally appeared in German in 1982
and was later included in *Draculas Vermächtnis: Technische Schriften*.
It is typically eccentric and also methodologically exemplary in
its treatment of Pink Floyd's 'Brain Damage' as a '[discourse] on
discourse channel conditions', with Roger Waters' song read as a
performance of its own technological conditions of possibility –
in this case advances in sound technology following the Second
World War. It also foreshadows many of the themes developed
in the late essay 'Preparing the Arrival of the Gods' (the second
translation featured in the collection), in which Kittler argues that
the rock stars of the 1960s were the first to be able to do with
music what Homer and Sappho had been able to do with language,
that is, to reinvoke the gods with media technology. These arguments are contextualized, glossed and critiqued by John Durham
Peters' vital assessment of Kittler's later, unfinished project, *Musik
und Mathematik*. Peters reveals to an Anglophone readership the
extraordinary scope of this work in a way that both appreciates and
keeps judicious distance from Kittler's polymathic but eccentric
scholarship; Peters also asks searching and acute questions of the
politics implicated within Kittler's Hellenism.

Stephen Sale further contextualizes the late turn by understanding Kittler's mathematical engagements to have been in
operation throughout his oeuvre and part of his extended engagement with Heidegger. Understanding Kittler through his place
in German philosophy rather than French poststructuralism or
Anglophone media theory, Sale's chapter reads Kittler as recon-
ceiving Heidegger's work for a digital age, while opening up
mathematics and the technical qualities of technology to the
humanities. Sale shows how Kittler precisely and productively
teases out an ambiguity in Heidegger's engagement with the question concerning technology – one which opens up the possibilities
for rendering visible and understanding 'calculative Being', but

which needs Kittler's thought to work through the implications. The chapters in this section are brought to a critical conclusion with Geoffrey Winthrop-Young's reading of the figure of recursion, or 'repetitive instances of self-processing that nonetheless result in something different', through Kittler's later work. The concept, used in mathematics and computer science, is frequently invoked by Kittler to account for the historical short circuit that he sees connecting the ancient Greeks to the present day. Winthrop-Young demonstrates the methodological importance of recursive historiography as Kittler moves away from his earlier 'artifactual bias' towards his work on cultural techniques in *Musik und Mathematik*. In contrast to younger media theorists such as Wolfgang Ernst and Markus Krajewski, however, Kittler uses the concept to structure his 'grand occidental narrative' and thereby presses it into the service of updating Heidegger's *Seinsgeschichte*, or history of Being.

The second section of the book moves backwards through Kittler's oeuvre, exploring the consequences of the differentiation of media that characterizes the 1900 discourse network. It comprises responses to Kittler's work from writers working broadly within the tradition of literary studies, with its acknowledged interest in interpreting the relationship between the history of media and the structural effects different technologies have on the form and content of 'writing'. Steven Connor's chapter takes us back to Kittler's reading of *Memoirs of My Nervous Illness* in *Discourse Networks*, exploring and extending the connection between Daniel Paul Schreber's madness and the new writing and recording technologies that both dominate and construct his imaginary. But where Kittler exults in Schreber's collapsing of mind into those new media capable of inscribing and storing the clicks and shudders of the real (Kittler reads the text as life-writing that registers human life itself as a form of writing, a processing of information), Connor suggests that Schreber's account of the inscription of his every move, thought, perception and sensation should be understood as the product of a powerful human fantasy. If this is true, Schreber's ideas do not simply reveal the technologically determined disappearance of 'man' and the reformation of the subject as a functional apparatus; rather, they demonstrate how the capacities of media need also to be understood as formed through and according to insistently human imaginaries.

Pursuing the more hermeneutic mode dominant in literary critical uses of Kittler, Katherine Biers' readings of film noir and early feminist theatre analyse the importance of the typewriter to the representation of women's identities in the first half of the twentieth century. Building on Kittler's account of the epistemic shift inaugurated by this new form of writing, alongside his sense of the gendering of the functioning of the typewriter (a term that refers suggestively both to the machine and to its operator), Biers then challenges Kittler's reading of women's place in the discourse network. By emphasizing women's interpretative work in the office, Biers offers an important complication of Kittler's tendency to collapse technology and gendered desire into automaticity. Gill Partington's close reading of the formal and conceptual qualities of Francois Truffaut's film *Fahrenheit 451* works in concert with Kittler's understanding of the way information and signification are constructed through the material qualities and potentialities of different media. Indeed, by reading with Kittler, Partington uncovers in Truffaut's film an allegory of how discourse networks might themselves function – a story of how particular historically determined technologies and institutions allow cultures to select, store, process and understand the weight, texture and significance of information.

The final section focuses on the re-emergence of a universal medium with the advent of digital technology and offers engagements with Kittler's work from writers concerned with theorizing 'new media'. It starts with Alexander R. Galloway, who pursues the same intuition troubling Connor: that Kittler's insistence on the idea of *techne* as fundamentally concerned with objects, with media hardware rather than the lived practices within which human subjects and objects are implicated, leads to mediation becoming the excluded middle of his thought. Galloway suggests that the computer, in particular, cannot be understood in these terms, for it is a medium that fundamentally 'instantiates a practice, not a presence'. Indeed, if, as Galloway has it, the computer remediates the world and even metaphysics itself into a dispersed network of practices, perhaps it makes more logical and more political sense to understand the computer not as an ontology (as an expression of Being), but as an ethic – as an articulation of *ethos*, of lived practice. Galloway analyses the specificity of the 'ethic' of the computer by reading it alongside the distanced/absorbed audience produced by cinema, and Caroline Bassett also uses the cinema as a counterpoint to her technologically determined, Kittlerian analysis of the screen and camera technologies of mobile/cell phones. Bassett demonstrates the clear value of reading in a way that analyses technical capacity and action away from those human investments and intimacies that have tended to dominate our understanding of these new technologies. Though Bassett is helpfully explicit that the human remains in the picture to the extent that the experiencing body is part of the network of operations through which the picture finds itself being taken, she nevertheless shows how Kittler's technological determinism assists in the production of a clear-sighted account of what it means to live through, within and across technologically distributed networks.

In the final chapter, Mark B. N. Hansen returns to his influential critique (on which Bassett builds) of Kittler's occlusion of the human in the technological scene. Here, though, Hansen finds what may always have been a residual humanism in Kittler's work – a humanism grounded in the sensory experience of the body. Hansen shows through and alongside Kittler how technologies are dependent on temporized embodied perception, even as they vastly expand the realm of the sensible for humans and contain modes of registration that are still absolutely opaque to us. In a way that might just have surprised Kittler himself, Hansen reveals the extraordinary potential in Kittler's thought for reading the functioning of new media when one understands 'human–machine co-functioning as the core of his legacy'.

Friedrich Kittler died in October 2011 and his theoretical legacy is still unfolding. The engagements included in this collection are intended to represent a snapshot of how Anglophone writers across the humanities are currently placing themselves in dialogue with Kittler's work, rather than simply applying or following it. Because of this, readers will find contributors using his thought to pursue their own critical projects – projects which, in many cases, ask questions of aspects of Kittler's radical message. Nevertheless, each contributor recognizes the startlingly new horizons Kittler opens up for the humanities, and, as such, we hope that this collection will be read both as a commemoration of his life and work, and as an avowedly Anglo-centric critical reflection upon what we can learn from him. In 'The God of Ears', we have one of the clearest statements of Kittler's method: put on your headphones, listen, then reflect. Surrender yourself to intoxication but afterwards investigate its causes. In urging us to adopt this strategy, Kittler did not expect us to regain control of ourselves, to come back into the fold of 'so-called Man'; he simply asked us to look with clear eyes, free from the solipsistic delusion that humans are always and everywhere at the beginning of things, instead of where we really are: *in media res*.

Notes

1 The book that introduced Kittler to many Anglo-American readers was Gumbrecht and Pfeiffer's 1988 edited collection *Materialities of Communication*.

2 Extensive bibliographic resources for Kittler's works are available online. See, for example, http://www.monoskop.org/ Friedrich_Kittler#Bibliography and http://hydra.humanities.uci.edu/ kittler/kittlerpub.html

3 See, for example, Rickels (68). An overview of the theory wars in Germany in the 1980s can be found in Hohendahl (187–97).

4 Friedrich Kittler in conversation with Stephen Sale at Kittler's home in Berlin, 23 November 2003.

5 See, for example, 'Media and Drugs in Pynchon's Second World War' and 'Media Wars: Trenches, Lightning, Stars', which are both in Kittler, *Literature, Media, Information Systems* (101–116; 117–129); 'Unconditional Surrender' (Gumbrecht and Pfeiffer 319–34); and 'The Flower of the Elite Troops'.

6 Originally published in German in 1991 and 1992, both essays are included in translation in Kittler's *Literature, Media, Information Systems*.

7 See, for example, Huhtamo and Parikka.
8 See, for example, the special issue on cultural techniques *Theory, Culture & Society* 30.6 (2013). It includes articles from leading figures in the field such as Markus Krajewski, Bernhard Siegert and Cornelia Vismann.

Works Cited

Armitage, John. 'From Discourse Networks to Cultural Mathematics: An Interview with Friedrich A. Kittler.' *Theory, Culture & Society* 23.7–8 (2006): 17–38.

Armstrong, Tim. *Modernism, Technology and the Body: A Cultural Study.* Cambridge: Cambridge University Press, 1998.

Braidotti, Rosi. *Metamorphoses: Towards a Materialist Theory of Becoming.* Cambridge: Polity, 2002.

Breger, Claudia. 'Gods, German Scholars, and the Gift of Greece: Friedrich Kittler's Philhellenic Fantasies.' *Theory, Culture & Society* 23.7–8 (2006): 111–34.

Cubitt, Sean, and Paul Thomas, eds. *Relive: Media Art Histories.* Cambridge: MIT Press, 2013.

DeLanda, Manuel. *War in the Age of Intelligent Machines.* New York: Zone, 1992.

Doane, Mary Ann. *The Emergence of Cinematic Time.* Cambridge, MA: Harvard University Press, 2002.

Elsaesser, Thomas. 'The New Film History as Media Archaeology.' *Cinémas* 14.2–3 (2004): 75–117.

Ernst, Wolfgang. *Das Gesitz des Gedächtnisses: Medien und Archive am Ende (des 20. Jahrhunderts).* Berlin: Kulturverlag Kadmos, 2007.

Fliethmann, Axel, ed. Special section on Friedrich Kittler, *Thesis Eleven* 107 (2011): 3–65.

Foucault, Michel. *Power/Knowledge: Selected Interviews and Other Writings 1972–1977.* Ed. Colin Gordon. Brighton: Harvester Press, 1990.

Gane, Nicholas. 'Radical Post-Humanism: Friedrich Kittler and the Primacy of Technology.' *Theory, Culture & Society* 22.3 (2005): 25–41.

Griffin, Matthew, and Susanne Herrmann. 'Interview mit Friedrich A. Kittler.' *Weimarer Beiträge* 43.2 (1997): 286–96.

Gumbrecht, Hans Ulrich, and Karl Ludwig Pfeiffer, eds. *Materialities of Communication*. Stanford: Stanford University Press, 1988.

Halliday, Sam. *Sonic Modernity: Representing Sound in Literature, Culture and the Arts*. Edinburgh: Edinburgh University Press, 2013.

Hohendahl, Peter Uwe. *Reappraisals: Shifting Alignments in Postwar Critical Theory*. Ithaca, NY: Cornell University Press, 1991.

Huhtamo, Erkki, and Jussi Parikka, eds. *Media Archaeology: Approaches, Applications, and Implementations*. Berkeley and Los Angeles: University of California Press, 2011.

Kahn, Douglas. *Noise, Water, Meat: A History of Sound in the Arts*. Cambridge, MA: MIT Press, 1999.

Kittler, Friedrich A. *Discourse Networks 1800/1900*. Trans. Michael Metteer with Chris Cullens. Stanford: Stanford University Press, 1990.

Kittler, Friedrich A. *Draculas Vermächtnis: Technische Schriften*. Leipzig: Reclam, 1993.

Kittler, Friedrich A. 'Global Algorithm: The History of Communication Media.' *ctheory* 30 July 1996. Web. www.ctheory.net/articles. aspx?id=45

Kittler, Friedrich A. *Literature, Media, Information Systems: Essays*. Ed. John Johnston. Amsterdam: G+B Arts International, 1997.

Kittler, Friedrich A. 'There Is No Software.' *Literature, Media, Information Systems: Essays*. Ed. John Johnston. Amsterdam: G+B Arts International, 1997. 147–55.

Kittler, Friedrich A. 'Protected Mode.' *Literature, Media, Information Systems: Essays*. Ed. John Johnston. Amsterdam: G+B Arts International, 1997. 156–68.

Kittler, Friedrich A. *Gramophone, Film, Typewriter*. Trans. Geoffrey Winthrop-Young and Michael Wutz. Stanford: Stanford University Press, 1999.

Kittler, Friedrich A. 'Computer Graphics: A Semi-Technical Introduction.' *Grey Room* 2 (2001): 30–45.

Kittler, Friedrich A. 'The Flower of the Elite Troops.' *Body and Society* 9.4 (2003): 169–89.

Kittler, Friedrich A. 'Universities: Wet, Hard, Soft, and Harder.' *Critical Inquiry* 31.1 (2004): 244–55.

Kittler, Friedrich A. *Musik und Mathematik I: Hellas 1: Aphrodite*. Munich: Fink, 2006.

Kittler, Friedrich A. *Musik und Mathematik I: Hellas 2: Eros.* Munich: Fink, 2009.

Kittler, Friedrich A. *Optical Media: Berlin Lectures 1999.* Trans. Anthony Enns. Cambridge: Polity, 2010.

Manovich, Lev. *The Language of New Media.* Cambridge, MA: MIT Press, 2001.

Parikka, Jussi. 'Dust and Exhaustion: The Labour of New Materialism.' *ctheory* 2 October 2013. Web. www.ctheory.net/articles.aspx?id=726

Rickels, Laurence. 'Spooky Electricity: An Interview with Friedrich Kittler.' *Artforum* December (1992): 66–70.

Shannon, Claude, and Warren Weaver, *The Mathematical Theory of Communication.* Urbana and Chicago: University of Illinois Press, 1963.

Sobchack, Vivian. *Carnal Thoughts: Embodiment and Moving Image Culture.* Berkeley: University of California Press, 2004.

Sterne, Jonathan. *The Audible Past: Cultural Origins of Sound Reproduction.* Durham, NC, and London: Duke University Press, 2003.

Thurschwell, Pamela. *Literature, Technology and Magical Thinking, 1880–1920.* Cambridge: Cambridge University Press, 2004.

Virilio, Paul. *War and Cinema: The Logistics of Perception.* Trans. Patrick Camiller. London: Verso, 1989.

Winthrop-Young, Geoffrey. *Kittler and the Media.* Cambridge: Polity, 2011.

Winthrop-Young, Geoffrey. 'Silicon Sociology, or, Two Kings on Hegel's Throne? Kittler, Luhmann, and the Posthuman Merger of German Media Theory.' *Yale Journal of Criticism* 13.2 (2000): 391–420.

Winthrop-Young, Geoffrey, and Nicholas Gane, eds. Special issue of *Theory, Culture & Society* 23.7–8 (2006).

Winthrop-Young, Geoffrey, and Larson Powell, eds. Special section on Friedrich Kittler, *Cultural Politics* 8.3 (2012): 359–464.

Winthrop-Young, Geoffrey, and Michael Wutz. Translators' Introduction. *Gramophone, Film, Typewriter.* By Friedrich A. Kittler. Stanford: Stanford University Press, 1999. xi–xxxviii.

Zielinski, Siegfried. *Deep Time of the Media: Toward an Archaeology of Hearing and Seeing by Technical Means.* Trans. Gloria Custance. Cambridge, MA: MIT Press, 2006.

Part I

Grecian 2000

1

The God of Ears

Friedrich A. Kittler

Translated by Paul Feigelfeld and Anthony Moore

The Greeks had a god who dwelt in the acoustic realm. With no warning whatsoever, when shepherds dreamt and the midday silence was overwhelming, Pan buzzed in every ear.

Pan, a cove of the auditory space [*eine Wöhlbung des Hörraums*], had always been closer to the Great Goddess than all her desperate lovers, those who pursued her by sight alone. Full of envy, Actaeon said:

> At times it seemed to me I saw, up there on the rock, the back of old Pan, who was also lying in wait for her. But from afar one might have taken him for a stone, or for some stunted old tree trunk. Then he was no longer discernible, though his pipes still rang out in the air. He had become melody. He had passed into the sighing of the wind, where she was sweating, where breathed the fragrance of her underarms and lower body, when she undressed. (Klossowski 30)[1]

'To look at a room or landscape' (no longer to speak of goddesses), 'I must move my eyes from one point to another. When I hear, however, I gather sound simultaneously from every direction: I am at the centre of my auditory world which envelopes me. You can immerse yourself in hearing, in

sound. There is no way to immerse yourself similarly in sight'
(Ong 72).[2]

The Great Pan, it is said, is dead. Yet gods of ears cannot
pass away. They return under the guise of our amplifiers and PA
systems. They come back as rock song.

Pink Floyd: Brain Damage

The lunatic is on the grass
The lunatic is on the grass
Remembering games and daisy chains and laughs
Got to keep the loonies on the path

The lunatic is in the hall
The lunatics are in my hall
The paper holds their folded faces to the floor
And every day the paper boy brings more

And if the dam breaks open many years too soon
And if there is no room upon the hill
And if your head explodes with dark forebodings too
I'll see you on the dark side of the moon

The lunatic is in my head
The lunatic is in my head
You raise the blade, you make the change
You re-arrange me 'til I'm sane
You lock the door
And throw away the key
There's someone in my head, but it's not me

And if the cloud bursts, thunder in your ear
You shout and no one seems to hear
And if the band you're in starts playing different tunes
I'll see you on the dark side of the moon.

(Words and music: Roger Waters)

The Dark Side of the Moon, Harvest LP I C 072–05–259: between
1973, when it was first released, and 1979, 8 million copies were

sold. According to the latest reports sales have reached 45 million. When streams of sound merge into streams of money, books and their editions become ridiculous. 'Brain Damage' doesn't need any description. The damage is done.

And yet everything started so easily – Roger Waters, Nick Mason and Richard Wright, three students of architecture in the 1960s, touring through England's suburban theatres with guitars and old Chuck Berry numbers. Their forgotten name: The Architectural Abdabs. Until, one day in the spring of 1965, a lead guitarist and singer invents Pink Floyd – the name and the sound. Overloaded amplifiers, the mixing desk as fifth instrument, tones circulating through the room and everything else made possible by a combination of deep-frequency technology and opto-electronics – with eyes like black holes, Syd Barrett exposes rock 'n' roll to the domain of astronomy.

The star above the London underground blazed for two years. We know Andy Warhol's words that in the age of electronic media we shall all become famous – everybody for 15 minutes. At Barrett's last gigs, if they took place at all, his left hand hung down while the right struck repeatedly on the same open string.[3] Monotony as the beginning and end of music, like dripping water torture. Then the man who invented Pink Floyd disappears from all stages somewhere into the diagnostic no-man's-land between LSD-psychosis and schizophrenia. Pink Floyd finds a new guitarist and the formula for their worldwide success. Furthermore, with record sales in seven figures, it remains true that the capitalist machine with its streams of money is fed by the decoded, deterritorialized current of madness which, in fact, is no more than electrical current.[4]

For six years Pink Floyd remained silent about the exclusion which made them possible. However, 'Brain Damage' speaks openly about outside and inside, exclusion and inclusion, and their annihilation. In the beginning all is well. There, in the house, is an owner, key in hand, being informed by newspapers of daily drivel. Here, on the lawn, possibly one of the beautiful lawns of southern England's countryside mansions and of Gottfried Benn's dreams,[5] the lunatic(s). This exclusion is required by a territorializing law, a law which tells the mad to stay on fenced paths and, above all, to keep out. It is the law of architects,[6] and in 1980/1 the former architecture student, Waters, will construct the barrier, materializing it as a giant wall across Earl's Court and the Westfalenhalle. That was my first visit to the region of the Ruhr.

Yet in the acoustic realm, things are not quite as simple as in show business. After all, '[i]n the field of the unconscious, the ears are the only orifice that cannot be closed' (Lacan 24).[7] Starting from the lawn, through the hallway and into the head – the irresistible advance of lunacy takes place via ears which are unable to defend themselves. By the end of the song, whether it is 'Brain Damage' or 'Another Brick in the Wall', the dam breaks, the head explodes and there is only howling with no reception. Because sound is the unwritable in music and is immediately its technology, no word, no wall, no barrier between the inside and the outside can resist it.

Foucault wrote *A History of Madness*, Bataille wrote *Story of the Eye*. But we have to thank Roger Waters who wrote the lyrics of 'Brain Damage' for the short history of the Ear and Madness in the Age of Media.

When the multiple inventor Edison built the first gramophone, following an idea of Charles Cros, the playback was merely a shadow of the recording. Even the insertion of a horn between source and cylinder could not reproduce mechanically recorded and mechanically played back vibrations louder than the original. It was not only Edison's near deafness that caused him to shout into his phonograph on that remarkable 6 December in 1877.[8] And it was only in the science fiction fantasies of the symbolists of that time that the magician of Menlo Park, using sound-space technology, connected his phonographs to arrays of loudspeakers to transport the singsong of his children into his office from the lawn outside.[9] In fact, the gramophone-loving citizens and emperors of the *fin de siècle* were more interested in voices than in the 'ritornello' which makes voices and identities dance. When in 1897 the Wilhelminian state poet Wildenbruch was, above all others, granted acoustic immortality, he (after lengthy explanations about how voices in contrast to faces cannot deceive and thus are ideal sources for psychologists) spoke the following sweet verse into the horn:

Vernehmt denn aus dem Klang von diesem Spruch
die Seele von Ernst von Wildenbruch.[10]

Hear, from the sound of this utterance,
the soul of Ernst von Wildenbruch.

From the sound to the saying, from the saying to the soul:
Wildenbruch tried so eagerly to reduce the real (his recorded, but
transient voice) to the symbolic (the articulated discourse on lyric)
and the symbolic to the imaginary (a creative poet's soul). Thank
God, the technicians chose precisely the other way around. Time
and fundamental research led to the drowning out of the last breath
of soul in sound and phon.[11]

Human voices were dominant only as long as recordings were
made and played back mechanically – no wonder, with a limited
frequency spectrum of just 200–2,000 Hertz. But with the wave
of innovation during the First World War that introduced the
principle of amplification, Edison's mechanical equipment could
become electrified. For the first time, frequency spectrum and
sound dynamic were in record grooves and loudspeaker coils. In
1926, in Respighi's 'Pini di Roma', a nightingale, electronically
recorded and amplified, stood its ground against the philharmonic
orchestra of Toscanini.[12]

To bring the magic of sound to perfection, just one more World
War had to break out. Its wave of innovation caused German
engineers to invent the tape machine, and British engineers the
hi-fi record, which made audible even the most subtle differences
in timbre between German and British submarine motors –
initially, of course, only apparent to the ears of aspiring RAF
officers.[13] Infused with war booty, America's record industry (slug-
gish through having been engaged with entirely different duties
between 1942 and 1945) was, thereafter, able to set a new standard:
tape recording. And only this allowed for acoustic manipulation in
the space between record production and reproduction.

British industry, around the same time, understood that its war-
driven progress in locating submarines had paved the way for a
peaceful application. In 1957, Electrical and Mechanical Industries
(EMI), which by no coincidence have Pink Floyd under contract,

released their first stereo record.[14] Since then, the two ears human beings happen to have are no longer just a caprice of nature, but a source of money: they are permitted to locate single voices and/or instruments between two living-room loudspeakers. And if these ears should happen to fail in locating where the sound is coming from, then this is only because a leading sound engineer had been even more artful. When John Culshaw, in 1959, produced Solti's wonderfully overloaded *Rheingold*,[15] every god and goddess found its audible place in the stereo mix. But the voice of the great technician Alberich, invisibly and drastically demonstrating the advantages of the Tarnhelm to his brother, came simultaneously from every possible corner.[16] And what remained a special effect for Culshaw, Syd Barrett turned into a rule. It is said that during recordings he turned the pots on the mixing desk wildly, as if the two stereo channels were themselves an instrument . . .

Since then, as we all know, there has been an explosion. So-called 'reproduction' turned into 'production', and the vow of loyalty to high fidelity, when confronted with all the existing possibilities, was reduced to a mere, pacifying formula. In 1974, purely for commercial and never technical reasons, the standard of radio and recording remains limited to mere preset sounds. There is no simulation of real or absolute sound spaces. But all limitations will fail where money and madness exist. Syd Barrett is the only one to have proved it. It was he who, with his Azimuth Coordinator, created a technical advantage for Pink Floyd over all the other bands. As the name implies, the Azimuth Coordinator is a PA system which makes it possible to bring to the listener's ear any event, track or slice inside the mass of sound, from any or all arbitrary, three-dimensional directions. 'Brain Damage' sings its glory.

Three times the song starts and three times sound production makes an historic step forward.

'The lunatic is on the grass . . .' Children's games and laughter come from outside the house, exactly what the Edison of the Comte de Villiers' science fiction novel wanted to intercept, muffled by the walls and, due to the distance, deprived of their space coordinates. Such effects may be simulated with filters. In another instance, using equalization with all the bass and high frequencies filtered out and copied over to a single track, a part on 'Wish You Were Here' simulates a simple transistor radio. The first verse, then, is the poor time of monaural reproduction.[17]

'The lunatic is in the hall. The lunatics are in my hall . . .' Step by step, phrase by phrase, monaural distance or abstraction vanishes. Because 'Dasein is essentially de-severant' and 'lets any entity be encountered close by' (Heidegger, *Being and Time* 105), the madman comes closer and closer.[18] With the subtly altered repetition of 'my hall', the meaning becomes personal; the hallway has a defined reference to the coordinates of both the listener and speaker. The hallway is close enough to distinguish left and right just by listening, and even close enough to distinguish the voices of many madmen. This is exactly how the acoustically built stairway works in the unforgettable ending of 'Grantchester Meadows', with steps running from left to right – from the vinyl directly into the rooms and ears of the listeners. So, the second verse is the time of high fidelity and stereophony.

'The lunatic is in my head. The lunatic is in my head . . .' To put it bluntly: the brain damage is done; an Azimuth Coordinator is at work. If sounds in the entire auditory space, controllable sounds, can appear from ahead and behind, right and left, up and down, then the space of day-to-day orientation disintegrates. The explosion of acoustic media turns into an implosion, toppling directly and immediately into the centre of perception itself. The head, as the real control desk of the nervous system and not only as the metaphoric site of what is thought of as thinking, becomes one with all the information pouring in; not just with so-called objectivity, but with actual sound.

At the end of 'Brain Damage' there are sounds of a synthesizer, perhaps to prove the point that, a long time ago, synthesizers had already replaced the synthetic judgements of philosophers.[19] A sound generator controlling and programming sound across the entire range of parameters – frequency, phase level, harmonic range, amplitude – transfers the conditions of possibility of alleged experience into the physiologically total simulacrum.

So, in the age of its possible technical impact, the history of the ear is always a history of madness, too. Brain damage music renders true what, in the form of dark anticipations, has been stalking many minds as well as the corridors of mental asylums. According to a dictionary of psychiatry 'the sense of hearing is, more than other senses, affected by hallucinations'.[20] Purported acouasms, perceived or caused by delusion, range from white noise, frizzling, the sounds of water drops and whispers to talking and screaming. It reads as if the dictionary of psychiatry wants to list Pink Floyd effects. White noise appears in 'One of These Days', frizzling in 'Echoes', water drops in 'Alan's Psychedelic Breakfast', screaming in 'Careful With That Axe, Eugene' and whispers everywhere . . .

Confronted with such keen ears, it remains astonishing that psychiatrists call it astonishing when acouasms nowadays are traced back to radio stations and radar screens and no longer to whispering devils or howling witches.[21] Madmen seem to be better informed than their doctors, for they realize that delusion, far from being the metaphorical meanderings of radio signals in the brain, is, in precisely the opposite sense, a metaphor for technology itself. Exactly because delusion is always scrutinized by the most modern means, its antenna registers the actual state of information processing with historical precision.

Only under the conditions of a culture which demands the reception of discourses as individual speech acts and the like do discourses on discourse channel conditions (white noise and frizzling, resonance and lingering sound) seem necessarily insane. But if speech acts in principle are mass media actions, anonymous and collective performances,[22] this madness is the truth and vice versa. A press statement, and therefore a mass media act, released by EMI in the days when Pink Floyd's song 'Let's Roll Another One' was banned, illustrates this beautifully.[23] At that time British newspaper readers learned: 'Pink Floyd have no clue what people mean by psychedelic Rock and they have no intention at all to exercise hallucinatory effects on their listeners.'[24]

Even if Barrett's glorious Azimuth Coordinator hadn't been reason enough for landing Pink Floyd listeners in hospital, sick with vertigo, such statements are an unerring means to drive people insane. Just saying that one doesn't intend hints at how easy it would be, because ears are impossible to shut. These mass media acts are drivel, but only to the regret of philosophers and to the pleasure of every ear. The plea, addressed to an unknown god or engineer in the song 'If' (using the same synthesizer tracks as in

'Brain Damage') remains unfulfillable: 'And if I go insane, please, don't put your wires into my brain . . .'.

Brain damage is inevitable. Unnoticed by psychiatrists, the antennas, before which insane fear and the fear of going insane cower, have long since invaded our brains. They keep transmitting on all frequencies, from LF to UHF. Above a thin layer of sound simulating the innocence of acoustic guitars, Waters sings solo only on the verses of 'Brain Damage'. The refrains are sheer walls of sound, innumerable tracks, one upon the other; chiming noisily they fill ears and brain. An 'I' recounts the verses. In the beginning it speaks of the madmen outside. In the end, after the collapse of distance created by the Azimuth Coordinator, it speaks directly to 'him'. With their if-sentences the choruses are answers – a discourse of the Other that turns the verses upside down. Barrett, now re-emerging, follows their words, 'You make the change, you re-arrange me 'til I'm sane.'

This cure is engineered very simply and concretely using acoustic arrangement and recording technology. In the first German 'dummy head' radio play[25] (and 'dummy head' stereophony is no more than an Azimuth Coordinator for daily use) all voices and sounds were recorded using stereo microphones – except for the one which was supposed to represent computer output as delusion input. In this elegant way, the radio play found a way to make its title 'Destruction' become true: if, among countless voices which can be located in three-dimensional auditory space, there appears one, and only one, single voice without coordinates, it will definitely be located in the listener's imploding head. Thus the most harmless and old-fashioned recording technology drives heroes and listeners insane. Under the conditions of perfect space-simulation, Culshaw's Alberich ruses are no longer necessary.

'Brain Damage' works in exactly the same way. Laughter is mixed over the third verse at the line, 'someone in my head who is not me'. It is a laughter which not only turns all fears of antennas in the brain into a big Nietzschean 'yes', but which is itself the antenna in the brain (because, in a beguiling exception, it has been recorded monaurally).

At the beginning of the record, when a triumphal voice announces it has always been insane and is well aware of it, the first, audible sentences vanish in laughter. At the end of the record, when it returns and the laughter of panic implodes in the head, Pink Floyd's madman wins out against the band. For there are two kinds of music: one acts as a quotation (and not as a memory) of voice and nature; the other – with reference to Paul Celan – acts as a song from beyond mankind.[26] 'I've always been mad, I know I've been mad . . .' (Pink Floyd, 'Dark Side of the Moon').

Brain damage means that the other music is going to triumph. 'Radio is far superior to nature, it is more comprehensive and can be varied' (Benn, 'Roman' 182). Nothing and nobody limits the possibilities of electronic media. There is always, beyond any angst of delusion, the possibility of making different music. When Barrett, years after his exclusion, returned to Abbey Road Studios and listened to the new tapes of his former band, he is reported to have mumbled, 'nice, but old-fashioned'. The end of 'Brain Damage' turns this mumbling into a big, laughing promise. When Pink Floyd play other music, their laughing madman will return. 'And if the band you're in starts playing different tunes, I'll see you on the dark side of the moon.' Or translated into French: 'Des dieux nouveaux, les mêmes, gonflent déjà l'Océan futur' (Foucault 396). Nietzsche who, of the other music knew only Wagner, dreamt of

> a deeper, mightier, perhaps wickeder and more mysterious music, a supra-German music which does not fade, turn yellow, turn pale at the sight of the blue voluptuous sea and the luminous sky of the Mediterranean, as all German music does; a supra-European music which holds its own even before the brown sunsets of the desert. (*Beyond Good and Evil* 169)

This is exactly the kind of music the madman of 'Brain Damage' transfers onto the dark side of the moon, the meeting point for other music. Against exactly this sunset, the legendary Pink Floyd concert at Pompeii took place. The four of them, close to the shore, held their ground, not moving for hours, only starting with the sound of a gong at precisely the second the red ball touched the edge of the sea.

Not surprisingly, the executives of EMI decided to hold the launch of *Dark Side of the Moon* in the London Planetarium. This would be the first opportunity for members of the press to hear it. However, on learning that the playback would only be in stereo and not fully spatialized as they had specified, the band members boycotted the event by simply not turning up. Only the more powerful and maybe even more evil music of our century has its antennas in the domain of astronomy. The control of all-encompassing, never-ending white noise through form and binary code (major/minor, consonance/dissonance etc.) was Europe's classical tone setting. Romantic music was and remains the decoding of such oppositional pairs: a *Lied von der Erde*, arriving at the word 'earth', broke, not in the least bit coincidentally, all triadic harmonies like 'decayed baubles [*morschen Tande*]' (Mahler).[27] But the music of our century also leaves earth or the living environment behind. Its two poles are cosmic ray sources and neurological energies – powers both beyond and on this side of mankind.[28] It is the short circuit in between that initiates them.

It couldn't be more clearly depicted than on the cover of *Dark Side of the Moon*. Pink Floyd's design team, Hipgnosis, depicts a ray of light on a black background refracted through a prism into the individual, spectral colours which become, once again, a single line. This turns out to be the ECG oscillogram of those heart beats with which the album begins and ends. This is how electronic technology catches up with those suspicions which, since time immemorial, short circuit the insane brain of lunatics with moon and stars.

And indeed, brain damage listeners become moonstruck. So many verses read, so many verses forgotten, but Pink Floyd remains in the head – 'I of today, who learns more from newspapers than from philosophies, who is closer to journalism than to the bible, to whom a classy song contains more of a century than a motet' (Benn, 'Probleme de Lyrik' 518).[29] Even if at the end of 'Brain Damage' a voice mumbles, 'I can't think of anything to say', even if books are ridiculous and descriptions of music outmoded, there is still something to write simply because something never ceases to write itself. 'Brain Damage' doesn't sing of love or other subjects – it is a single and positive feedback between sound and the listener's ears. Sounds speak of what is done by sounds. And this is more than all the effects old Europe had hoped to evoke through the Book of Books or the immortal poets.

The simple secret of any kind of lyric is to wrest words from their transience. When the Greeks invented the hexameter, they had nothing else in mind. Through 'the rhythmic tick-tock' (Nietzsche, *The Gay Science* 84), certain words become inescapable for people's ears and carry over even longer distances to gods' ears. (The first are so oblivious, the latter are so deaf.)

Nietzsche, who rediscovered this technology of channelling discourses, also gave the philological proof: in contrast to modern times, Greek rhythm measured syllables not according to their significance in the word, but simply by their acoustic length or shortness. Therefore, and for only this reason, antique lyric remains linked to a foot, the literal foot of dancing bodies. If, on the contrary, the accentuation and rhythm of the verses are determined by the significance of a word, as in modern European languages, then the music, together with the memory of the body, evaporates.[30] It becomes impossible to tell, from the lyrics alone, how they should be sung or danced. It is pure chance how they might then be fixed with some mnemonic technique.[31]

Maybe this is why the classic-romantic lyric, more than any other form of poetry, was directly linked to the experience and psychology of its author. In the imaginary, before all composition, it became possible to invent inner music even to verses read silently. Because phantasmagoric voices were whispering between the lines (for male readers, the mother's voice; for female readers, the author's), poetry stayed in the amorous memory. *Classical Forget-Me-Not* [*Klassisches Vergißmeinnicht*] was the name of a tiny book of Goethe's poems. Not until conditions turned highly capitalistic and consumers started to yawn when confronted with such psychology, preferring stronger drugs, did the lyric change its mnemonic technique to the cold medium of writing. Baudelaire's *Fleurs du Mal* starts with an assertive address to the reader, telling the whole story from the yawning to the water pipe.

Thus, modern lyric is a special pleasure of alphabet fetishists at a time when the one and only symbolic tone storage of Old Europe – letters and music notation – is being displaced by electrical means. Serious then Light culture . . .

There was a reason why Wildenbruch was so moved, the day he was permitted to utter his phonographic verses into the phonograph. That day the death knell tolled for lyric which had stood for love for so long and for so many. Is there still need of poetry in these technical times? Media are far too effective to limit their memory capacities to the sound, sayings and soul of someone like Wildenbruch. When record grooves and magnetic tapes are able to capture the unwritable that is sound, then mnemotechnical, auxiliary constructions such as authorship or individuality become superfluous. After millennia, the old linkage between word and music in the culture of entertainment returns, not only via the feet of verses and dancers, but as an inscription into the real.[32] Pink Floyd remains in the head – precisely because people no longer need to have a memory made for them, when machines themselves *are* a memory. And for that reason alone it becomes possible to save, not only words and melodies, but also instrumental colours, sound spaces and even the unfathomable stochastic of white noise.

Respighi's little nightingale carved out a career. The mad laughter of 'Brain Damage' and the blessed noises of a summer day in 'Grantchester Meadows' are not simply sung of; you can actually hear them. With all its noises, a meadow near Cambridge gives the primary colour to the song which at the same time recalls it. What in books or scores could only be hinted at with pedantic gimmickry (duets, changes of perspective, quotations of nature) becomes an event in the absolute space of sound. In this way they return: the midday silence, the meadow, the laughter of a god.

And since, in recording studios, rock bands themselves started to put parameter upon parameter, layer upon layer, and words upon sounds instead of following record company directives by playing standard singles written by hacks and arrangers, the watchdogs were chased out of the sound space of late 1960s records. 'There's someone in my head, but it's not me.' Only atavisms like the copyright law deriving from (where else) the age of Goethe still enforce the mentioning of lyricists and composers (as if there were such things in the space of sound). It would make much more sense to list the circuit plans and the model numbers of the synthesizers used (as appeared on the cover of *Dark Side of the Moon*). But this is exactly the way many things still are.

The famous personalization of power is like a territoriality that accompanies the deterritorialization of the machine, as its other side. [. . .] One sometimes has the impression that the flows of capital would willingly dispatch themselves to the moon if the capitalist State were not there to bring them back to earth. (Deleuze and Guattari, *Anti-Oedipus* 258)

But who knows what is moon and what is earth. 'So you think you can tell Heaven from Hell', mocks a song on *Wish You Were Here*. Whispered into the almost inaudible vanishing heartbeats, the last sentence on *Dark Side of the Moon* says the same: 'There is no dark side of the moon, really. Matter of fact, it's all dark' (Pink Floyd, 'Eclipse').

Even a heart attached to contact microphones and oscilloscopes becomes still. And when, with loud and quiet, light and dark, Heaven and Hell, all differences disappear, another realm (possibly known as Satori by other cultures) is coming closer. The media explosion of our days, therefore, should not only be heard in the media-theoretical manner of its prophets. According to Marshall McLuhan, the message of the synthesizer is simply the synthesizer. But even if the darkness is so overwhelming that no dark side of the moon exists, electronic media might yet invoke a still darker presence. Original sound – Waters: 'the medium is not the message, Marshall . . . is it? I mean, it's all in the lap of the fucking gods . . . (Pause for laughter)' (Sedgewick 13).

Translator's Note

Without the invaluable contributions of Paul Feigelfeld and Kerstin Bergmann simply nothing would have been achieved. For their sake it is necessary to point out that an eccentric decision was taken when it came to the style of the translation. Wanting still to hear the dear, German voice of its creator, I made a deliberate attempt not to render the text as if it were emerging from an English throat. Instead I thought the translation should simulate (if at all possible) a transcription of a recording of the author, speaking a language not his own. In some sense, then, the translation is dictated, so that what is inscribed is still first heard. In all the time that has passed since I came across this essay, that same 'voice' has informed much of my inner reflections, particularly with regard to the 'acoustic realm', the shift from orality to literacy and the history of recording. As an approach to translating 'The God of Ears', perhaps there might be some method in this madness.

Anthony Moore, Arles, February 2011

Notes

A first version of this text was published in 1982 in Lindemann (467–76). The volume was based on the idea of picking and interpreting one German, one English and one French poem for every twenty-five years between 1775 and 1975. It was aimed at school and university students. This is how Roger Waters and 'Brain Damage' ended up appearing next to such illustrious names as Goethe, Wordsworth, Eliot or Yeats – as the reality of lyric today. The original German version of this current chapter is available as: 'Der Gott der Ohren' in: Friedrich A. Kittler, *Das Nahen der Götter vorbereiten*. With a preface by Hans Ulrich Gumbrecht. Wilhelm Fink Verlag, Paderborn 2011, p. 48–61.

1 See also Barrett.

2 The exact quotation reads: 'Vision comes to a human being from one direction at a time: to look at a room or landscape, I must move my eyes around from one part to another. When I hear, however, I gather sound simultaneously from every direction at once: I am at the center of my auditory world, which envelopes me, establishing me at a kind of core sensation and existence. This centering effect of sound is what high-fidelity sound reproduction exploits with intense sophistication. You can immerse yourself in hearing, in sound. There is no way to immerse yourself similarly in sight' (Ong 73).

3 David Gilmour (Pink Floyd's new guitarist), quoted in Leduc (54).

4 See Deleuze and Guattari (*Anti-Oedipus* 240, 374).

5 See Benn ('Roman' 174).

6 On architects, see Scherer.

7 See also Bernhardi (24).

8 See the details in Bruch.

9 See Comte de Villiers de l'Isle-Adam (29).

10 Wildenbruch's dictum can be found as a phonograph transcript in Bruch. It cannot be found in his *Gesammelte Werke*.

11 A phon is a unit of perceived loudness equal to the loudness of a 1,000-Hertz tone at 40 dB above threshold.

12 See Gelatt (234).

13 See Gelatt (282).

14 See Chapple and Garofalo.

15 Editorial note: In *Das Rheingold*, the first part of Richard Wagner's Ring cycle, Alberich, a Nibelung dwarf, forges a magical ring which gives the possessor power over the world. To help fulfil his plans for domination he orders his brother Mime to make the Tarnhelm, a magical helmet that gives invisibility to the wearer.

16 'Thus in Scene three, Alberich puts on the Tarnhelm, disappears, and then thrashes the unfortunate Mime. Most stage productions make Alberich sing through a megaphone at this point, the effect of which is often less dominating than that of Alberich in reality. Instead of this, we have tried to convey, for thirty-two bars, the terrifying, inescapable presence of Alberich: left, right, or center there is no escape for Mime' (John Culshaw, quoted in Gelatt 316).

17 'When a track disappears into a thin, reedy transistor radio sound which is then joined by a plainly recorded acoustic guitar, there has obviously been a lot of thought behind the end product. How did they tackle that one? – "When it sounds like it's coming out of a radio, it was done by equalisation. We just made a copy of the mix and ran it through eq. to make it very middly, knocking out all the bass and most of the high top so that it sounds radio-like"' (Cooper 77).

18 'In Dasein there lies an essential tendency towards closeness. All the ways in which we speed things up, as we are more or less compelled to do today, push us on towards the conquest of remoteness. With the "radio", for example, Dasein has so expanded its everyday environment that it has accomplished a de-severance of the "world" – a de-severance which, in its meaning for Dasein, cannot yet be fully overlooked' (Heidegger, *Being and Time* 140) (translation slightly altered). One decade later, however, Heidegger realized that radiophonic de-severance lies not in the essence of an inhuman Dasein of whatever nature, but in technology: 'The gigantic presses forward in a form which seems to make it disappear: in destruction of great distances by the airplane, in the representations of foreign and remote worlds in their everydayness produced at will by the flick of a switch' (*Off the Beaten Track* 71). From Dasein to technology as sentence subjects of de-severance – Heidegger's 'Kehre' is nothing else.

19 See Deleuze and Guattari (*A Thousand Plateaus* 106, 378–9).

20 See 'Halluzination' (Müller).

21 For example, Bleuler (32).

22 Deleuze and Guattari (*A Thousand Plateaus* 104).

23 See Dister, Woehrle and Leblanc.

24 Quoted in Sahner and Veszelitis (23).

25 Editorial note: 'Dummy head' or binaural sound recording uses a replica of the human head with a microphone mounted in each ear to capture the audio frequency adjustments as sounds wrap around the head and into the ear canal. Playback through headphones offers listeners an immersive experience that accurately reproduces the distance and direction of recorded sounds. The technique was patented in 1927 but enjoyed a resurgence following a broadcast by Berlin radio station RIAS in 1973.

26 See also *The Wall* for these two musics, where at the end the maximization of Watts is followed by a little piece with accordion, clarinet and children's drums – just, once again, Merry Old England.

27 Translation author's own.

28 See Deleuze and Guattari (*A Thousand Plateaus* 372–82).

29 Translation author's own.

30 See my essay on Nietzsche in Turk (200–4).

31 Georgiades (224–44) explains this using Schubert's musical versions of Goethe.

32 See Lescure (1705–8). Nothing can prove the technical linkage of word and music more beautifully (and more philologically) than two hidden quotes on *Dark Side*. The line 'Look around and choose your own ground' refers of course to Don Juan's first order to his pupil Castaneda. But also the enigmatic order 'Run, rabbit, run!' is a literal Don Juan quote (see Castaneda 154). That way, the record (like 'Revolution 9') becomes a memory of secret messages.

Works Cited

Benn, Gottfried. 'Roman des Phänotyp.' *Gesammelte Werke in Vier Bänden: Zweiter Band.* Ed. Dieter Wellershof. Wiesbaden: Limes, 1958. 152–204.

Benn, Gottfried. 'Probleme der Lyrik.' *Gesammelte Werke in Vier*

Bänden: Erster Band. Ed. Dieter Wellershof. Wiesbaden: Limes, 1959. 494–532.

Bernhardi, August Ferdinand. *Sprachlehre*. Vol. I. Berlin: Frölich, 1801–3.

Bleuler, Eugen. *Lehrbuch der Psychatrie*. 11th edn. Ed. Manfred Bleuler. Berlin, Heidelberg and New York: Springer, 1969.

Bruch, Walter. 'Von der Tonwalze zur Bildplatte. 100 Jahre Ton- und Bildspeicherung.' Special issue of *Funkschau*, 1979.

Castaneda, Carlos. *Journey to Ixtlan: The Lessons of Don Juan*. Harmondsworth: Penguin, 1973.

Chapple, Steve, and Reebee Garofalo. *Rock'n'Roll is Here to Pay: The History and Politics of the Music Industry*. Chicago: Nelson-Hall, 1978.

Comte de Villiers de l'Isle-Adam, Philippe August Mathias. *L'Ève future*. Paris: José Corti, 1977.

Cooper, Gary. 'An Interview with David Gilmour.' *Pink Floyd, Wish You Were Here [Songbook]*. London: Pink Floyd Music, 1975. 73–81.

Deleuze, Gilles, and Félix Guattari. *Anti-Oedipus: Capitalism and Schizophrenia*. Trans. Robert Hurley, Mark Seem and Helen R. Lane. Minneapolis: University of Minnesota Press, 1983.

Deleuze, Gilles, and Félix Guattari. *A Thousand Plateaus: Capitalism and Schizophrenia*. Trans. Brian Massumi. London and New York: Continuum, 2004.

Dister, Alain, Udo Woehrle and Jacques Leblanc. *Pink Floyd*. Bergisch-Gladbach: Böhler, 1978.

Foucault, Michel. *Les mots et les choses: Une archéologie des sciences humaines*. Paris: Gallimard, 1966.

Gelatt, Robert. *The Fabulous Phonograph: From Edison to Stereo*. New York: Appleton-Century, 1965.

Georgiades, Thrasybulos. 'Sprache als Rhythmus.' *Sprache und Wirklichkeit: Essays*. Ed. Clemens Podewils. Munich: Deutscher Taschenbuch, 1967.

Heidegger, Martin. *Being and Time*. Trans. John Macquarrie and Edward Robinson. Oxford: Blackwell, 1962.

Heidegger, Martin. *Off the Beaten Track*. Ed. and trans. Julian Young and Kenneth Haynes. Cambridge: Cambridge University Press, 2002.

Klossowski, Pierre. *Diana at her Bath: The Women of Rome*. Trans. Sophie Hawkes and Stephen Sartarelli. New York: Marsilio, 1998.

Lacan, Jacques. *The Four Fundamental Concepts of Psychoanalysis*. Ed. Jacques-Alain Miller. Trans. Alan Sheridan. London: Hogarth Press, 1977.

Leduc, Jean-Marie. *Pink Floyd*. Paris: A. Michel, 1973.

Lescure, Jean. 'Radio et literature.' *Encyclopédie de la Pléiade: Histoire des littératures*. Vol. III. Ed. Raymond Queneau. Paris: Gallimard, 1958. 1705–8.

Lindemann, Klaus, ed. *europaLyrik 1775–heute: Gedichte un Interpretationen.* Paderborn: Schöningh, 1982.

Mahler, Gustav. *Das Lied von der Erde: Vocal Score.* Vienna and Leipzig: Universal-Edition, 1912.

Müller, Christian, ed. *Lexikon der Psychiatrie: gesammelte Abhandlungen der gebräuchlichsten psychopathologischen Begriffe.* Berlin: Springer, 1973.

Nietzsche, Friedrich. *Beyond Good and Evil: Prelude to a Philosophy of the Future.* Trans. R. J. Hollingdale. Harmondsworth: Penguin, 1973.

Nietzsche, Friedrich. *The Gay Science.* Ed. Bernard Williams. Trans. Josefine Nauckhoff. Cambridge: Cambridge University Press, 2001.

Ong, Walter J. *Orality and Literacy: The Technologizing of the Word.* London and New York: Methuen, 1982.

Pink Floyd, 'Careful With That Axe, Eugene.' *Ummagumma.* Harvest/ Capitol, 1969.

Pink Floyd, 'Grantchester Meadows.' *Ummagumma.* Harvest/Capitol, 1969.

Pink Floyd, 'Alan's Psychedelic Breakfast.' *Atom Heart Mother.* Harvest/ EMI, 1970.

Pink Floyd. 'If.' *Atom Heart Mother.* Harvest/EMI, 1970.

Pink Floyd, 'Echoes.' *Meddle.* Harvest/Capitol, 1971.

Pink Floyd, 'One of These Days.' *Meddle.* Harvest/Capitol, 1971.

Pink Floyd. 'Brain Damage.' *Dark Side of the Moon.* Harvest/Capitol, 1973.

Pink Floyd. 'Dark Side of the Moon.' *Dark Side of the Moon.* Harvest/ Capitol, 1973.

Pink Floyd. 'Eclipse.' *Dark Side of the Moon.* Harvest/Capitol, 1973.

Pink Floyd. 'Wish You Were Here.' *Wish You Were Here.* Harvest/EMI, 1975.

Pink Floyd, 'Another Brick in the Wall.' *The Wall.* Harvest/EMI, 1979.

Sahner, Paul, and Thomas Veszelitis. *Pink Floyd: Elektronischer Rock in Vollendung.* Munich: Heyne Discothek, 1980.

Scherer, Wolfgang. *BAB(B)ELLOGIK: Sound und die Auslöschung der buchstäblichen Ordung.* Basel: Roter Ster, 1983.

Sedgewick, Nick. 'A Rambling Conversation with Roger Waters Concerning All This and That.' *Pink Floyd, Wish You Were Here [Songbook].* London: Pink Floyd Music, 1975. 9–23.

Turk, Horst, ed. *Klassiker der Literaturtheorie: Von Boileau bis Barthes.* Munich: C. H. Beck, 1979.

2

Assessing Kittler's Musik und Mathematik

John Durham Peters

'*Nun de ta megista tōn agathōn hēmin gignetai dia manias*'. [And now the greatest of the goods come to us through madness.]

Plato, *Phaedrus*.

'Unorganised Innocence: An Impossibility'

William Blake

The Puzzle of Late Work

Friedrich Kittler's death leaves his vast project *Musik und Mathematik* incomplete. Two books comprising the first volume have been published, and it is unclear whether anything remains to be published. The outline for the project was grand:

I Hellas
  1 Aphrodite
  2 Eros

II Roma aeterna [eternal Rome]
  1 Sexus [sex]
  2 Virginitas [virginity]

III Hesperien [Europe]
  1 Minne [Courtly Love]
  2 Liebe [Love]
  3 Sex

IV Turingzeit [The Turing Age]

Kittler is in good company: some of the greatest works of German thought were fragments. The central question animating the project is how 'Europe' came to couple music and mathematics technically. Kittler's story is simultaneously a history of sexuality, though he preferred the less clinical term 'love'. Music, 'the delight and art of singing dancing playing' (*Aphrodite* 15), calls us mortals not only to couple our theoretical knowledge of counting with the practice of making beautiful sounds via voices and instruments, but also to couple sexually with each other in *Liebesnächte* or 'nights of love', odd-numbered men and even-numbered women entwining rhythmically in a cosmic rounddance. *Aphrodite* and *Eros* constitute a reverential hymn to music, mathematics and sex, and a lament for the Western disease of suppressing such joys that first broke out in ancient Athens, only to spread among the Romans and become a roaring contagion among the Christians. (The homecoming in this odyssey was to occur in the last volume dedicated to the digital era.) Kittler celebrates the primal unity of music, mathematics and love as it arose in the Sirens' voices.

The tone of piety and gushing enthusiasm is only one of many surprises awaiting readers familiar with Kittler's previous work. In some ways an abrupt shift in tone and topic, *Aphrodite* and *Eros* nonetheless continue Kittler's life-long interest in music, and more particularly, in the privileged relationship that sound, whose essence Hegel said is to vanish (Kittler, 'Real Time Analysis' 182), has to being and time. There are several other ties with his earlier work, including his fabled crotchetiness. Though these strange, fascinating books defy full summary or appreciation, my aim here is to situate them in the context of Kittler's thought, sketch their argument, and assess their contributions to media theory. How I wish he were still around to contest or at least ignore my interpretation!

Musik und Mathematik poses a puzzle for Kittler's international reputation. In English-language scholarship his name has probably never been bigger. The recent collection *Critical Terms for Media Studies* (Mitchell and Hansen), for instance, bears a strong Kittler imprint but shows only the most minimal engagement with his two recent books. In the German-speaking world, *Musik und Mathematik* has been met largely with bafflement, scorn or neglect. German *Medienwissenschaftler* (media scholars) can be astonished at the figure Kittler cuts abroad, knowing all too intimately his foibles and quirks. In the 1980s and 1990s, Kittler was an absolutely central player in German media studies; his blockbuster book *Aufschreibesysteme: 1800/1900* (1985; translated as *Discourse Networks*) in many ways founded that field. The psychedelic, wry, ultra-hip 'punk Germanist' of yore lives on in English-language scholarship, but is hardly to be found in the earnest, oracular, rhapsodic voice of *Musik und Mathematik*. Such reputational discrepancies, of course, are not unusual in intellectual life. In both intellectual and organic evolution, the closer you get to the point of origin, the more intense the competition and more variegated the gene pool. Many German media scholars regard Kittler as having gone off the deep end in his late years, and his most sympathetic critics, such as Hans Ulrich Gumbrecht, David Wellbery and Geoffrey Winthrop-Young, tend to have one foot in, one foot out of German-language debates. In Kittler's case, distance focuses.

Critics have pointed to three main objections. First, the project proposes a retrograde vision of Europe. The quest for origins in the purity of ancient 'Hellas' replays a German obsession with Greece that goes back to the late eighteenth century. Though this fascination inspired diverse political visions ranging from Schiller to Marx to Nietzsche, Kittler's Greece fits in a particular conservative lineage linked to the later Heidegger, to whom Kittler loudly swore his fealty in his later years. Greece for both thinkers is the *Ursprung* (origin) of the *Abendland* (West; lit. 'evening land'). Kittler's Hellas is anything but multicultural – Phoenicians, Egyptians, Jews, Babylonians play little role – and he implicitly disdains both the free-trade, multicultural Europe coming out of Brussels, and the Europe of non-renewable Judaeo-Christian moral resources endorsed by both Pope Benedict XVI and Jürgen

Habermas. Instead, European history is a cover-up of the *Ursprung*. We have to return to the ever-renewable 'recursive' resources found in Greece before its ruinous *Übersetzung* (translation) into Rome (Heidegger; Hörl). This translation was an *über-setzen* – a 'setting over' – that made the West oblivious to Being. While Heidegger's legacy also ranges wildly across the political spectrum, Kittler follows the would-be-Hellene who speaks in gnomic incantations based on the writings of the pre-Socratic philosophers and the poetry of Friedrich Hölderlin. Though this dialect can be very evocative, it can also seem a rather lofty mode of circumnavigating history. Heidegger's fourfold relation among mortals, gods, heaven and earth can seem a retreat from more ordinary clarity about politics and ethics. Habermas, for instance, whom Kittler long regarded as a sworn enemy, has since the 1950s criticized Heidegger for not coming into the light of responsible public communication and sees Heidegger's poetics of Being as complicit with his unmastered Nazi past. With his Graeco-German reveries and tainted rhetorics Kittler stepped on many toes with a seemingly gleeful political incorrectness, as Breger and Winthrop-Young (52–81) demonstrate.

The second issue is the curious scholarship. The erudition is massive and the mastery of primary texts and secondary literature is very impressive. Kittler's original translations from the Greek, sometimes from excruciatingly difficult texts such as Sophoclean odes, show great facility and seem free of Ezra Pound-like howlers (though this, like much else, awaits expert evaluation). *Musik und Mathematik* wears its learning like a frigate bird, providing original texts in Greek, Latin, German, French, English, Italian and Spanish. He seems to have read everything. From the massive book-learning to the veneration of the Greeks as the alpha point, the project is resolutely retro. Rather like Heinrich Schliemann, who excavated the site of ancient Troy from the 1870s, Kittler wants to localize Homer. He claims to have discovered the Sirens' island and recreated their song experimentally with modern singers; like Wagner, he takes his myths seriously. *Aphrodite* and *Eros* include extended quotations – long a hallmark of Kittler's practice – from some of Hellas's greatest hits, with the original Greek typically followed by Kittler's '*Verdeutschung*' (German translation). The books are the quirky record of a late-life classical education. Though his readings are often highly original, the canon remains largely intact. There is little source criticism of his Greek scriptures, let alone a deconstructive scepticism about textuality or authorship. Kittler is certainly no more a humanist than he ever was, but his edgy post-structuralism has given way to something else; Larson Powell calls him 'a born-again logocentric' (98). Kittler proclaims the Gospel of musical-mathematical erotic bliss.

If there is little palaeographic self-reflection, there is plenty of bickering. Kittler can be as vituperative and foul-tempered in his polemics as a church father. The footnotes are Schmittian musterings into friends and enemies. John Winkler is hot, Wilamowitz is not (*Aphrodite* 158), and the latter, a giant of classical philology, is one of many classicists Kittler sees as accomplices in the cover-up (Wilamowitz wins further demerits for having bashed Nietzsche). Not only classical scholars and monks, whom Kittler blames for mutilating the historical transmission of Greece by book-burning and prudishness, but many pillars of the Western canon are the targets of Kittler's ire. Socrates is 'the fool from Attica' (a label taken from Cicero with evident relish), 'the clueless one', 'the chatterbox' or 'the Pederast'; Romans and Christians are 'dense' (*dumm*). Isaac Newton is feeble-minded (recycling an insult from Goethe), Karl Marx and Ludwig Feuerbach are numb-skulls (*Dummköpfe*), Jacob Burckhardt cries his blindness to the heavens, Max Horkheimer and Theodor W. Adorno are 'hobby philosophers', Habermas is 'unspeakably unlearned' and Jacques Derrida, Kittler wickedly claims, only consults the Greek text in case of emergency (*Eros* 100). Even Foucault, another late-life student of sex in ancient Hellas, gets spanked occasionally for not getting it right.[1] For an advocate of love, Kittler rarely handles enemy combatants gently. The criterion for sorting the sheep and the goats is the primal unity of music, mathematics and love: Jim Morrison of The Doors gets it, Habermas doesn't. (It is hard to imagine Habermas inciting a throng of Florida concert-goers to engage in a sexual orgy as Morrison did, an event Kittler approves of.) The 'truth' is more important than the facts. Lightning flashes of insight take precedence over historical contextualization; poets are as likely as classicists to be called in for explanatory duties. As

Gumbrecht suggests, Kittler is best read as a mythographer in the Wagnerian mould. His grand tale is the structural transformation of the pubic sphere.

Third, the style is odd – nothing new for Kittler. There are times when one has little clue about what is going on or what logic connects one chunk of exposition to the next, despite the intricately numbered outline which includes, for instance, the key section 2.2.2.2.2.2. Kittler still enjoys zingy one-liners, and his German fortunately tends towards fragments and condensation rather than long-windedness and syntactic sprawl. Kittler can be aphoristic and poetic, and, like Wagner, can have some great moments. He loves to juxtapose snippets and allusions in the spirit of T. S. Eliot, another Wagner-inspired mythographer with whom Kittler shares a method (learned montage) and a theme (sexual degeneration in the West) but not an outlook (Eliot saw the only salvation in the Church). Kittler might not recognize Eliot as a forebear, but Lacan, whom he does recognize, loved Eliot and practised the art of erudite allusion constantly, and there is plenty of learned perplexity and modernist hinting in *Musik und Mathematik*.

A particular interpretative challenge comes from the regular but apparently random interruptions of the exposition by apostrophes to a woman who is Kittler's (or at least the authorial) beloved. In the first book, the unnamed addressee may be Aphrodite, and in antiquity, interrupting the textual flow now and then to invoke the patron or deity was common (as in Saint Augustine's *Confessions*). By the second book, the mystery lady seems a long-time lover, a latter-day Diotima to his Hölderlin. We learn about their travels, meals and shopping in Greece, overhear some pillow talk, and learn what German dialect she speaks, among many other things. Though lyric poetry calls to an absent other and the modern novel emerges from letters turned public (especially love letters), readers might be surprised to find Kittler the author rather than analyst of such practices. That he includes such intimate communications shows what a fiercely proud project this is. Kittler doesn't care what anyone thinks – he is moved by *mania* (madness) and *philautia* (pride). His contempt for notions of *Öffentlichkeit* (the public sphere) extends to his literary practice. The narrator is always 'we', whether from royal pretention or from collective claim, or perhaps

inclusion of his lady-love (cf. *Aphrodite* 307). The mode is that of
a devotee who reveres the gods indifferent to the milling crowd.
These books are written from intoxication and, indeed, manifest
the double toll of drunkenness: heights of divine inspiration and
fist-fights about trifles.

Despite – and sometimes perhaps thanks to – these challenges,
I think the books are worth the trouble. The project is definitely
not mad, or rather, it *is* mad, in the inspired sense: music and
mathematics are both at the very heart of the human condition;
music is a human universal and mimes the emotions more directly
than any other art form; and it is a cliché to observe that digital
media are, in their guts, mathematics (zeroes and ones). Moreover,
you don't have to buy into the Heideggerian filter to think that
the ancient Greeks are pretty interesting. Kittler has once again
provided us with a rich archive for grappling with media by offering fresh readings of texts that have ossified into classics, much
as he did in his earliest forays into German literature at the time
of Goethe. He is the latest in a tradition of ancient Greek media
studies in which we might place such scholars as Milman Parry,
Harold Innis, Eric Havelock, Jesper Svenbro, Deborah Steiner,
Simon Goldhill, John Miles Foley and Barry Powell. The Greeks
are a well-studied bunch and they can tell us a lot about how to
write the media histories of other cultures that have not reaped
equivalent scholarly attention. Any project so ambitious on a topic
of such inherent interest from a thinker so provocative deserves the
benefit of the doubt.

Musik und Mathematik is an old man's work, as the late, much-
missed Cornelia Vismann once noted in conversation. Late work
is often hard to interpret. Beethoven, Heidegger, Wittgenstein,
Stravinsky and Foucault all made late turns that left their followers gasping. (You at least have to admire Kittler's willingness to
destroy his fan base.) Long after his career was made Kittler dove
into something new and dangerous. The project is ambitious,
interdisciplinary, original, feisty to the point of prickliness, outra-
geous, erudite, weird, tender, sentimental, self-indulgent, gutsy,
flamboyant, philologically expert, intensely personal, strung out
and packed with interesting stuff. It sets a high bar for a would-be
interpreter. One must be able to manage all the major European

languages, ancient and modern musical theory, mathematics, philosophy, literature and much more. I believe it will be some time before we know what to do with *Musik und Mathematik*; it takes time to build the right readers for texts like this.

The Books

Early McLuhan was interested in the history of the trivium, but late Kittler was interested in the history of the quadrivium. McLuhan dedicated his 1943 dissertation to the study of grammar, rhetoric and dialectic, whereas *Musik und Mathematik* concerns music, arithmetic, geometry and astronomy, the four sister disciplines first grouped together by Kittler's new hero Archytas and later dubbed the *quadrivium* by Boethius. Both media theorists fight against our tendency to produce smokescreens and alibis that keep us from seeing our technical conditioning: McLuhan calls us 'somnambulists', invoking the Greek myth of Narcissus to explain our media-narcosis, and Kittler declares that no discourse network lets itself be laid bare while it prevails (*Eros* 160). But otherwise the two media theorists part company, as their preferences for the trivium and quadrivium suggest. McLuhan complains that Descartes, mathematics and the printing press wrecked the unity of our sensorium, but Kittler complains that the humanities forgot how to count, embracing the delusion that they had no need to calculate (*Aphrodite* 220). *Au contraire*: 'For the humanities there is nothing nontechnical to teach and research' (Kittler, 'Universities' 251). His story about the fate of the humanities is not one of violation by *technē* but rather one of the crippling divorce of the technical-mathematical from the beautiful. Technology does not sunder subjects from objects; it yokes humans and things together dangerously, that is, productively (Kittler, 'Lightning and Series' 72). The humanities – and humans – are nothing without mathematics. The arts of song, poetry and dance all rest on measure, metre and number. It is counting, as anyone who has ever taken music lessons knows, that makes music such a difficult discipline. The 'tale' of our existence lies in numbers. ('Tale' once meant 'sum' and is cognate with the German *Zahl* or number.) Since the Being of mortals is in time, and time is a rhythm that we count, the twin counting (telling) arts of music and mathematics are keys to disclosing our existence.

So what does Kittler mean by music and mathematics? He takes 'mathematics' in the most existential sense. It is the most fundamental kind of learning, one that combines thinking, thanking and remembering – '*denken, danken, und gedenken*' (*Aphrodite* 15). (*Mathēma* in modern Greek means 'lesson'.) Kittler follows the Pythagoreans in seeing mathematics as the science of the elements of Being, a science that consists in counting and measurement, arithmetic and geometry. (So does sex: three plus two makes one, a point Kittler belabours in his discussion of the *tetraktys*, a Pythagorean device.) Kittler defines music with similar scope: it is the art of the Muses, that which records all things. Like arithmetic, which Kittler sees emerging from the art of weaving (*Aphrodite* 71), music comes from female sources – Sirens, nymphs, Muses and goddesses. The Sirens and their song are central to *Aphrodite*; for Kittler their combined erotic and musical allure sets the gold standard for music: 'the singing of the Sirens promises us mortals the ultimate most beautiful thing in the world: knowledge that is simultaneously music' (*Aphrodite* 241). Aphrodite, as the books often remind us, is the mother of Harmonia, a term that first meant joining, as in ship-building (*Aphrodite* 70) or, of course, intercourse. Already we spot three long-standing themes in Kittler's work: that sound and especially music have a special way of revealing the relation of Being and time; that apparently minute changes in the infrastructures of cultural storage and transmission have far-reaching effects; and that such effects include not only our eyes, ears and nervous systems but also our erotic organs.

Kittler's subject in *Musik und Mathematik* is what he calls '*Seinsgeschichte*', the history of Being. Being is disclosed in practices, algorithms and programs. Kittler revels in a certain kind of simple-mindedness – we might use Bertolt Brecht's term '*plumpes denken*' (crude thought) if the two figures were not otherwise so different – that hunts for obvious, literal, explanations: *Klartext*, as he likes to say. He loves to introduce thinkers, for instance, by their father's occupations: Heidegger, we learn, was the son of a sexton, that is, a man responsible for upkeep of a church, including the ringing of bells and digging of graves. Kittler implies a certain paternal legacy in Heidegger's preoccupations. The point is to offer as unfancy an explanation as possible – *schlicht* (plain) is one of Kittler's favourite words. In this push to the basic, Heidegger himself is Kittler's guide. Kittler reads Heidegger as anything but a cultural pessimist or technophobe; he is the great thinker of the infrastructures of Being. Clocks, calendars, points, lines, planes, solids, weights, measures, ploughs, shoes, typewriters, phonographs, radios, computers all contribute to what is. Apparatus is the precondition, not the corruption, of the world. Kittler likes to invoke Lacan's famous saying that 'the slightest alteration in the relation between man and the signifier [. . .] changes the whole course of history by modifying the moorings that anchor his being' (174). This dictum serves Kittler as a methodological mandate. If history is the history of apparently inconspicuous transformations in our relations to the signifier, *Seinsgeschichte* and media history are one. This means a complete revaluation of cultural history from talk to techniques, from narratives to devices. The task is to find epochal tipping points in the elements or *stoikheia* of signifying systems.

The Greek 'vowel alphabet' is the momentous shift in Being's history analysed in *Aphrodite*. The ability to write vowels brings about a tectonic shift in existential possibilities. 'AEIOU: What is that? In your, my, our ears? A pure miracle, for the world dawns. We hear that we hear. AEIOU, invented in one night' (*Aphrodite* 108). Just as Edison's phonograph made sound writable, the Greek alphabet is an all-purpose processor of cultural data. The Greek alphabet is an *Urmedium* which unites voice, sound and number (*Aphrodite* 207) and is thus the recursive prefiguration of the Turing era, in which Kittler claims all media melt into a universal digital alphabet. In accounting for the stunning cultural achievements of the ancient Greeks, Kittler sees Plato's ideas as so much blather. But a new method of writing capable of articulating vowels? Ah, there you can see and hear the world change. As usual, Kittler's analysis rests on a 'medial *a priori*' that alters materialities of communication. Building on the work of Barry Powell, Kittler argues that the Greek alphabet was invented by one man to store Homer's hexameters. Systematic vowel graphemes

were invented to represent Greek poetic metre, which scans in
intricate patterns of short and long vowels that are unwritable in
the syllabic scripts of Semitic, Linear B or Egyptian hieroglyphs.
Needless to say, scholarly debates about the why, how and when
of the Greek alphabet are very involved, and Kittler's position is
typically extreme in emphasizing a clean rupture with previous
writing practices. 'Wine, women, and song' were the mothers of
invention (*Aphrodite* 113), not trade or politics. (He thus defends
his beloved Greek alphabet from the ignoble political-economic
motives to which scholars typically attribute the emergence of new
writing systems.) Among the many women he has in mind are the
Sirens of the *Odyssey*, and Sappho, the inventor of vowels, which
yoke letters together into connubial bliss (in this he follows Anne
Carson). The alphabet emancipated beautiful female voices to bear
truth: 'Being is Knowing, and Knowing Being. Goddesses express
what was, what is, and what will be. Since the vowel alphabet has
been unconcealed, truth resounds from women's voices' (*Aphrodite*
225).

For Kittler the greatness of the vowel alphabet lies not only in
its ability to represent the sung or spoken voice. It is also a system
for storing and processing numbers and musical notes. The Greek
alphabet was a 'writing system for sounds, numbers and notes'
(*Eros* 29). He celebrates the first recursive script. Convergence
between media platforms thus came not only late in history, but
early. For Kittler, an alphabet must both represent all the vocal
sounds of a language and maintain an invariant order among letters
(*Aphrodite* 115). An alphabet must rank its elements ordinally:
alpha is always first, beta second, gamma third, etc. The alphabet's invariant order makes it usable as a system for representing
numbers. Lacking numerals, the letters of the alphabet represented
numbers: alpha is 1, beta is 2, gamma is 3, etc. (In 'Number and
Numeral', Kittler reminds us that numbers and numerals are not the
same.) The vowel alphabet was secondarily a device of arithmetic
calculation.

Third, with the Pythagorean discovery that musical tones can
be represented as ratios between numbers, the vowel alphabet was
also a kind of musical notation. A *logos* meant a ratio between two
numbers: 1:1 is the unison, 2:1 an octave, 3:2 a perfect fifth, 4:3

a perfect fourth, and so on. Thus on a stringed instrument, fret-
ting a string at its precise midpoint will produce a note that is one
octave higher than the open string (2:1). (Every violinist's fingers
implicitly reproduce Pythagorean ratios.) Writing 'delta to gamma'
(4:3) or 'gamma to beta' (3:2) thus denotes tones. (Exotic as this
practice may seem, we still name notes by letters, A to G, and
the Germans use H and S as well.) While medieval and modern
Europe had to make do with three non-communicating systems
for words, numbers and sounds – Roman letters, Hindu-Arabic
numerals, and musical notation – the ancient Greeks combined
all three in one (*Aphrodite* 207). The Greek alphabet liberated and
recorded the harmonies within poetry, numbers and music, but it
also embodied the harmony between them; it enabled the singing
and stringing of Being. In turn, this cosmic harmony was a vast
mimesis of 'how the gods sleep with each other' (*Aphrodite* 285).
All music, says Kittler, is an imitation of the gods, 'and the gods
made love'. (Jimi Hendrix as much as Hölderlin serves as Kittler's
gateway to the dead Greeks.) Orgasm is the music of the spheres.

Kittler proudly acknowledges his debts to Nietzsche and
Heidegger – who Winthrop-Young quips (110) might almost be
considered co-authors of *Musik und Mathematik*. To Nietzsche's
narrative that something marvellous (music) and something awful
(Socrates) occurred in ancient Greece, and Heidegger's story that
the pre-Socratics were the first to hear the mystic rumblings of
Being, Kittler adds at least two original touches: mathematics
and Aphrodite. Pythagoras offers a way to re-establish Europe
after a long Roman-Christian deviation that supposedly prized
neither music nor mathematics. Kittler styles himself his disciple
and, following an ancient custom, refers to Pythagoras throughout
as 'HE'. Pythagoras, whose name means something like 'disclo-
sure of the oracular', was the first to hear the music of Being.
For Kittler as for Heisenberg, the Pythagorean discovery of the
numerical structure of harmony was one of the most consequential in history. Pythagoras discovered the existential hum, the
'*Rauschen*' or rustling at the heart of all things, and taught us that
our ears are buzzing with love (*Aphrodite* 235ff). (One of Socrates'
or Plato's several crimes was to shift the organ of love to the eye.)
Without Pythagoras, hardly anything that matters would have ever

happened (*Eros* 214). Kittler is not concerned to sort out the large measure of legend and obfuscation around this mysterious figure, relying heavily on Iamblichus, a Neo-Platonist who lived over eight centuries after Pythagoras. Kittler celebrates the instruments of the Pythagoreans – the *tetraktys* and *kithara* – as 'epistemic things' (a term borrowed from Hans-Jörg Rheinberger's work on the history of scientific instrumentation). The *kithara*, source of our word for guitar, was a lyre or lute, and the *tetraktys* (pictured here) consisted of ten stones that revealed mystic harmonic, arithmetic and sexual relations.

The first book concludes by introducing a new hero, Archytas, a late Pythagorean contemporary of Plato, and the apparent model for Plato's philosopher-king. In Archytas, Kittler espies an ancient analogue to his beloved Renaissance artist-engineers such as Leon Battista Alberti, Filippo Brunelleschi, Albrecht Dürer and Simon Stevin (Stevin is explicitly compared with Archytas). Archytas lived at once as a musician, philosopher and strategist, was the first experimentalist, invented percussion as a musical form (including the baby's rattle), combined geometry and strategy in the field of mechanics, was the progenitor of all engineers, and has the honour of being the first person in history to be called a mathematician. He went beyond the Pythagorean interest in music alone and studied sound and even noise as such, thus founding the field of acoustics. Acoustics had a strong bond with ballistics (Kittler claims that musical notions of 'sharp' and 'flat' come from projectiles launched from catapults), and Kittler milks this link throughout the book. (If he has shifted from war to love as his main focus, he still loves to find military origins for technical innovations.) The bow – as lyre, as catapult – is a central device in *Aphrodite*. In a characteristic sentence, he describes Odysseus' vengeance against Penelope's suitors: 'Struck by the arrows of his bow, the suitors fall loud and hard to the ground, but the bowstring itself sings as beautifully as a swallow' (*Aphrodite* 323). The act of stringing a bow, whether to kill or make music, also has a strong sexual sense for Kittler; *tonos* (tone) comes from *teino*, meaning to stretch, spread or span (*Aphrodite* 50, 85, 256). Indeed, throughout *Aphrodite* and *Eros*, Kittler leaves no sexual etymology untickled.

Aphrodite ends with an axial choice: two compatriots, both of whom served the king of Syracuse. Plato offered philosophy, packaged into written dialogues and utopian books like the *Republic*; Archytas offered science and engineering, couched in short, clear propositions that could be demonstrated with mathematical rigour. Plato won, at least with the philosophers, and sent the history of the West down the wrong path. Plato misunderstood how numbers dwell mimetically with mortals. For him all the real circles we make on earth were but fake versions of the ideal ones. Thus Plato pulls the rug out from under everything beautiful: 'For our dances, round-dances, nights of love there is no more ground' (*Aphrodite* 334). But Archytas anticipates those who write and program (*Aphrodite* 335). As always, Kittler favours a counterhistory of those who make the algorithms (and 'hardly anything is more algorithmic than music'; *Eros* 213).

Eros takes up where *Aphrodite* ends, with Athens wrecking everything. Athens tears *mathēsis* (learning) from the Muses and turns sex into chastity: 'Athenian inanity knows no bounds' (1.2:50). If Kittler loves Pythagoras, Sappho and greater Greece, he hates Athens for its treatment of women. Though he knows all the scholarship on Greek homosexuality, Kittler is no queer theorist, marking one of his sharpest contrasts with Foucault: the shift away from heterosexual coupling is part of his *Verfallsgeschichte* (narrative of decline). Athens banished Aphrodite, preferring the chaste Athena (whom Kittler calls a fake virgin). In contrast to Sparta, which Kittler praises at length – it is a city always dear to counterculturalists – Athens excluded women both from the most sacred religious rites and from schools. The illness starts with Euripides, whom Nietzsche derided as the murderer of tragedy and art. Kittler ratchets up the diagnosis: Euripides was the first misogynist, a proto-Christian, the inventor of pornography and illegitimacy, and of faith, hope and the guilty conscience (among many other notions later 'plagiarized' by Paul of Tarsus). Having dispatched

Euripides, Kittler piles onto Socrates. Socrates knows nothing of
art, stops his ears before women's voices, doesn't write because he
probably doesn't know how, can't do mathematics and does not
play the guitar. He invents meaning as a mental entity, and even
invents the definite article, *to kalon* (the beautiful), instead of taking
a young woman naturally as the most beautiful thing (*Eros* 106).
In a primal cover-up, Socrates explains the origin of music and the
alphabet in the *Phaedrus* without any mathematical knowledge,
attributing them to the Egyptian Thoth as if Pythagoras had never
existed. In a typical illuminating reorientation, Kittler's interest
in the last days of Socrates is not in his notion of the immortality
of the soul, but in his efforts to learn to compose poetry and play
music. Here Kittler spots a collision of tectonic plates in the history
of Being, with Socrates finally embracing in a kind of deathbed
repentance the things that made Greece so special: music, poetry
and mathematics. At Socrates' death the music of greater Greece
also breathes its last.

We can predict how Plato will fare at Kittler's hand: Plato
moves music and mathematics to the sky, where they remain for
another sixteen hundred years. Metaphysics is a form of cow-
ardice; it marks a cosmos without music; it is a forgetfulness that
always points to music and mathematics without being about to
think them (*Eros* 139, 129, 164). The Pythagoreans embodied
music in epistemic things – 'machines saturated by number' (*Eros*
213) such as the lyre, bow and *kithara* – and not in the heavens,
but Plato's music is left without a body, thoroughly stripped of
its ties to the arts of Aphrodite. Aristotle is treated with more
nuance. For one thing, Kittler cannot but admire his sobriety and
precision. Though Aristotle is a refugee from numbers, he understands mimesis and has a residual or crypto-Pythagorean streak.
Aristotle's conception of humans as '*logos*-animals' means that the
ears remain our most important organ; his conception of language
sees us as imitative animals who imitate each other's imitations,
thus making the *polis* a 'phonomimetic' community. (Aristotle is
thus favoured as one who understands Heidegger's '*mitsein*'.) In
Aristotle's school, drawing is optional but music is required. Of all
of Aristotle's lost books it is not those of the *Poetics*, as Umberto
Eco's *Name of the Rose* suggests, but the *Metrics* and the *Symmetrics*

that Kittler wishes we possessed. So far so good: Aristotle sees us mortals as tied together through the sounds, words and music that come through our ears, which provide our unique capacities for learning. But the deviation lies in Aristotle's concept of analogy without arithmetic. Relations among diverse things are metaphorical instead of mathematical. Aristotle's notion of analogy fosters a kind of metaphorical thinking that launches a bad split between the spiritual and the sensual. Metaphor bids farewell to numerical ratios, and ushers in the disenchantments of Christianity and mere literature; ontology is left without mathematics; music is gutted of algorithms.

The rest of *Eros* chronicles the decline. Aristoxenus, the supposed founder of musicology, is actually the one who cements it in its a-mathematical stupor. Like Socrates and Plato, he is commonly praised as the origin when he is actually the decadent preserver of a mistake. The Sirens fall from grace, and the gods start to live in the real like animals or humans, while the 'logos' of the Gospel of John ascends triumphantly into the Christian heaven (*Eros* 263, 276). Mortals no longer imitate the gods in their love-making; they imitate the birds and the bees, and become obsessed with virginal bleeding, blending sex and injury. How the mighty are fallen!

Questions

Many questions remain, and I ask but a few. How to situate this venture in Kittler's corpus? The tone may be new, but the themes are not. *Musik und Mathematik* descends most clearly from *Gramophone, Film, Typewriter* – a book that endorsed mating with the dead as reading the ancients, and included a story from Maurice Renard about a seashell that holds the Sirens' voices (Kittler, *Gramophone* 8, 51). Even more, that book equates sexy women and music in several images (not to be found in the English translation due to copyright troubles, much to Kittler's dismay), such as the soft-core cover of Jimi Hendrix's *Electrical Ladyland* LP or the image inside both covers showing the pubic

powering of a turntable. The climactic spot in the acknowledge-
ments to *Gramophone, Film, Typewriter* is 'Agia Galini', a village
on the southern coast of Crete whose name comes from Galēnaiē,
'the goddess of the quiet sea' (*Aphrodite* 49), that is, Aphrodite.
The themes of *Musik und Mathematik* were there all along, like the
sounds in Renard's shell, but the more recent books amplify their
faint signals. Aphrodite has long presided over Kittler's texts.

Are the Greeks as interesting if they don't play an axial role?
Once you reject, as I do, the view that the Greeks are history's
chosen people for revealing Being, what remains? The Greeks
still have plenty to offer to the history of media, as does the field
of classical studies, but deserve to be placed in a more comparative frame. Kittler slights the ancient Hebrews, for instance, in
part because they weren't much on mathematics – he mocks the
biblical account of the building of Solomon's temple for treating
'pi' and '3' as equivalents (*Aphrodite* 262). But the Jews did have
a lively vision of sexuality and of song. The prophets denounced
Aphrodite-like idols, but they didn't denounce sex: the anti-
sex animus in Western thought is the legacy of Athens, not of
Jerusalem. No tradition ever quite celebrated fertility as vigorously as the rabbinical – but it saved Aphrodite for the marriage
bed. Though Kittler would surely disapprove of ordering sex by
patriarchal law, taking account of the Jewish tradition would make
the story very different. For my part, I want no part of a Western
world without a Hebraic element; its absence here is telling (if not
alarming). Kittler mentions the Indians occasionally but they too
would nuance his story. In the Sanskrit tradition the discipline of
grammar – the queen of all sciences – is always described in sexual
terms. Polytheistic Hinduism was generally frank about sexuality and free of the neuroses infesting the West. '*Om mani padme
hum*' – hail the jewel in the lotus: the erotic implications of this
mantra would surely please Kittler. Other literatures of the subcon-
tinent celebrated dance, number and sexuality as much as did the
Sanskrit. In China, Confucius considered music central to a well-
ordered state, but quite without the phallogocentrism of the West.
Other cultures could be added. Or why not draw on evolutionary
biology's interest in the role of song and sound in attracting mates
and defending territory? Voice, song, dance and rhythm play a role

in sexual reproduction in many species besides the human (indeed, birds and bees). Wouldn't this approach put Kittler's triad of love, war and music onto even deeper footings?[2] In response to these and other alternative stories, Kittler would probably defend the uniqueness of Greeks as the only ones who made algorithms out of music, put mating songs into a form that can be stored, transmitted and processed, and mimed the gods with numbers. The singularity of the Greek technical achievement is attested in the fact that most languages still use the Greek terms *music* and *mathematics* for these fundamental practices. By any standard the ancient Greeks did do amazing things, and Kittler is onto something relevant in the age of the human genome – the algorithmic character of life itself.

How much of a roadblock are Kittler's metapolitical and rhetorical antics? *Caveat lector*, as always, but I do not think Kittler's theory is a package deal with his politics or postures. Indeed, media theory, like critical-cultural theory in general, has had to become quite good at coping with retrograde politics and grandiose gestures. One of the specialities of the field is the art of reading crafty conservatives critically but profitably, as shown by such masters of the genre as Walter Benjamin (reading Jung, Ludwig Klages or Schmitt), Derrida (reading Heidegger or Schmitt) or Raymond Williams (reading Edmund Burke, Matthew Arnold or D. H. Lawrence). None of these readers gave troubling texts a free pass, but all were willing to do considerable work for the sake of quality of mind. McLuhan readers have to bushwhack through jungles of outrageousness to get at the mineral deposits. Innis' oil seems available only by fracking. Kittler is one in a long line of media and cultural theorists who require and repay creative reading.

What of Kittler and gender? He is an enthusiastic lover of women, but his love has its limits. Kittler's a feminist when the women are young, sexy and great singers, or Sirens, Muses and nymphs; when it's a bus of elderly women tourists unloading at Delphi or a name that sounds like mother's milk – horrors! (*Eros* 39; *Aphrodite* 202). Women, like music itself, are subject to a sustained idealization. (Indeed, we never get any sense of what Greek music actually sounded like; it might as well be Pink Floyd.) Sex, for that matter, is also idealized. (Isn't there such a thing as bad music or bad sex?) The idea that Greece could ever have been a sexual paradise requires amazing powers of concentration.[3] The ability to ignore a significant chunk of human experience takes a certain kind of genius. John Stuart Mill, the author who coined the term 'patriarchy' (a term for which Kittler seems to have little use), praised 'one-eyed men' for the special vision they can achieve: 'Almost all rich veins of original and striking speculation have been opened by systematic half-thinkers' (351). Kittler's one-eyed defence of the goddess and her sweet ways is inspiring, perhaps even arousing, but completely unsustainable. It is joyfully one-sided. You won't find much in *Musik und Mathematik* about rape, jealousy, menses, morning sickness, the pains and dangers of childbirth, nursing or toilet-training. (These are not facts that the Christians made up!) Kittler's praise of *Liebesnächte* seeks to provide the strong poetry he berates the post-Hellenic West for having forgotten, with its greater concern for the morning after. Kittler is doubtless a systematic half-thinker of the first rank. Certainly much of what the Romans and Christians said about sex was destructive and one-sided, but it had some empirical basis: sex does have consequences. As one of the greatest of all whole-thinkers said, '[t]he idea of love sinks to mere edification if it lacks the seriousness, the pain, the patience, and labour of the negative' (Hegel, 20). Recursion for Kittler means not only looping back in a 'meta-' way, but ever-renewable resources; it means that every kiss should be like the first. His notion of love lacks the labour of the negative.

Kittler can have an uncanny resemblance to D. H. Lawrence, another cranky pro-sex visionary. Lawrence modelled sex protoplasmically on the elephants, and Kittler mathematically on the gods, but both want it free of the unhappy consciousness, like Adam and Eve before the serpent showed up. The question in reading both writers is whether their tender lechery should be taken as female-friendly or macho phallophilia. Kittler likes the technical but not the social processing of sex. He laments that the Christians invented an institution of marriage requiring mediators – priests and witnesses. Here again, the public sphere be damned. For my part, I think love sometimes *should* involve third parties. It's the only way to assure a bulwark against the abuses that so readily sneak into romance. Fidelity requires the thirdness of law, a check against the fickleness of our hearts. Romantics sometimes think two are enough for love, but the apple has already long been eaten. The discovery that love and sex implicate power, history and ethics is not a fall from Aphrodite's paradise, but a step forward into decency and responsibility. (Kittler might have called me a 'US-Puritan' for this: *Eros* 66.) To say so might be boring, but that does not make it untrue. Sex as justice is a more urgent task than sex as beauty. (To take love as the aesthetic instead of the ethical, as Kierkegaard showed, is the attitude of the seducer.) Nature or the grace of the gods have already seen to sexual beauty in all its excessive abundance, but the gods – even the Greek ones – gave people laws as well.

In the end, what we have in *Musik und Mathematik* is religious warfare. Kittler uses monotheistic weapons against those who do not see the polytheistic splendour of Greece's vision of love. He fought as ferociously as a deuteronomist for the true god(dess). He calls monotheism idiotic, and sees it as the source of the world's disastrous political situation (*Eros* 231ff), but his pantheon does not have room for Aphrodite and Athena both, let alone any other deities. Monotheism in large part is about gender differentiation, that is, patriarchy, and Kittler is forever belatedly coming after, seeking a primal polymorphous perversity. How should we understand a polytheist iconoclast, an Aphrodite-worshipper who fights like a Protestant image-smasher? As Kate Southworth noted in conversation, Kittler takes a phallic approach to the feminine, and you can't get there from here. The 'matrixial' remains inaccessible. The message of *Musik und Mathematik* is to enjoy the full pleasures of love, mathematics and music without corruption. The medium of the books, however, is, as always, wiser and clearer than their message: Kittler's garden of earthly delights is full not only of roses but also of thorns and thistles. His gospel of love comes wrapped in a sometimes caustic package – a phenomenon not unknown in the history of monotheism. The rapid cycling between pettiness and grandeur in Kittler's texts reveals what he doesn't acknowledge: that the effort to imagine loving like the gods remains tethered by our most ungodlike conditions. The emancipation of love requires an ethical and social theory, not only a technical one; even more, it requires an ethical and social practice that few seem able to manage. Some heavenly airs and arias waft through *Musik und*

Mathematik and I am always tempted to linger awhile by their beauty. But the bile that occasionally spouts up warns of other fates that might await those who heed the songs of the Sirens.

Notes

For comments, criticism, correction and inspiration I am grateful to Amit Pinchevski, Alexander Rehding, Stephen Sale, Kate Southworth, Katie Trumpener and Geoffrey Winthrop-Young.

1 For a comparison of Foucault's and Kittler's Greek projects, see Breger (120–30) and Winthrop-Young (106–7).

2 See Hartshorne.

3 Anyone who thinks of Greece like this should read Storace.

Works Cited

Breger, Claudia. 'Gods, German Scholars, and the Gift of Greece: Friedrich Kittler's Philhellenic Fantasies.' *Theory, Culture & Society* 23.7–8 (2006): 111–34.

Carson, Anne. *Eros the Bittersweet*. Princeton, NJ: Princeton University Press, 1986.

Gumbrecht, Hans Ulrich. 'Friedrich Kittler setzt seinen Roman übers abendländische Denken fort.' *Frankfurter Allgemeine Zeitung* 18 November 2009.

Hartshorne, Charles. *Born to Sing: An Interpretation and World Survey of Bird Song*. Bloomington: Indiana University Press, 1973.

Hegel, Georg Wilhelm Friedrich. *Phänomenologie des Geistes*. Hamburg: Meiner, 1952.

Heidegger, Martin. *Der Ursprung des Kunstwerkes*. Stuttgart: Reclam, 1960.

Heisenberg, Werner. 'Die Bedeutung des Schönen in der Exakten Naturwissenchaft.' *Quantentheorie und Philosophie: Vorlesungen und Aufsätze*. Ed. Jürgen Busche. Stuttgart: Reclam, 1979. 91–114.

Hörl, Erich. 'Heidegger und die Römer.' *Römisch*. Ed. Walter Seitter and Cornelia Vismann. Berlin and Zurich: Diaphanes, 2006. 103–10.

Kierkegaard, Søren. 'The Seducer's Diary.' *Either/Or*. Trans. Howard V. Hong and Edna H. Hong. Princeton, NJ: Princeton University Press, 1987. 301–445.

Kittler, Friedrich A. *Discourse Networks 1800/1900*. Trans. Michael Metteer with Chris Cullens. Stanford: Stanford University Press, 1990.

Kittler, Friedrich A. 'Real Time Analysis, Time Axis Manipulation.' *Draculas Vermächtnis: Technische Schriften*. Leipzig: Reclam, 1993. 182–207.

Kittler, Friedrich A. *Gramophone, Film, Typewriter*. Trans. Geoffrey Winthrop-Young and Michael Wutz. Stanford: Stanford University Press, 1999.

Kittler, Friedrich A. 'Universities: Wet, Hard, Soft, and Harder.' *Critical Inquiry* 31.1 (2004): 244–55.

Kittler, Friedrich A. 'Lightning and Series: Event and Thunder.' Trans. Geoffrey Winthrop-Young. *Theory, Culture & Society* 23.7–8 (2006): 63–74.

Kittler, Friedrich A. *Musik und Mathematik I: Hellas 1: Aphrodite*. Munich: Fink, 2006.

Kittler, Friedrich A. 'Number and Numeral.' *Theory, Culture & Society* 23.7–8 (2006): 51–61.

Kittler, Friedrich A. *Musik und Mathematik I: Hellas 2: Eros*. Munich: Fink, 2009.

Lacan, Jacques. *Écrits: A Selection*. Trans. A. Sheridan. New York: Norton, 1977.

Lawrence, D. H. 'The Elephant is Slow to Mate.' *Literature*. Ed. X. J. Kennedy. Boston: Little, Brown, 1976. 821.

Mill, John Stuart. *Early Essays*. London: George Bell, 1897.

Mitchell, W. J. T., and Mark B. N. Hansen, eds. *Critical Terms for Media Studies*. Chicago: University of Chicago Press, 2010.

Powell, Barry B. *Writing and the Origins of Greek Literature*. Cambridge: Cambridge University Press, 2002.

Powell, Larson. 'Musik und Mathematik: Friedrich Kittlers gegenkulturelles Deutschland.' *Musik und Ästhetik* 48 (2008): 94–100.

Storace, Patricia. *Dinner with Persephone*. New York: Pantheon, 1997.

Winthrop-Young, Geoffrey. *Kittler and the Media*. Cambridge: Polity, 2011.

3

Thinking By Numbers: The Role of Mathematics in Kittler and Heidegger

Stephen Sale

Martin Heidegger was one of the most divisive figures in the twentieth-century culture wars between the sciences and the humanities. He was deeply critical of scientific modernity and its claims to truth, which he believed to be the negation rather than the fulfilment of authentic philosophy. His arguments that scientific knowledge is reductive and partial, and that philosophy should be refounded on hermeneutic not transcendental grounds, met with strong opposition in the politically charged climate of the 1920s.[1] Following the famous Davos debate with Ernst Cassirer in 1929,[2] Heidegger's attacks on the foundations of science came to be seen as aligned with a dangerous irrationalism that sat in opposition to liberal democracy – a viewpoint consolidated after the war when his support for the Nazis (as rector of the University of Freiburg in 1933–4) cast a long shadow over his reputation. His increasingly mystical later work is generally taken to be a retreat from technological modernity into a nostalgic union of poets and craftsmen.[3]

This technophobic caricature of Heidegger contrasts sharply with the thrillingly techno-savvy figure of Friedrich Kittler, a thinker who seems equally at ease with physics and philology. As the leading proponent of German *Medienwissenschaft*, Kittler led an attempt to reconfigure academic disciplines and to bring scientific methods to bear upon the cultural objects that are often claimed as the preserve of the humanities. Yet Kittler was heavily indebted to Martin Heidegger, and his allegiance became increasingly overt towards the end of his career. Kittler is a thinker who takes seriously Heidegger's later work, seeing an ambiguity in Heidegger that opens up a more productive engagement with modern science and technology. This can come as something of a surprise to Anglo-American readers who assume that Kittler's contribution to techno-cultural theory will follow a broadly 'critical' approach more familiar in the work of continental thinkers such as Adorno, Marcuse and, indeed, Foucault.

This chapter examines the 'question concerning technology' posed by Heidegger in the post-war period and its recasting by Kittler at the end of the twentieth century. Heidegger's legacy means that this question is heavily laden with philosophical and political baggage and Kittler's role in developing it has not yet been adequately assessed. Most secondary literature has been devoted to explicating Kittler's relationship to poststructuralism (particularly Foucault and Lacan) and media theory (mainly McLuhan), but little attention has been paid to Kittler's relation to Heidegger and the German tradition. The main thread used to trace the differences between the two thinkers is their different approaches to mathematics.

Heidegger and the *Grundlagenkrise*

In the early twentieth century, mathematics was undergoing what became known as a crisis in foundations (*Grundlagenkrise*). The basic assumptions of classical mathematics had been challenged by three major developments: the discovery of non-Euclidean geometries, the introduction of imaginary elements into geometry, and Cantor's set theory. At the same time as mathematicians were trying to rethink the grounds of their practice, the neo-Kantians were trying to extract Kant's method from its imbrication with mathematical physics, which he had offered as the very paradigm of knowledge. Heidegger, who was for a period in Freiburg's mathematics faculty before moving to philosophy, was well acquainted with the intersecting debates.

In the 1920s, the leading mathematician David Hilbert was pursuing a formalist programme of axiomatization. The model for Hilbert was Euclidean geometry, which proceeded from ten basic postulates. According to Hilbert's programme, once a revised set of axioms was in place to secure its foundations, mathematics would unfold almost mechanically, with deductions then proceeding as manipulations of symbols. He believed that he could extend these foundations to ground even seemingly elusive problems such as Cantor's theory of infinite sets. When formulating the new axioms, the only part of mathematics that Hilbert took to be epistemologically secure was elementary arithmetic. Where Kant had taken arithmetic to be grounded in the spatio-temporal structure of experience, Hilbert took it more narrowly to be the structure of finite arrangements of objects: numerals (*Ziffern*). For Hilbert, at its most basic level, arithmetic was the manipulation of finite strings of strokes: 'the objects of number theory are [. . .] the signs themselves' (202). In this view, mathematics was a formal discipline, abstract, symbolic and without reference to meaning.

The main opposition to Hilbert came from the intuitionists led by Brouwer and Weyl.[4] They completely rejected axiomatics and, drawing inspiration from Husserlian phenomenology, believed that the logical principles of mathematics must conform to 'correct intuitions' about objects. Truths had to be experienced in order to be recognized. Basing their new constructions on the self-unfolding of fundamental intuitions, Brouwer and Weyl attempted to rebuild the foundations of mathematics. They viewed mathematics very much as a human activity and an accretive historical process. It composes truths rather than derives implications of logic.

Though no longer active as a mathematician, Heidegger took great interest in the philosophical implications of the crisis in mathematics. He was opposed to contemporary attempts to conceive philosophy as a kind of 'transcendental logic', notably by the Marburg School of neo-Kantianism, and thought that the *Grundlagenkrise* weakened such claims. For Heidegger, the intuitionists, following the insights of phenomenology, had shown that what was 'prima facie the most firmly established science' is shifting towards 'new and more original foundations' (*History* 3). The metaphysical assumption of science handed down by Descartes and Kant – that of the human as a self-posited and autonomous thinking substance standing opposed to a world understood as extended matter – is 'unimpeachable in its facticity' (Heidegger, *Being and Time* 86) but is irredeemably partial and leaves us in the dark ontologically. For Heidegger, mathematical research into fundamental intuition opens up questions that science had concealed for two thousand years: namely, that truth is a kind of revealing and is always relative to human existence. In his most significant early engagement with mathematics, a lecture series from 1924–5 published as *Plato's Sophist*, Heidegger argues that investigations into the nature of number serve to show that behind mathematics 'a still more original discipline is predelineated, a discipline which studies the basic constitution of beings: *Sophia*' (*Plato's Sophist* 83). Immanent crises in physics, biology, theology and history also represent advances being made 'toward an original relationship to the matters themselves' (*History* 4) and show that science must ultimately defer to philosophy. One of the tasks Heidegger sets himself in *Being and Time* is to put aside the metaphysical reductionism of modern science and elucidate a phenomenological method by which we can reintroduce the question of human existence to philosophy. In so doing, we can open ourselves up to the horizons of meaning which explicate life itself. This is Heidegger's 'fundamental ontology'.

Heidegger's Critique of 'the Mathematical'

The theme of the relationship between philosophy and science is picked up once more in the 1930s, after the so-called 'turn' where Heidegger shifted his attention away from a phenomenological analysis of the human situation towards a historical analysis of the relationship of man to 'Being' in general (*Seinsgeschichte*). In *What is a Thing?*, a lecture course given in 1935, Heidegger discusses the conceptual models employed in the sciences from the Greeks to the present. The implicit epistemological positions taken towards 'things' in Plato, Aristotle, Galileo, Newton, Leibniz and Kant are each conceived as 'the execution and consequence of the historical mode of [B]eing at that time' (Heidegger, *What is a Thing?* 96). Heidegger identifies a crucial conceptual shift as ancient and medieval science gave way to the modern: modern science is *mathematical*. The mathematical here is not numerical and Heidegger is less and less concerned with specific debates within mathematics. Rather, Heidegger identifies what he calls the 'essence of the mathematical project' (*What is a Thing?* 89).

The mathematical is, for Heidegger, who interprets the Greek *mathemata* as 'learning what one already knows', the 'fundamental presupposition of the knowledge of things'. Numbers are merely the most familiar form of the mathematical because numbers, as the expressions of the 'how much', 'are the closest to that which we recognise in things without creating it from them' (Heidegger, *What is a Thing?* 75). In the sixteenth and seventeenth centuries, modern science installed the mathematical as a determination of things that is no longer based on learned experience, as it was assumed to be for the Greeks, but is derived from a theoretical 'basic blueprint' (*Grundriss*). This axiomatic thought posits itself as the conceptual frame for the world and then begins to turn in on itself with Descartes, as the *res extensa* comes to be grounded by the *res cogitans*. The mathematical, as that which is knowable, relies upon the *cogito*.

In Heidegger's work on Nietzsche in the 1930s and then with the *Beiträge zur Philosophie (Vom Ereignis)*, translated as *Contributions to Philosophy (From Enowning)*, a treatise written in 1936–8 and first published in 1989, the theme of the mathematical is developed into a critique of calculation in an explicitly political context: the looming Second World War. Heidegger's onto-historical diagnosis of the contemporary moment was as the nihilistic culmination of European metaphysics, recognized but not overcome by Nietzsche. In Heidegger's view, humankind has forgotten its role as the 'situation-constitutors' of Being; far from being mere observers, we are active participants in the revelation of Being. In the *Beiträge*, Heidegger suggests that this forgetting of Being is the corollary of the reductive understanding of Being characteristic of the modern era. This is made manifest in the 'growing validity' of several strategies of concealment, the most important of which is 'calculation'. Calculation, as 'the basic law of [human] comportment' (Heidegger, *Contributions* 84) towards the world, is grounded in the mathematical but takes on political import as the unrestrained domination of 'machination' expands into planning, management and the organization of beings. Machination is here dependent on calculation, itself dependent on a particular way of thinking the mathematical. The sway of the mathematical as the ontological foundation of the modern era results in 'a hollowing-out of beings' (Heidegger, *Contributions* 91) and, adopting the terminology of Ernst Jünger, a technologized 'total mobilization' that ultimately leads to the devastation of Europe.

The treatment of machination in the *Beiträge* foreshadows Heidegger's better-known work on technology which he produced after the war. In 'The Question Concerning Technology' (1955) Heidegger's conception of modern science as setting 'nature up to exhibit itself as a coherence of forces calculable in advance' (Heidegger, *Question* 21) consists in subjecting to calculation and planning all that can be accessed through experimentation. As Heidegger quotes, for physicist Max Planck, the real is 'that which can be measured' (Planck, quoted in Heidegger, *Question* 169). This way of thinking prepares the way for technology and, more importantly, for the *essence* of technology now characterized as 'enframing' (*Gestell*).

A recurring theme in his later work is the marking of the development of self-referential, cybernetic systems as a decisive break in the history of Being. Heidegger makes little reference to the mathematical developments behind cybernetics, to which we will return, focusing instead on what he sees as an increased 'withdrawal' of the essence of technology. Cybernetics is viewed as the culmination of the dominant form of thought in Western history, earlier conceived as 'the mathematical'. This form of thought is, for Heidegger, the only strict form of philosophy for the modern age, because it works solely in the service of the 'technological universe'. In language reminiscent of the *Beiträge*, Heidegger tells us that 'the essence of technology assumes dominion – because that essence wills and therefore needs absolute univocity' (*What is Called Thinking?* 26). Cybernetics makes possible a completely homogeneous and universal calculability; it employs a universal language that can be applied to all spheres of life and knowledge. As Norbert Wiener emphasized, in the cybernetically represented world the difference between automatic machines and living things is erased. With cybernetics, *everything* is mobilized into increasing the power of the technological system. Its colonizing impulses are reaching beyond the natural sciences to co-opt other disciplines – psychology, psychoanalysis and sociology – and are mounting a charge on the humanities (*Geisteswissenschaften*). In Heidegger's words: cybernetics is 'beginning today to seize power over the spirit' (*What is Called Thinking?* 21). Soon all the sciences will be 'determined and regulated by the new fundamental science that is called cybernetics' (Heidegger, 'The End of Philosophy' 434).

Hölderlin and the 'Other Beginning'

Heidegger suggests that with the universal implementation of Aristotelian logic in cybernetics comes the end of philosophy. He calls instead for a proper meditation on technology, one that does not assume mastery, but that 'achieve[s] an adequate relationship to the essence of technology' ('Only a God Can Save Us' 111). In the *Beiträge*, Heidegger discusses the notion of machination and describes it as a mode of human comportment towards the world and increasingly towards humankind itself. Machination, if we recall, signifies the covering over of the truth of Being. But machination (*Machenschaft*) is derived from making (*machen*) and Heidegger relates it to *poiēsis* and *technē*, the simple bringing forth of objects into truth and beauty. It is, then, a mode of revealing, albeit a reductive and self-effacing one, but one that neverthe-less 'yields a faint hint of the truth of [B]eing itself' (Heidegger, *Contributions* 88). And so, for Heidegger, the ambiguity of the essence of technology holds within it a 'saving power': the secret of revealing and concealing. His remedy, then: 'to look with yet clearer eyes into the danger' (Heidegger, *Question* 29). In place of philosophy, what is required now is 'genuine thought', which, in its proximity to art, can establish a free relation to technology.

In the *Beiträge* Heidegger describes the 'other beginning' of

Western culture, where the dominant metaphysics is overcome and what is 'ownmost to thinking' (*Contributions* 119) is regained. Machination, or the 'first beginning', is the history of how the event of presencing, or the articulation of Being, is erased in favour of brute presence. For Heidegger this represents an 'echo' of the event of Being and it is only by tuning in to the echo that humankind can make the leap to the 'other beginning'. Alternatives cannot be sought elsewhere, for example in Eastern thought, but must come from where the modern technical world originates: the West as an unfolding of ancient Greek culture. Certain individuals are said by Heidegger to be attuned to this 'other beginning'. These 'ones to come' include Nietzsche, the Romantic poet Hölderlin and Heidegger himself. These poets and thinkers are the hermeneuts who will usher in the new epoch.

Hölderlin, to whom Heidegger devoted three lecture courses, is highlighted as the most significant guide to the future, for on the other side of technology is poetry. Cybernetics, as we have seen, is predominantly viewed as a phenomenon of language but figured as the imposition of a universal language under the sway of the mathematical. It is *logos* in the standard reading as 'reason' or 'logic'. Ever since *Being and Time*, Heidegger has rejected this standard reading, arguing that in Aristotle the *logos* in *zoon logon echon* ('the rational animal') refers to speech/discourse or conversation (that is, *Rede* or *Gespräch*). *Logos* is derived from *legein*, which Heidegger translates as 'to make manifest what one is "talking about" in one's discourse' (*Being and Time* 56). In this view, discourse lets things be seen; it is a singular and privileged mode of revealing Being. But in the cybernetic world of standardized information exchange, even language becomes assimilated to the computer (Heidegger, *Zollikon* 214). Heidegger, then, attempts to retrieve a different *logos*, not one that is subordinate to 'the doctrine of thinking called logic' (*What is Called Thinking?* 168) but one that is true to the broader meanings evident in the Greek root. An essential resource in making the leap to the 'other beginning' is a reclamation of language as 'the instituting-naming of the truth of [B]eing' (Heidegger, *Contributions* 124) instead of cybernetics' tool of estrangement. And this is precisely what poetic language is to Heidegger. It is no mere representation; it is an ordering and a placement of things, like technical-scientific thinking. But, unlike technical-scientific thinking, it allows Being to be revealed: it reinstates man's forgotten role as situation–constitutor, or articulator, of Being. Hölderlin's hymns are exemplary here. In their poetizing of the essences of the Rhine and the Danube, Heidegger tells us that the hymns stand outside Western metaphysics and instead demand 'a transformation in our ways of thinking and experiencing' (*Hölderlin's Hymn* 166), as we open ourselves to long-concealed relations between ourselves and the world.[5] Heidegger surely had Hölderlin in mind when he offered his famous prognosis in the 1966 *Der Spiegel* interview:

> Philosophy will not be able to effect an immediate transformation of the present condition of the world. This not only true of philosophy, but of all merely human thought and endeavour. Only a god can save us. The sole possibility that is left for us is to prepare a sort of readiness, through thinking and poetizing, for the appearance of the god or for the absence of the god in the time of foundering; for in the face of the god who is absent, we founder. (Heidegger, 'Only a God Can Save Us' 106)

Without the cultivation of alternative modes of comportment through reflective thought and poetic language, Heidegger tells us that we will be unable to make the crossing to the 'other beginning'.

Kittler and Turing's Machinization of Number

Heidegger is often taken to be pessimistic in his view on technology, but the ambiguity in his inquiry into the 'question concerning technology' opens up a productive avenue for investigation. In Heidegger's *Seinsgeschichte* the fundamental assumptions that characterize each epoch are not readily apparent. Instead, it is to the 'essential relations' that we must turn, and in the modern era the transformation of the relation of Being to man is played out in the '"metaphysical" instrumentarium' (Heidegger, *Parmenides* 86) of media technology. Heidegger's claim that '[t]echnology is entrenched in our history' (*Parmenides* 86) is a methodological call to arms for media historians such as Kittler. Kittler, indeed, became increasingly vocal in his admiration for Heidegger but stopped short of signing up as a full-blown Heideggerian. One of Kittler's major criticisms is what he calls 'the phenomenological circumvention of technology and science' ('Thinking Colours' 46) in Heidegger (and in Husserl before him). Where Heidegger adopted an increasingly dismissive attitude towards actual developments in science after *Being and Time*, taking the *geisteswissenschaftlich* route and opening up a disciplinary divide, Kittler has led an engagement with the sciences. Where Heidegger sought to protect the 'spirit' of the humanities from the encroachment of cybernetics, Kittler has gleefully led efforts to 'kick the human out of the humanities' (Kittler, quoted in Winthrop-Young 365). One way to approach these opposing positions is through their accounts of the *Grundlagenkrise* and its aftermath. As we have seen, Heidegger allied himself with the intuitionists, but Kittler is more interested in the opposing side: Hilbert and, in particular, Alan Turing.

In 1936, Turing was working on the third problem in David Hilbert's programme to ground mathematics as a purely formal discipline. In his 'Incompleteness Theorem', Kurt Gödel had already refuted Hilbert's first two demands – completeness and consistency – by mathematizing the procedures of mathematics and producing defiant paradoxes. Gödel suggested that the operations of proof were themselves arithmetical in nature and were effectively procedures of counting and comparing. His innovation was to mathematize the very syntax of mathematics to produce meaningful arithmetical statements that referred to themselves. He found examples that could belong to a particular system of axioms but not be provable within that system. One such statement is 'This statement is unprovable', which could not be proved true or false. What then remained was the question of decidability, or how to distinguish between provable and unprovable statements. Turing's paper 'On Computable Numbers, with an Application to the *Entscheidungsproblem*' answered this question by turning metaphors of mechanical rules for mathematics into hypothetical plans for a machine that did mathematics; that is, it could read a mathematical assertion and return an answer as to its provability or otherwise. The breakthrough for Turing was his conception of computable numbers: numbers that are defined by rules and can therefore be calculated. All these numbers can in principle be listed in a particular order. Cantor had previously done this with the rational numbers expressed as infinite decimals. Reading across the table diagonally produces a 'diagonal number' and shifting the diagonal one position to the right generates a new number. In Cantor's example, the generated number would be an infinite decimal that could not be rational because it would differ from each rational number in the list. Following the same procedure with Turing's list of computable numbers would produce an uncomputable number, which corresponds to an unsolvable problem. Turing then posited the existence of a machine that would use sets of instructions to produce the tables of numbers. While there might be a method for checking whether a particular instruction table would produce the required infinite sequence, there was no mechanical procedure that would work on all instruction tables. There was no way to mechanize the production of the table that would generate the required diagonal. This number really was uncomputable and Turing had found an unsolvable problem. Turing's 'mechanical procedure' with the recursive function followed directly on from Gödel's mathematization of mathematics and Hilbert's initial abstraction of the formal truth procedures of mathematics. This, of course, was anathema for the intuitionists, who held that mathematics is a strictly human affair. It was, nonetheless, the first technical implementation (or at least conception in these terms) of a mathematical-theoretical problem and, together with contributions from John von Neumann and Claude Shannon, was a foundation for the emerging discipline of computer science and the related fields of combinatorics and applied logic. For our discussion of Kittler, Turing's innovation opens up three main areas of interest: first, it marks an epistemological break enabling a new conception of human being and allowing Kittler to break from Heidegger in important ways; second, it offers Kittler the conceptual basis for a recuperation of 'number' and a renewed pursuit of Heidegger's goals; and third, it provides Kittler with an alternative set of theoretical tools for a political engagement with cybernetics.

Epistemological Break

In *Gramophone, Film, Typewriter*, Kittler describes the invention of
the computer in the wake of Turing's breakthroughs in explicitly Heideggerian terms: it was a 'techno-historical event' which
'alter[ed] (strictly following Heidegger) the relationship of Being
to man' (229–30). Kittler, however, does not identify cybernetics with a withdrawal of the essence of technology from Dasein.
Rather he sees computing as freeing us of the solipsistic illusions
that characterize the humanities and which Heidegger was unable
to overcome. Kittler relies heavily on Jacques Lacan's work on
cybernetics in his account. In brief, the major text for Kittler is
Lacan's *Seminar II*, where he argues that our philosophical conceptions are much more deeply entwined with our technologies
than we might care to think: machines are not 'simple artefact[s]
[. . .] They are something else. They go much further in the
direction of what we are in reality' (74). When Lacan calls for
a 'return to Freud' and a focus on language as the site of human
symbolic activity, he also moves to historicize this symbolic activity by aligning it with specific technological systems. He argues
that the supporting models for Freud's elaboration of the psychic
apparatus, such as repression, displacement and condensation,
could only emerge with the invention of the steam engine. Lacan
claimed to advance on Freud by incorporating the lessons of 'a
mutation taking place in the function of the machine' (32): the
mechanical innovations of the nineteenth century were giving
way to a new industrial revolution: the invention of the computer and its theorization in cybernetics and information theory.
Human symbolic activity, for Lacan, should now be understood
as 'the discourse of the circuit' (89) rather than that of thermo-
dynamics. This insight about the importance of computers allows
Kittler to grant Lacanian psychoanalysis the status of a privileged
discourse: 'Under high-tech conditions, therefore, psychoanalysis no longer constructs psychic apparatuses [. . .] merely out of
storage and transmission media, but rather incorporates the entire
technical triad of storage, transmission and computation' (Kittler,
'The World of the Symbolic' 135). Psychoanalysis alone was able

to adapt its conceptual model to embrace the implications of Turing's innovations.

Drawing on Lacan, Kittler offers an account of the shift in technological development from the nineteenth century to the twentieth. In the nineteenth century, machine functions were able to replace some of the functions of the hand and mouth, but, until the invention of computers that were able to process information, 'human being[s] still appeared to be doing the transmitting' (Kittler, *Gramophone* 245). With Hilbert and then Turing, a narrower definition of human intelligence was conceived, one that computers were equally, if not more, able to perform. Kittler is not suggesting here that brains are computers, though he is claiming that their primary functions are equivalent. The main difference between them, he tells us, is that computers, while much faster at processing data, are restricted to serial processing. The brain, on the other hand, can process large amounts of data in parallel. The apparent complexity of the brain's parallel processing meant that many mathematicians (including Gödel) remained committed to a transcendental view of human intelligence, but Kittler glosses any such objections by claiming that it was not Gödel's beliefs that won the day but 'Gödelization that [. . .] emerged victorious' (*Gramophone* 247) with Turing and the computer. Turing's arguments for machine intelligence were foundational for the emerging discipline of Artificial Intelligence (AI) and its gains in the latter part of the twentieth century.[6] For Kittler, this emerging technical reality put paid to the last vestiges of humanism and its valorization of 'so-called thinking'.

Kittler tells us that Heidegger, too, was susceptible to this lingering humanism. Unlike Lacanian psychoanalysis, Heideggerian phenomenology remained embedded in the assumptions of a previous discourse network. In *Gramophone, Film, Typewriter*, Kittler comments on the Romanticism in Heidegger's account of the typewriter in *Parmenides* and suggests that Nietzsche is more attuned than Heidegger to the transformations wrought by the new writing technology (xl, 198–200). A more detailed interpretation of the trajectory of Heidegger's thought is offered in Kittler's essay 'Thinking Colours and/or Machines', originally published in 1996. There, Kittler argues that in his early work Heidegger inherits Husserl's phenomenological error: the creation of a philosophically

autonomous life-world of cultural techniques as a defence against
the inroads that science was making into the interpretation of
cultural data. Kittler tells us that institutional changes in the wake
of Kant installed philosophy as the universal arbiter of cultural
data. The chief threat to its position in the second half of the
nineteenth century was posed by Gustav Fechner's psychophysics,
which was working to isolate the functions of human perception
in laboratories. Mathematicians were then able to use logarithmic
functions to analyse the laboratories' output: sense data, which had
previously been synthesized by a Kantian transcendental ego (in
Kittler's parlance, 'so-called Man'). Kittler's claim is that Husserl's
concept of the life-world was an attempt to circumvent the findings of psychophysics by asserting the role of self-observation
in the interpretation of cultural data. If scientific facts conflict
with philosophical findings then the phenomenologist can trump
the experimental data by an appeal to the mediating role of the
life-world of the scientist and the experimental subjects (Kittler,
'Thinking Colours' 42). It was this tenet of phenomenology that
Heidegger developed into a wholesale critique of modern science
and its methods in *Being and Time*, and that Kittler suggests was at
least in part motivated by a 'claim to power' ('Thinking Colours'
43) later revealed in Heidegger's involvement with the Nazis.[7]
When Heidegger, in response to the *Grundlagenkrise*, attempted
to turn mathematics into an object of philosophical investigation,
this was part of a broader institutional subjection of the sciences
by hermeneutic philosophy (Kittler, 'Thinking Colours' 43).
Though he has little to say about the political implications of the
turn towards irrationalism, Kittler joins Heidegger's contemporary
opponents in deriding this move as undermining any claims on the
part of philosophy to universal validity. Like Goethe's dismissal
of Newton's frequency theory of colour on aesthetic grounds,
the continued resistance of Heideggerian phenomenology to the
lessons of cybernetics amounted to a rejection of objectivity, and
with it of the ability to address the complexities of modern technology adequately, the consequences of which we return to later.

Kittler does, however, identify a crucial insight in Heidegger's
phenomenological focus on the local site of scientific activity that
he claims provides impetus for Heidegger's later work. In *Being*

and Time, Heidegger noted that the tools of scientific investigation include writing materials, which were 'by no means ontologically indifferent' (quoted in Kittler, 'Thinking Colours' 47). Kittler draws parallels between this line of inquiry of Heidegger's and Hilbert's abstraction of mathematics to the mechanics of proof: 'Hilbert, much like Heidegger, turned the mathematical signs themselves into the ontological foundation of his science' ('Thinking Colours' 47). For Kittler, it is this insight that is later developed by Heidegger when he foregrounds technology as a 'mode of revealing'. The description of modern technology offered in 'The Question Concerning Technology' as 'unlocking, transforming, storing, distributing and switching' (quoted in Kittler, 'Thinking Colours' 47) gestures towards an engagement with information theory and the cybernetic technological *a priori*. Indeed, elsewhere Kittler ascribes Heidegger's 'turn' to Turing's breakthrough:

> Evidently numbers had to leave humans behind and become part of machines that run on their own in order for technology to appear as a frame that conjoins [B]eing and thought. This turn was completed by Alan Turing when he devised his paper machine, the principal switch of all possible discrete computers. ('Number and Numeral' 58–9)

In his later work, Kittler suggests, Heidegger comes close to realizing the lessons of Turing.

Despite Heidegger's stated allegiance to Brouwer and the intuitionists, Kittler insists on reading Heidegger with the eventual victors of the *Grundlagenkrise*: Hilbert, Turing and cybernetics. If philosophy, after cybernetics, is finished for Heidegger, who opts instead for 'thinking', one of Kittler's responses is to contest philosophy. Philosophy's mistake, for Kittler, is to continue to ground consciousness in self-consciousness. It should instead follow the example of Lacanian psychoanalysis and accept that 'consciousness is only the imaginary interior view of media standards' (Kittler, 'World of the Symbolic' 132). Heidegger's destructive contribution to this debate was to replace philosophy's age-old alliance with the sciences with a national-Romantic alliance with craftsmen (Kittler, 'Thinking Colours' 43). Instead of cybernetics representing the end of philosophy, Kittler believes that an awareness of its dependency on technical media can help rejuvenate philosophy (Gane and Sale 328). Instead of building ontologies on outdated dichotomies such as form and matter, Kittler urges philosophy to analyse commands, addresses and data. In this manner, Kittler hopes to reverse the disciplinary ascendance of hermeneutics and restore philosophy's alliance with the sciences. Naturally, media science will lead the way.

The Recuperation of Number and Another 'Other Beginning'

Kittler identifies one of the main causes of Heidegger's 'phenomenological circumvention' of technology and science as his (Romantic) misconception of language, which led to the exclusion of number from his investigations. When Heidegger lamented the assimilation of language to the computer in cybernetics he failed to acknowledge the import of Hilbert and Turing's discoveries. As already discussed, Hilbert started his axiomatization by conceiving numbers as numerals and treating mathematics as an abstract symbolic system. This material abstraction allowed Turing to conceive of words and numbers as interchangeable, and with the universal discrete machine it was proven for the first time that 'formal languages exist as technologies' (Kittler, 'Thinking Colours' 47). Armed with this reconception, Kittler revisits a question of Heidegger's, namely: 'why philosophic logic as invented by Aristotle finally led to its machinization by Turing, Shannon, and others' (Kittler, 'Towards an Ontology' 24). As we have seen, Heidegger's answer to this question, as outlined in *What is a Thing?*, the *Beiträge* and elsewhere, takes a very critical position on 'the mathematical'. But Kittler sets out to correct Heidegger's error by tracing a technical history of signs and in so doing providing an alternative 'media history of Europe' (Kittler, 'Towards an Ontology' 29).

In 'Number and Numeral' Kittler offers his own history of number from the Greeks to the present day, one that is attentive to the signifying systems and technological apparatus with which it is imbricated: 'the media of mathematics' ('Number and Numeral' 54). Drawing on the work of Barry Powell, Kittler argues that the Greek alphabet, the first alphabet to include vowels, was developed to allow the transmission of Homer's sung poetry. Music, not trade or the law, was there at the inception of Western culture and its founding cultural code: the phonetic alphabet. The importance of the Greek alphabet for Kittler is that a single signifying system was used to denote letters, numbers and musical notes. With the addition of vowels, the alphabet was able to mark out individual sequences of sounds (syllables). A sequence of letters that did not correspond to syllables could readily be identified as numbers. The same characters were also used both to identify musical notes and to specify the ratios that allowed fingers to play notes on the strings of musical instruments such as the lyre, 'a magical thing that connects mathematics to the domain of the sense' (Kittler, 'Number and Numeral' 56). Musicians could pluck a string at the point that marks the ratio 4:3 to sound the fourth note in the scale, at the point that marks 3:2 for the fifth, and so on.

In Kittler's media-historical account of the Greek alphabet, he is also able to find traces of the *logos* that Heidegger found in Aristotle. As we have already seen, *logos* means both speech and reason, what Kittler elsewhere describes as 'the words spoken as well as the relations that hold them together' (Khayyat 13). Kittler suggests that what we call meaning is the 'manifestness' of these relations. This resembles the revelation that Heidegger finds in poetic language ('the instituting-naming of the truth of [B]eing' and the opening up of long-concealed relations, as exemplified by Hölderlin's hymns), but instead of Heideggerian appeals to essential Being, Kittler dismisses such philosophical inquiry as wrong-headed. Media are not simply the means of transmission for preconceived meanings or interpretations. Rather, meaning is conjured in association with media when, for example, the harmony of a set of strings is connected with the ears of listeners. This, for Kittler, is what Heidegger missed when he described 'Man as the shepherd of Being': an attunement of humankind, the bearers of ears, as witnesses to recursivity. Truth claims are not necessarily relative to human existence, as they are for Heidegger, but neither are they universal and absolute. Knowledge of harmony is revealed in the feedback between historically variable sign systems, their technological objects and our sense apparatus. Truth claims are circumscribed as resonant medial configurations within the historical *a priori*.

In Kittler's media history of Europe, just as it did for Heidegger, *logos* became corrupted. The fall from grace occurred with Aristotle and Plato, and was cemented by the Romans who consolidated philosophical error with the split of originary *logos* into *oratio* and *ratio*. Then, during the Middle Ages, European culture retained the Latin alphabet for letters but adopted the stave system for musical notation and Indian numerals for numbers. Greek harmonies and their musico-technical origins were forgotten. In the realm of number, the import of zero as a digit and placeholder led to the invention of decimal notation. Simon Stevin then used decimal fractions to divide the Greek octave into twelve equal parts: the pitch varied by the twelfth root of two (approximately 1.05946). The resulting system (the equal-tempered chromatic scale) eventually became the standard for musical instruments such as the valve horn, piano and guitar, and the music composed for them: symphonies and sonatas, the dominant forms of European music in the second millennium. That this musical system is based not on the elegant harmonies of whole numbers and their ratios, as it was for the Greeks, but on potentially infinite real numbers is crucial for Kittler.[8] Human culture has imposed its own organizing principles on the configuration brought forth by the mathematical sea of real numbers and the 'epistemic things' (Rheinberger) or technological media that connect them to the human sensorium. These organizing principles – God, Meaning or Man (generally prepended by Kittler's characteristic 'so-called', *sogenannt*) – are dangerous fantasies in Kittler's opinion, and the latter two are the main targets of his post-hermeneutic media philosophy (though monotheism also comes in for a good deal of criticism in his later work).

There is, however, an 'other beginning' for Kittler, just as there was for Heidegger, but in this version Turing creates the conditions for the 'ones to come'. When he developed the idea of computable numbers a new, pure alphabet emerged to replace the fragmented sign systems of the Middle Ages and their arbitrary organizing principles. In Kittler's view, the 'power of this alphanumerical explosion can hardly be exaggerated' (Kittler, 'Thinking Colours' 48). Computable numbers are a definable subset of the real numbers: for each computable number or sequence of numbers there is a closed algebraic expression. And for each closed algebraic expression there is (potentially) a computer. Once more, concealed relations are able to emerge in the feedback between sign systems, technological objects and their human witnesses. In modern computing, based on von Neumann's specifications for a universal discrete machine, the self-referential manifestness of technical configurations can again resound and we can hear the echo of ancient harmonies. Furthermore, the binary notation system used by Turing and his successors is equally able to encode words and numbers (and, latterly, sounds and images, as they too are digitized). For Kittler the universality of binary coding represents a reincarnation of the Greek alphabet and allows us to 'unfold the essential unity of writing, number, image and tone' (Kittler, 'Number and Numeral' 52). It is in the unlikely assemblage of the personal computer that the supposed plenitude of Greek culture returns: 'In the Greek alphabet our senses were present – and thanks to Turing they are so once again' (Kittler, 'Number and Numeral' 59). And in place of Hölderlin and his poetry, Kittler's authentic heroes are the musicians and artists that are able to master the technical possibilities made available in the cybernetic age.

Kittler's Politics of Calculation

We have already seen that Heidegger's exclusion of number was based on his critique of 'the mathematical'. He aligned the mathematical, negatively conceived, with modern science and its reliance on theoretical models of knowledge instead of experience. Man came to be 'the measure of all things' in the era of Descartes's cogito and Kant's transcendental ego. The domination inherent in this model of modern science culminates in total mobilization, world war and the cybernetic era. Many thinkers have followed Heidegger in viewing the mathematics of procedural technique or game theory represented by computer science as starkly reductive and have called for alternatives.[9] How, then, do politics feature in Kittler's siding with what is often regarded as an 'ultimately technical project' (Badiou 9) and is generally cast in opposition to democratic goals?

In his early discourse analytical work, Kittler followed Foucault in examining the structures that control the articulation of statements within different discourse networks. Kittler, however, claims that, given the changing conditions of the discursive formation, Foucault's discourse analysis is unable to penetrate the twentieth century and its new information systems. Kittler draws attention to the fact that Foucault's analyses end at around 1850, arguing that his archive, the library, loses its monopoly around this time. Instead, Kittler proposes that '[a]rchaeologies of the present must also take into account data storage, transmission and calculation in technological media' (*Discourse Networks* 369). Following Turing and cybernetics, Kittler tells us that politics is already inside the 'black box' of modern technology and that our ability to analyse the structures that control the articulation of statements is receding: 'data flows once confined to books and later to records and films are disappearing into black holes and boxes that, as artificial intelligences, are bidding us farewell on their way to nameless high commands' (Kittler, *Gramophone* xxxix). Like Heidegger in the late 1930s, Kittler suggests that a fundamental political shift accompanied the epistemological shift of cybernetics. Kittler tells us that the analogue media that previously structured information flows were harder for 'the powers that be' to control. Turing's discrete media, however, are algorithmic; they are subject to both logic and control. They can be transcoded, operated upon and negated. Technical media, developed in the crucible of war, as they were for Heidegger, are being pressed into service by a totalizing and increasingly technological organization. The computer 'always already speaks the language of the upper echelons' (Kittler, *Gramophone* 250). Kittler implies that just as philosophy needs to learn the lessons of information theory, so does political analysis. A good place to start is John von Neumann's standard computer architecture, which provides the necessary functional separation of data, addresses and commands for the structuring of dedifferentiated digital data streams.

Kittler's best-known work on the political implications of cybernetics is in the essay collection *Draculas Vermächtnis: Technische Schriften* from 1993. In 'There Is No Software' Kittler argues that programming languages, having toppled the monopoly of ordinary language, are now multiplying in order to obfuscate the technical decisions made at a hardware level. It is hardware that has been built to 'house some notation system' ('There Is No Software' 153) and that, as we have seen from the Turing discussion, is decisive. What is often referred to as 'interface' is merely 'eyewash' to distance users from hardware and bring them under the command and control of Microsoft. Power is being locked down in microchips and rolled out to unwitting customers of IBM and Intel (now Apple and Samsung). To analyse the new discursive formations, Kittler tells us that 'one should attempt to abandon the usual practice of conceiving of power as a function of so-called society, and, conversely, attempt to construct sociology from the chip's architectures' (Kittler, 'Protected Mode' 162). For Kittler, 'society' is another of the bogus organizing principles mistakenly applied by the humanities (alongside 'God', 'meaning' and 'Man'). As an explanatory model, it is being made redundant as data flows disappear into technical media. For Foucauldian discourse analysis to retain any relevance it must attempt to penetrate the black box, which is increasingly where political decision-making is being implemented. In the wake of Kittler, many media archaeologists have taken up the challenge of making technological artefacts transparent to social and political analysis.[10]

Kittler's response to the political changes that he identifies is to champion a certain kind of political resistance: challenges to technical hegemony from within the technical community. In a technical culture of mass mediality, political activity consists purely in interception, scrambling and feedback. Turing as master code-breaker is exemplary (despite working for the British government!), but he is also praised in counter-cultural terms. In *Gramophone, Film, Typewriter*, for example, Turing is held up as a hero of the resistance, not for his role in defeating the Nazis, but for opening up the 'craft of thinking' to workers such as the machine operators at Bletchley Park. In this respect, 'he was an anti-technocrat, subversively diminishing the authority of the new priests and magicians of the world' (Hodges, quoted in Kittler, *Gramophone* 246). Other counter-cultural heroes include Linus Torvalds, the creator of the Open Source operating system Linux, but most commonly it is rock stars that substitute for political leadership in Kittler's work. Lennon, Hendrix and Pink Floyd are repeatedly singled out for praise. In a world where technology acts to conceal, the most urgent task, in Kittler's view, is to keep technical possibilities alive; all that is required is technical knowledge (*Gramophone* 110). Rock musicians in their recording studios are using and abusing media technologies that were developed in the Second World War and subsequently rolled out as propagandist entertainment systems. In the hands of Syd Barrett et al., vocoders and Magnetophones are used to 'sing of the very power that sustains them' (Kittler, *Gramophone* 111). In the cybernetic era of control, 'or, as engineers say, negative feedback', the principal form of resistance is 'positive feedback'. Kittler, quoting Marx, tells us that we must 'play to the powers that be their own melody' (Kittler, *Gramophone* 110).

This model of resistance is in line with that of William Burroughs. In 'Playback from Eden to Watergate' (Odier and Burroughs) quoted at length in *Gramophone, Film, Typewriter*, Burroughs urges the dissemination of tape splicing as a disruptive force, one capable of countering the political control of the Nixon administration. He called for millions of people to perform their own Watergate buggings, splicing sex tapes with hateful, disapproving voices and playing them to politicians and their constituents. To counter distraction, Kittler calls for mobilization (*Gramophone* 111), but we should ask 'to what end?' Politics beyond this narrow view of resistance becomes hard to conceive when the individual is dissolved into technological mediation. His closed systems offer little space for positive conceptions of politics. Normative appeals to freedom, justice or equality can all be dismissed as yet more bogus organizing principles. In Kittler's later work, the only appeal is to the supposed plenitude of ancient Greece. And here he follows the template for conservative revolution that so appealed to Heidegger's philosophy and politics: the restoration of a lost past with an energizing promise of a new dawn.

Conclusion

As we have seen, Kittler's teasing out of the ambiguity in Heidegger's account of technology does offer the humanities a form of rapprochement with the sciences. Heidegger opens up the question of the historical conditions for calculative Being but is unable to bear down on the problem. Kittler, on the other hand, places Heidegger in the Romantic disjunction of mathematics and philosophy and in so doing is able to reconceive his legacy for the digital age. This makes Kittler better able to show us the danger of 'number', while also offering the promise of alternative modes of comportment towards technology, as Heidegger started to do in the 1930s. Furthermore, Kittler has made important strides towards prising open the black box of technology and putting its contents on display to the humanities. But Kittler doesn't seem to have taken us far from the problems surrounding Heidegger's politics and its relationship to his thought. Recent engagements with Carl Schmitt have deployed his critique of liberalism for various ends,[11] whereas Kittler's technological update of Heidegger remains within a radical conservative position. This can take the form of conservative worries about American influence (for example, Microsoft, George W. Bush), which can be productive, but also of the need to roll back the corruptions of culture to the ancient Greeks, which is less so.

Looking beyond the polarity of Heidegger's politics, many of the accusations of theoretical shortcomings levelled at Heidegger can also be applied to Kittler. Kittler's statement in an interview that his 'work on the military–industrial complex is not interested in the details of people's lives or how it really was, for example, in the Weimar Republic' (Armitage 29) reminds one of Heidegger's disdain for the 'merely ontic'. Kittler goes on to admit that 'the relationship between human agency, technology and autonomy is a complex one' but does very little to address this issue. This highlights one of the major problems with his position: it offers a circumscribed account of command and control within technical systems with little or no reference to their imbrication with other systems. Instead, readers are invited to insert Kittler's work into their own narrative. Like Heidegger, Kittler is attuned to changes wrought at the micro level of the subject and at the macro level of the epoch but is less able to account for the bits in between. Specific political configurations always disappear behind virtuoso descriptions of ears, loudspeakers and 'the powers that be'.

One way to approach Kittler is to view his work as polemic that aims to address the technological blind-spot of the humanities. With this in mind, we can see that his bravado can also serve to obfuscate the theoretical choices that he makes when engaging with the sciences. As we have seen, Kittler sides with the axiomatic project of Hilbert and Turing, but there are myriad other positions that are available in mathematics. For example, Badiou finds radical uncertainty in set theory and the axiom of choice. Many find his position politically untenable, but the example serves to highlight the fact that there are other positions available. Kittler's rhetorical brilliance should not prevent us from returning to the questions that he opens up in the quest for alternative answers.

Notes

1 One of Heidegger's early public clashes was with the logical positivist Rudolf Carnap. Carnap had objected to the reasoning in Heidegger's inaugural lecture (*'Was ist Metaphysik'*) at Freiburg in 1929 and famously singled out the phrase 'the nothing nothings [*das Nichts nichtet*]' for derision. Carnap was at that time trying to bring philosophy within the realm of a universal mathematical logic where it could then be applied in fulfilment of the aims of international socialism.

2 The debate between the leading philosophers of the time was staged in Davos, Switzerland. Cassirer, representing the dominant Marburg School of neo-Kantianism, was a staunch liberal and a supporter of the Weimar Republic. Heidegger was a radical conservative thinker who had recently published *Being and Time* (1927) and was eager to contest the established positions of German philosophy. Carnap was also present at the debates.

3 See, for example, Adorno for an influential critique of Heidegger.

4 See Brouwer and Weyl for the main texts of intuitionism.

5 The value of poetic language for Heidegger lies in the excess of the materiality of language over its informational content. It is this

resistant weight of excess that conjures possible relations to the world and opens us to language as an encounter of Being and beings. Heidegger suggests that language is 'a site of dwelling', not just an instrumental tool of information exchange.

6 Turing's major contribution to the AI debate was 'Computing Machinery and Intelligence'. In it Turing admits that the model of the brain as a 'discrete controlling machine' is one of several alternative views. He claimed, however, that his model was 'relevant to what was called "thinking"'.

7 Kittler here refers to Heidegger's famous Rectorial Address.

8 Real numbers can be expressed as (potentially infinite) decimals and comprise both the rational numbers (integers and fractions) and irrational numbers (such as the square root of two). The twelfth root of two is an irrational number. The ancient Greeks only recognized whole numbers as numbers.

9 Notable adherents to this view include Foucault, Agamben and Badiou. Badiou has engaged most directly with many of the issues raised here. He also argues for the ontological centrality of mathematics, but categorizes the axiomatic approach of Hilbert as having been appropriated by an ideology of number that is wedded to capital.

10 See, for example, the work of Wolfgang Ernst, Bernhard Siegert and Siegfried Zielinski.

11 See Müller (221–43) for a discussion of applications of Schmittian thought from both Left and Right.

Works Cited

Adorno, Theodor W. *The Jargon of Authenticity*. Trans. Knut Tarnowski and Frederic Will. London: Routledge & Kegan Paul, 1973.

Armitage, John. 'From Discourse Networks to Cultural Mathematics: An Interview with Friedrich A. Kittler.' *Theory, Culture & Society* 23.7–8 (2006): 17–38.

Badiou, Alain. *Number and Numbers*. Trans. Robin Mackay. Cambridge: Polity, 2008.

Brouwer, Luitzen E. J. 'On the Foundations of Mathematics.' *Collected Works*. Vol. 1. Amsterdam: North-Holland, 1975. 15–101.

Gane, Nicholas, and Stephen Sale. 'Interview with Friedrich Kittler and Mark Hansen.' *Theory, Culture & Society* 24.7–8 (2007): 323–9.

Heidegger, Martin. *Being and Time*. Trans. John Macquarrie and Edward Robinson. Oxford: Blackwell, 1962.

Heidegger, Martin. *What is a Thing?* Trans. W. B. Barton Jr. and Vera Deutsch. Chicago: Henry Regnery, 1967.

Heidegger, Martin. *The Question Concerning Technology and Other Essays*. Trans. William Lovitt. New York: Harper & Row, 1977.

Heidegger, Martin. *History of the Concept of Time: Prolegomena*. Trans. Theodore Kisiel. Bloomington: Indiana University Press, 1985.

Heidegger, Martin. *Parmenides*. Trans. André Schuwer and Richard Rojcewicz. Bloomington and Indianapolis: Indiana University Press, 1992.

Heidegger, Martin. '"Only a God Can Save Us": Der Spiegel's Interview with Martin Heidegger.' *The Heidegger Controversy*. Ed. Richard Wolin. Cambridge, MA, and London: MIT Press, 1993. 91–116.

Heidegger, Martin. 'The End of Philosophy and the Task of Thinking.' Trans. J. Stambaugh. *Basic Writings*. Ed. David Farrell Krell. London and New York: Routledge, 1993.

Heidegger, Martin. *Hölderlin's Hymn 'The Ister'*. Trans. William McNeill and Julia Davis. Bloomington and Indianapolis: Indiana University Press, 1996.

Heidegger, Martin. *Plato's Sophist*. Trans. Richard Rojcewicz and André Schuwer. Bloomington and Indianapolis: Indiana University Press, 1997.

Heidegger, Martin. *Contributions to Philosophy (From Enowning)*. Trans. Parvis Emad and Kenneth Maly. Bloomington and Indianapolis: Indiana University Press, 1999.

Heidegger, Martin. *Zollikon Seminars: Protocols – Conversations – Letters*. Trans. Franz Mayr and Richard Askay. Ed. Medard Boss. Evanston: Northwestern University Press, 2001.

Heidegger, Martin. *What is Called Thinking?* Trans. J. Glenn Gray. New York: Perennial, 2004.

Hilbert, David. 'The New Grounding of Mathematics.' *From Brouwer to Hilbert: The Debate on the Foundations of Mathematics in the 1920s*. Ed. Paulo Mancosu. Oxford: Oxford University Press, 1998. 198–214.

Khayyat, E. 'The Humility of Thought: An Interview with Friedrich A. Kittler.' *boundary* 2 (2012): 7–27.

Kittler, Friedrich A. *Discourse Networks 1800/1900*. Trans. Michael Metteer with Chris Cullens. Stanford: Stanford University Press, 1990.

Kittler, Friedrich A. *Draculas Vermächtnis: Technische Schriften.* Leipzig: Reclam, 1993.

Kittler, Friedrich A. 'The World of the Symbolic: A World of the Machine.' *Literature, Media, Information Systems: Essays.* Ed. John Johnston. Amsterdam: G+B Arts International, 1997. 130–46.

Kittler, Friedrich A. 'There Is No Software.' *Literature, Media, Information Systems: Essays.* Ed. John Johnston. Amsterdam: G+B Arts International, 1997. 147–55.

Kittler, Friedrich A. 'Protected Mode.' *Literature, Media, Information Systems: Essays.* Ed. John Johnston. Amsterdam: G+B Arts International, 1997. 156–68.

Kittler, Friedrich A. *Gramophone, Film, Typewriter.* Trans. Geoffrey Winthrop-Young and Michael Wutz. Stanford: Stanford University Press, 1999.

Kittler, Friedrich A. 'Number and Numeral.' *Theory, Culture & Society* 23.7–8 (2006): 51–61

Kittler, Friedrich A. 'Thinking Colours and/or Machines.' *Theory, Culture & Society* 23.7–8 (2006): 39–50.

Kittler, Friedrich A. 'Towards an Ontology of Media.' *Theory, Culture & Society* 26.2–3 (2009): 23–31.

Lacan, Jacques. *The Seminar of Jacques Lacan: Book II: The Ego in Freud's Theory and in the Technique of Psychoanalysis 1954–1955.* Trans. Sylvana Tomaselli. New York and London: Norton, 1988.

Müller, Jan-Werner. *A Dangerous Mind: Carl Schmitt in Post-War European Thought.* New Haven and London: Yale University Press, 2003.

Odier, Daniel, and William S. Burroughs. *The Job: Interviews with William S. Burroughs.* New York: Grove Press, 1974.

Rheinberger, Hans-Jörg. *Toward a History of Epistemic Things: Synthesizing Proteins in the Test Tube.* Stanford: Stanford University Press, 1997.

Turing, Alan. 'Computing Machinery and Intelligence.' *Mind* 59 (1950): 433–60.

Turing, Alan. 'On Computable Numbers, with an Application to the *Entscheidungsproblem.*' *The Essential Turing: Seminal Writings in Computing, Logic, Philosophy, Artificial Intelligence, and Artificial Life.* Ed. B. Jack Copeland. Oxford: Clarendon Press, 2004. 58–90.

Weyl, Hermann. *The Continuum.* New York: Dover, 1994.

Winthrop-Young, Geoffrey. '"Well, What Socks Is Pynchon Wearing Today?" A Freiburg Scrapbook in Memory of Friedrich Kittler.' *Cultural Politics* 8.3 (2012): 361–73.

4

Siren Recursions

Geoffrey Winthrop-Young

Recursive Hardcore Arcadian Porn

Among the more dubious historical figures for whom Friedrich Kittler has expressed a certain affection is Tiberius Julius Caesar Augustus, second emperor of Rome. Tiberius has endured centuries of bad press. He had the particular misfortune of incurring the wrath of Tacitus, master of the laconic invective and supremely skilled in the historian's black art of reviving the dead to kill them once more with words. Knowing that denunciations work best when they cater to stereotypes, Tacitus assimilated the life of Tiberius to established literary models of the promising young ruler who turns into an ageing tyrant. As a result, we remember Tiberius as the plummeting *princeps*: he starts out with the virtues of his predecessor Augustus only to end up with the vices of his successor Caligula. If Tacitus provided the story, Suetonius added the sleaze. It is thanks to him that Tiberius ranks among the dirtiest of antiquity's dirty old men. And that makes him interesting to Kittler.

In 26 CE Tiberius left Rome for good. He was in his late sixties and had another decade to live, most of which he spent on

Capri, an island known for the hospitality it extends to figures of questionable repute (from Tiberius himself all the way to Norman Douglas and Curzio Malaparte). According to Suetonius, Tiberius turned Capri into an adult adventure park featuring – in Kittler's words – an abundance of Arcadian 'hardcore porn' (*Eros* 253):

> On retiring to Capri he [Tiberius] devised 'holey places' [*sellaria*, a 'place for seats', aka latrines] as a site for his secret orgies; there a select team of girls and male prostitutes, inventors of deviant intercourse and dubbed analists, copulated before him in triple unions to excite his flagging passions. Its many bedrooms were furnished with the most salacious paintings and sculptures, as well as with books of Elephantis [a Greek erotic writer], in case a performer should need an illustration of a prescribed position. Then in Capri's woods and groves he contrived a number of spots for sex where boys and girls got dressed up as Pans and nymphs and solicited outside grottoes and sheltered recesses; people openly called this 'the old goat's garden' [*Caprineum*], punning on the island's name.
>
> He acquired a reputation for still grosser depravities that one can hardly bear to tell or be told, let alone believe. (Suetonius 371–3)

At which point Suetonius launches into a meticulous account of all the depravities he, for one, can very much bear to believe and tell. Fortunately we can dispense with the particulars because we have read enough to understand Kittler's fondness for Tiberius. The Old Goat of Capri appears to have been obsessed with matters that are also of central importance to Kittler's later work: sex and the Greeks – more precisely, sex *of* the Greeks. The affinities, however, go beyond the carnal domain. Tiberius's Graecophilia included more refined matters that required the services of philologists rather than prostitutes:

> [H]is special aim was a knowledge of mythology, which he carried to a silly and laughable extreme; for he used it to test even the grammarians [. . .] by questions like this: 'Who was Hecuba's mother?' 'What was the name of Achilles among the maidens?' 'What were the Sirens in the habit of singing?' (Suetonius 409)

Quid Sirenes cantare sint solitae – readers who have navigated the depths and shallows of *Musik und Mathematik* know that Kittler cannot let this pass. His enterprise revolves around the fact that thanks to the invention of the Greek vowel alphabet we know *exactly* what the Sirens sang, at least when Odysseus came their way. It is recorded verbatim for all to read and repeat in Homer's *Odyssey*:

> Come closer, famous Odysseus – Achaea's pride and glory –
> moor your ship on our coast so you can hear our song!
> Never has any sailor passed our shores in his black craft
> until he has heard the honeyed voices pouring from our lips,
> and once he hears to his heart's content sails on, a wiser man.
> We know all the pains the Achaeans and Trojans once endured
> on the spreading plain of Troy when the gods willed it so –
> all that comes to pass on the fertile earth, we know it all!
>
> (Homer 277)

Kittler chooses an intriguing term to describe how Tiberius and other Romans processed and recycled the cultural, intellectual and sexual achievements of Greece: *recursion*. The moment *Musik und Mathematik* crosses over from Greece to Rome, the word crops up everywhere. Tiberius's philhellenic pornotopia? A recursion. The sad reappearance of the Euboean sybilla in Petronius's *Satyricon*, or Longos' retelling of the tale of Daphnis and Chloe: ditto. Roman reverse engineering of Archimedes' war machines: 'also a form of recursion' (*Eros* 244). Indeed, the reappearance at the beginning of Eliot's *The Waste Land* of the sybilla that had already reappeared in Petronius signals that we are dealing with *Rekursionen über Rekursionen* – 'one recursion after the other' (*Eros* 256). To emphasize the importance of the concept Kittler dedicates a section to it that culminates in the assurance: 'For this new way of writing history there is only one way, one name: recursion' (*Eros* 245).[1]

What new way? What history? Is this transfer of a concept from mathematics and informatics to cultural history worth the effort? Modern theory is littered with the remains of defunct technobabble (remember Baudrillard's 'precession of simulacra'?), so why bother? The first thing to note is that Kittler is not alone. Over the last few years there have been many recursions in the media-technologically informed variant of German *Kulturwissenschaften* indebted, in no small part, to Kittler's work. Ana Ofak and Philipp von Hilgers have edited an excellent volume on recursions with a roster of high-profile contributors (including Kittler himself) that probes the carrying capacity of the concept. While there is no clear agreement on what exactly the term implies and how it should be employed in the colder humanities, there is a common understanding that it has the potential to solve some very basic quandaries. What I would like to offer are a couple of examples and ideas – a recursion sampler with a certain entertainment and provocation value – before concluding with the question: why was the older Kittler so recursively inclined?

Serving Time

Programmers define a recursive function as one that calls itself during its execution. This has a certain tautological ring to it, as do the visual examples that invariably accompany explanations: mirrors mirroring each other, nested Russian dolls, Fibonacci sea-shells, broccoli, or Escher's hands drawing Escher's hands drawing Escher's hands. In order to avoid simple circularity, a recursive algorithm must specify a base case and thus a termination point that will prevent a program from getting lost in an endless loop. But although the same keeps happening to the same, it does not have the same outcome. In an early paper on the epistemological implications of programmability, repetition and recursion, Hartmut Winkler highlighted this particular point:

> Recursion is defined as the reapplication of a processing instruction to a variable that is itself already the result, or interim result, of that processing instruction. The variable changes with every iteration, and the effect of the repetition is not the production of identity but a predefined variation. Recursion is thus not simple but expanded reproduction; it brings together repetition and variation with the goal of producing something new that cannot be executed in advance. (235)

Recursions involve repetitive instances of self-processing that nonetheless result in something different. Put differently, variation arises from algorithms that command repetition without themselves containing the repetition. Note, however, that this expanded reproduction involves a Janus-type double movement. The recursion runs back, it 'takes recourse', as it were, to itself, but at the same time it runs ahead to a predefined result (which, however, could not come about without the running back). 'We "run back" in time from today to the Greeks', Kittler notes, 'but simultaneously we also run ahead, from the first beginning to its repetitive overcoming [*Verwindung*]' (*Eros* 245).[2]

A brief (though highly recommended) example: in a study entitled *Der Diener* ('The Servant'), Markus Krajewski, a media theorist of the K-3 generation (i.e., scholars who studied with Kittler in Berlin in the 1990s and early 2000s),[3] traces the structural correlation between human *servants* – butlers, attendants, lackeys, domestics – and electronic *servers* – bots, web-crawlers, mail delivery systems, search engines. What exactly links Bertie Wooster's know-it-all Jeeves to find-it-all search engines, one of which used to be called Ask Jeeves? For conventional histories of technology the name is a skeuomorph, the retention of a design feature in a new technical environment in which it no longer serves any function other than to create a sense of familiarity. Krajewski, however, insists on systemic connections. As we know from countless eighteenth-century domestic tragedies and repeated viewings of *Upstairs, Downstairs*, servants are not simple humanoid tools; instead they are liminal beings that straddle and negotiate the boundaries between private and public, inside and outside, the master's domain and life on the street. Clever servants like Jeeves are able to store, anticipate, communicate and even withhold knowledge in such a way as to influence and determine the actions of those they are supposed to serve.

> The three aspects that make the servant a privileged custodian and navigator of knowledge are his function as a hinge and intermediary between different spheres; a certain logic of economy that his services carry; and his institutionalization in the form of designated spaces that are consolidated into privileged contact points for the distribution of information. (Krajewski, 'Ask Jeeves' 10)

Exchange *his* for *its* and you have a pretty accurate description of, say, an electronic mail server. Krajewski's basic point is that the protocols and procedures that determine the exchanges of helpful demons in cyberspace contain the protocols and procedures that determine the exchanges in the old human service domain, and vice versa. As he points out, the interaction between a mail client and a mail server in cyberspace in part imitates a dialogue 'in everyday language' (Krajewski, *Der Diener* 265) – which would not be the case had the protocols for this particular technical setting been developed completely from scratch (if, in other words, servers had not been preceded by the servants they replace). In order to understand the servers of today, then, the analyst must retrace the iterations of the protocols and procedures back in time to a predetermined reversal point (in Krajewski's case, the mid-eighteenth century), and then, equipped with the knowledge gained from this movement backwards, turn around and retrace the iterations forward in time to the present. The trick is that retracing the iterations backwards (which in each and every case involves the observation of how servant protocols process them-selves) will change the reversal point. If we step by step trace the history of servers and servants back to the eighteenth century, we will arrive at a new description of the latter. This means that our iterations forward to the present will start in a past that is differ-ent from the one we had targeted when we set out. The iterative process – Winkler's expanded reproduction – changes the goal. As a result, the present we return to will also change. And one of the main aspects of this change is a new insight into the structural cor-relation between past and present serving entities.

> The result of such a recursive historiography is the mutual explanation of all stages of iterations. Ultimately, it enables a symmetrical insight: in a certain way, the eighteenth-century servant functions like a mail server which, in turn, exhibits some of the specific functional elements of the classic servant figure that are further differentiated with every iteration. (Krajewski, *Der Diener* 274)

Krajewski speaks of 'recursive historiography', which appears to imply a new approach that can be added to the arsenal of established historiographical procedures. However, there are things at work here that may not fit into our historiographical toolboxes because they are at odds with conventional notions of history. The more technical the story gets (that is, the more we move from servants to servers), the more we are dealing with a mushrooming techno-logical structure which, increasingly oblivious to its socio-human environment, changes itself by constant recursive self-processing. Also, how do we reconcile this performative recursive analysis of nested structures with more conventional understandings of diachronic processes, given that each iteration can only be ana-lysed as always containing past and future states? With this in mind, Krajewski provides the most succinct definition possible: '*Die Rekursion ist ein Vorgriff auf den Rückgriff*' – 'recursion is a pro-lepsis of an analepsis' (*Der Diener* 271). It enables us to apprehend the *Gleichzeitigkeit des Ungleichzeitigkeiten* ('the contemporaneity of the non-contemporaneous'). However, this is where matters get serious, since we are faced with history-defying juxtapositions and short circuits that are outside the provenance of time – *human* time, that is.

Tempus Ex Machina

The basic reason for the rising profile of recursion as a (counter-) historiographical procedure is the increased fracturing of time. We do not live under the rule of one absolute time; we live in and through different temporal habitats that are every bit as varied as our spatial environments. Needless to say, this is nothing new. Time is not one and indivisible; it never was. Medieval theologians happily assigned varying scales, shapes and speeds of time to humans, angels and animals; and modernity (including all its prefixed breeds and variations) can be described as an ongoing chronomachia in which attempts to install a homogenized industrial time face off against recalcitrant allo-, micro- and counter-temporalities. However, what has caught the attention of German media scholars working in the wake of the Kittler effect is the fact that, when it comes to media, established historiographical narratives are unable to handle non-human temporalities. Historiographical emplotments cannot capture *machine time*.

Nobody has expressed this view more vigorously than Wolfgang Ernst. Following and at times radicalizing Kittler, Ernst insists that the social construction of technical artefacts reveals little about their technical make-up. While there is nothing wrong with either affirmative tales about the rise and fall of media technologies or more critical accounts of how media should be used, these culturally inflected narratives will not enable us to understand media fully. Media are not what we do with them, neither are they what they do with (or to) us. Regardless of social background, usage or impact, media are what they do, no more and no less (faint existentialist echo intended). To pick up on one of Ernst's examples, take an ancient Greek vase and a 1930s radio, both on display in a museum. From a conventional archaeological and/or historical point of view they are of interest because they have both defied time by still being around.

> But what drastically separates an archaeological object from a technical artifact is that the latter *discloses its essence only when operating*. While a Greek vase can be interpreted simply by being looked at, a radio or computer does not reveal its essence by monumentally being there but only when being processed by electromagnetic waves of calculating processes. If a radio from a museum collection is reactivated to play broadcast channels of the present, it changes its status: it is not a historical object anymore but actively generates sensual and informational presence. (Ernst, 'Media Archaeography' 241; my emphasis)

Which is why a 1930s radio on display in a museum invariably plays Glenn Miller rather than Lady Gaga: measures are taken to ensure that the artefact is confined to its original temporal habitat. (Just like zoos, museums want their displays to feel at home and their visitors to feel safe.) But Ernst is not talking about any old radio; he has in mind the *Volksempfänger*, the low-priced, Bakelite-encased 'people's receiver' first mass-produced in the 1930s to establish a permanent link between Hitler's mouth and German ears.

[The *Volksempfänger*] receives radio programs when operated today, since the stable technological infrastructure of broadcasting media is still in operation. There is no 'historical' difference in the functioning of the apparatus now and then (and there will not be, until analogue radio is, finally, completely replaced by the digitised transmission of signals); rather, there is a media-archeological short circuit between otherwise historically clearly separated times. ('Media Archaeography' 240)

The fact that the radio was primarily used to transmit Joseph Goebbels' ranting about total wars reveals little; its history-defying 'media-archeological short circuit' becomes apparent when it is used, for instance, to broadcast George W. Bush's celebration of missions accomplished.

At this point we could enter on a lengthy discussion of Ernst's theory background(s). The notion that media reveal their essence only in operation is an interesting twist on Heidegger's elaboration of *Zeug* or equipment in *Being and Time*. The emphasis on the *Eigenzeit* of media – the fact that they have, and produce, their own time – continues and expands Kittler's emphasis on the importance of analogue and digital time axis manipulations. More fundamentally, it is a further radicalization of Foucauldian archaeology. If Foucault insisted on subjecting history to vertical cuts that sliced it into epistemic discontinuities, and if Kittler's update of Foucault consisted in relating these *epistēmēs* to techno-discursive networks grounded in epoch-specific materialities of data processing (if, to update Ranke, every epoch is immediate to its machines), then Ernst is adding horizontal cuts that transfer these materialities into their own temporal domain – a xenochronia fundamentally out of synch with human time. Many, no doubt, will lament this as yet another step in the regrettable disemplotment of the world. *Libera nos, machina, a furore narrandi.*

We could also launch a time-honoured conceptual sabotage operation by exposing certain metaphysical underpinnings (which is the media-theoretical equivalent of catching a 'family values' politician in a strip joint). Like the theological dwarf hidden inside in Walter Benjamin's historico-materialist chess automaton (Benjamin 253), Ernst's 'materialist diagrammatics' (Parikka) has a few metaphysical goblins frolicking underneath its cool veneer. Obviously, history-defying short circuits presuppose that the physical and electromagnetic laws known to the designers of the *Volksempfänger* are still in operation today. Mathematically encoded laws of nature, then, occupy the place once held by the music of the spheres. It is a higher zone, one of quasi-angelic timelessness, into which those of us equipped with the required computational expertise can momentarily escape our dull sublunary existence.

Of course matters are not that simple. Take the fact that both access to and execution of these media short circuits – for those adventurous readers patrolling the slippery pathway between science and science fiction: these media-enabled wormholes or Einstein–Rosen bridges that cut across the human time-space continuum – are themselves increasingly mediated. Starting in 1902, Enrico Caruso made a large number of disc phonograph recordings most of which have been re-engineered and released over the last century. It is one of the most persistent (and lucrative) instances of sonic remediation, as Caruso's voice migrated from shellac to vinyl to CDs and iPods, while all around his voice orchestral accompaniments were enhanced, removed and overdubbed. Closer to Ernst's terminology, the posthumous career of Caruso is a sequence of archival transformations. All media technologies are 'archives of cultural engineering' (Ernst, 'Media Archaeography' 243), and in ways which give a lot of additional meaning to McLuhan's mantra that the content of one medium is always another medium, each archive recursively processes another.

As a result, these recursive remediations are not only aesthetic and commercial undertakings; they are also archaeological endeavours. If, for instance, the inscribed phonographic traces on wax cylinders from Edison's days are opto-digitally retraced, inaccessible sound recording becomes audible again. 'Frozen voices, confined to analogue and long-forgotten storage media, wait for their (digital) unfreezing' (Ernst, 'Media Archaeography' 248). Media are the new capital-S Subjects of media archaeology; we, the former subjects, can sit back and enjoy the 'blessing of the media-archaeological gaze' (Ernst, 'Media Archaeography' 249). For this reanimation of dead sounds and images Ernst even goes so far as to use the word 'redemption' ('Media Archaeography' 248). Cue, once again, Benjamin. Or should we phrase it the other way round? That Benjamin's awkward phrasing is now itself redeemed?

Let us summarize three Kittler-related points before we wormhole back to antiquity:

1 Kittler readers will recall that his history of the early analogue media is structured by the Disability Theme: '[T]echnical media like the telephone and the gramophone were invented in the nineteenth century for and by the deaf, and technical media like the typewriter were invented for and by the blind [. . .] Cripples and handicaps lie like corpses along the path to the present' (Kittler, *Optical Media* 120). Frequently dismissed as a Kittlerian snarkasm, the idea is in fact based on a straightforward observation: it was, above all else, the isolation of cognitive subroutines resulting from injuries and impairments that allowed for the decisive nineteenth-century psychophysical mapping procedures, in the course of which these subroutines and the new analogue media were modelled on each other. Ernst adds an a-human twist. In Kittler's earlier narrative, media that help us see, hear and write better were developed by and for those who saw and heard less; now we have a sequence of intermedial prosthetics: media with superior storage, processing and communication facilities come to the help of their disabled brethren.

2 Kittler readers will further recall that he was a great promoter of unknown quotations. Among the best-known is the observation by the newly mechanized Friedrich Nietzsche, who, reflecting on the impact that his Malling Hansen Writing Ball had on his style, noted in a letter: '*Unser Schreibzeug arbeitet mit an unseren Gedanken*' – 'our writing tools too are working on our thoughts'. Unearthed by Kittler (*Gramophone* 200), the quotation has had a great afterlife. The obvious self-reflexive twist – our writing tools are also working on our thoughts about our writing tools – contains in a nutshell the recursive epistemological dilemma that has haunted media theory since the days of Harold Innis. By referring to the new opto-digital rewriting of old phonographic traces, Ernst is tightening the loop: our writing tools are (re)writing our

writing tools – without any human assistance or interference. The evolution behind our backs which fully revealed itself with the arrival of media 'able to read and write by themselves' (Kittler, *Literature* 147) is complemented by the intimacy between media subjects processing each other without human interference.

3 It was, I believe, Thomas Steinfeld who first spelled out Kittler's hidden Hegelianism. Unwittingly or not, Kittler encouraged this reading by providing sound bites which turned media history into an updated German Idealism downloading itself into cyberspace:

> What I keep dreaming of and what people don't like to hear because they believe that technology and science are mere tools made for people in the street [. . .] is that machines, especially the contemporary intelligent machines as conceived by Turing in 1936, are not there for us humans – we are, as it were, built on too large a scale – but that nature, this glowing, cognitive part of nature, is feeding itself back into itself. (Kittler, *Short Cuts* 270)

The increasing miniaturization and acceleration of digital technologies allow for an ever deeper and finer processing of matter down to its crystalline structure, which, in turn, feeds back into the refinement of ever faster and more powerful technologies. The ultimate vanishing point is a quasi-Lacanian holy grail of establishing a direct micro-physical and temporal link between the real and symbolic at the complete expense of the imaginary. On this level of processing, humans are about as helpful and necessary as horse-drawn carriages are for space travel. Pushing the envelope, we can see something similar in Ernst's xenochronic scenario: a whole infrastructure of links and short circuits is emerging next to and beyond human history – it may indeed obsolesce history as we know it. And make no mistake, the medial recursions extend far beyond minor century-old short circuits connecting turntables to iPods; they go back millennia. The greatest media-based madeleine moment will lead us – you guessed it – all the way to the Sirens.

Gulf Excursion: Storing the Sirens

Musik und Mathematik I/2: Eros concludes with an eighty-seven-page chronology covering 35,000 years of Kittlerian history (293–380). The first entry reads: '33,000: Five-hole flute made from the hollow bone of a griffon vulture, discovered 2008 in the Achtal close to Ulm' (293). The year 2008 also happens to be the chronology's final one; in fact, Kittler's very last entry notes the death of Richard Wright (380). History started with the earliest musical instruments and ended with the impossibility of Pink Floyd ever reuniting. Even the greatest recursions must terminate.

The Sirens are part of the grand chronicle. Zeus 'lies with' Leda in 1245 BCE (*Eros* 299). Helen is born in 1244 and abducted by Paris in 1220. The Trojan War ends in 1209 and three years later, in 1206 BCE, 'Odysseus listens to the Sirens' (300). For 27 CE Kittler records Tiberius' move to Capri 'in order to indulge in young flesh in the Blue Grotto and ask his grammarians what the Sirens sang on the neighbouring islands' (333). So far, so exact. But fast-forward to 1943, another important Siren year. Kittler notes the birth of Janis Joplin and Jim Morrison, Albert Hofmann's first LSD trip, Heinz von Foerster's largely unknown work on radar engineering for the German Luftwaffe, and the occupation by US Marines of 'Europe's first island: Lampedusa' (376). No wonder Kittler himself was born in that year. So much of what came to dominate his thinking was born or took shape then: sex, drugs and rock 'n' roll; the spirit of free love (incarnated by Dionysus redux Jim Morrison); the technical achievements of the Wehrmacht; and the ambiguous blessings of European Americanization. But he omits one important item. Serving on HMS *Exmoor in* early September 1943, Ernle Bradford (who following the war spent years tracking Odysseus' voyage across the Mediterranean) heard the Sirens sing:

> The music crept by me upon the waters [. . .] I cannot describe it accurately, but it was low and somehow distant – a natural kind of singing one might call it, reminiscent of the waves and the wind. Yet it was certainly neither of these, for there was about it a human quality, disturbing and evocative. (Bradford 130)

The *Exmoor* was patrolling the Gulf of Salerno in support of a
seaborne invasion. Acting on Bradford's warning, the ship steered
towards the nearby Li Galli islands of Gallo Lungo, Castelluccio and
La Rotonda, known since antiquity to be the home of the Sirens
and now a possible hideout for enemy vessels. As the destroyer
circled the islands nobody else heard or saw a thing, but Bradford
kept hearing and seeing more:

> I had now reached a point when the singing somehow began to make
> sense. First of all it was very old [. . .] And secondly, it had a direct
> bearing on *me* – of that I felt sure. It began to draw on me so that I
> wanted to join it – and this 'joining it', I knew in some obscure way,
> meant going back into the past [. . .] It meant, I knew, going back in
> time, retreating in some way or other into a different world. I kept
> getting a picture, as it were, of temples by the shore: white shores
> under the sun and, where the waves ran up to the land, there was a
> small temple. (133)

Note the switch from aural to visual, song to temple. Note
also how the former is located in a grey zone between natural
sounds and specifically addressed messages with a 'human quality'.
Meaning emerges from noise and reinforces its content by acti-
vating a cultural memory of antiquity – a Lacanian transfer from
the real (waves) over the symbolic (encoded communication) to
the imaginary (picturesque temples). Ironically, Bradford's clas-
sically embellished vortex into the past appears to channel the
famous analysis proposed by Kittler's principal competitors in Siren
matters, Max Horkheimer and Theodor W. Adorno. In *Dialectic
of Enlightenment*, the two Frankfurt 'hobby philosophers' (Kittler,
Aphrodite 263) noted that the main 'allurement' of the Sirens 'is
that of losing oneself in the past' (Horkheimer and Adorno 25) –
a regression that threatens the very foundations of subjectivity.
Odysseus resists the tempting song by tying himself to a mast;
Bradford is protected by the command structure of the Royal
Navy. (But how close are the Siren recursions explored in Berlin
to the Siren regressions analysed in Frankfurt?)

Fast-forward sixty-one years. In April 2004 Kittler and Ernst
headed a 'sound-archeological' research expedition to the Li Galli

islands (Ernst, 'Lokaltermin Sirenen'). The basic premise was unqualified trust in the ability of Homer's and Bradford's words to describe Siren songs and a qualified distrust in the ability of human ears to understand them fully. Several experiments involving human organs and technical apparatuses were conducted. On the human side, mouths sung and spoke Homeric verses at and from the islands while being listened to by human ears. The result was additional proof of Odysseus' well-known mendacity. His tall tale of ropes, mast and wax-stuffed ears turns out to be an Ithacan sailor's yarn. Consonants do not carry far, so in order to understand the Sirens' invitation to step ashore Odysseus must have left the boat. A similar procedure was carried out on a technical level: sound-producing technologies were used to project sounds to and from the islets while being recorded by storage devices. The subsequent (technical) analysis of the (technical) recordings produced an interesting insight: sounds emanating from the main island, Gallo Lungo, hit the Siren rocks Castelluccio and La Rotonda and, much like a ball caught between the flappers of a pinball machine, started to echo between the two, resulting in the disorienting sonic phenomenon experienced by Bradford: 'It seemed to have moved, for the sound which I could have sworn originated near this particular rock was now masked by it and seemed to come from the other' (132). The special twist of this forensic Siren story, however, is the fact that one of the sound-producing devices used to reveal the ancient Sirens was an aerophone, a noise-maker that produces signs by interrupting the air flow – in other words, a modern siren.

Sirens track Sirens. At first glance this recalls Tiberius' 'silly and laughable' attempt to determine what the Sirens used to sing; it makes Krajewski's recursions involving twenty-first-century electronic servers and eighteenth-century servants sound like the epitome of respectable common sense. But let us follow the example of Kittler's Odysseus, abandon the safe boat of scholarly probity, and go along on the Siren field trip.

Both Ernst and Kittler subscribe to the idea that the Greek vowel alphabet was invented to transcribe Homeric verse. With this in mind, one of the major differences between the two epics becomes especially important. As Philipp von Hilgers notes, 'Homer's *Odyssey* – unlike the earlier *Iliad* – plays its games with the Greek vowel alphabet by speaking of and with voices that, detached from the bodily presence of heroic figures, have various traceable effects on their audience' (197). First off, this alludes to one of the well-known, self-recursive *Tristram Shandy* moments of the *Odyssey*. At the court of the Phaeacians the grief-stricken Odysseus listens to Demodocus sing about the exploits of Odysseus.[4] It is recursive nesting at its Homeric best: the epic anticipates the setting in which it is customarily performed, and it then tightens the screw by having its audience listen to the hero – who has temporarily crossed over to the side of the audience – listen to his own epic.

This metafictional component is linked to the epic's awareness of its medial underpinning. Von Hilgers' claim that the *Odyssey* is 'speaking of and with detached voices' points to the fact that a new symbolic notation system can store the poet's voice in such a way as to enable verbatim reproductions that no longer require the special skills of bards (who will never give verbatim performances anyway). The effectiveness of the notation system arises from its ability to capture the constituent components of sound production: it encodes how we speak rather than what we hear. The *Odyssey*, however, is ambivalent about its own medial effects, and the Sirens are the epitome of the ambivalence. On the one hand, they sing that they 'know all that comes to pass on the fertile earth' and are eager to share their knowledge. This omniscience has led many interpreters to identify them with the Muses. Read through the Kittler effect, the ritual appeal to the Muses to grant a song that exceeds more than any one singer can faithfully remember is the invocation of a new storage technology which enables this astounding feat. On the other hand, the deadly allure of their song, the way in which their disembodied voices assail the body of Odysseus, indicates a fundamental loss of autonomy of those who read and listen. In order to speak, the perfectly stored songs need bodies as much as the underworld shadows consulted by Odysseus need blood. From the point of view of the vowel alphabet, humans are voice machines composed of lungs, lips and larynx necessary for the performance and propagation of texts. As Jesper Svenbro has brilliantly analysed in *Phrasikleia*, the ancient Greeks (just like the young Kittler) were very much aware of the degree to which reading is a hostile takeover of bodies and subjects by texts. The greatest leap forward in the history of communications technology becomes indistinguishable from the deepest fall into a media-induced heteronomy.

Ernst adds a twist by arguing that this medial awareness also acts in preparation of future media:

> The ancient Greek practice of the vowel alphabet sensitises the culture of knowledge [. . .] From the point of view of the archaeology of knowledge, this beginning of the technology of vocal culture already contains [. . .] its teleo-archaeological end. The true message of the phonetic alphabet as a cultural technique is the desire to achieve an indexical relationship to the sound of the voice, but this outstrips the capabilities of symbolic notation. The phantasm is only realised by a genuine media technology, the phonograph. ('Der Appell der Medien' 182)

Sound familiar? We are back in Benjamin territory – to be precise, section XIV of 'The Work of Art in the Age of Mechanical Reproduction'. Reflecting on the fact that Dadaism employed literary and artistic means to achieve effects that now can easily be had in cinemas, Benjamin noted that every historical era 'shows critical epochs in which a certain art form aspires to effects which could be fully obtained only with a changed technical standard' (237). Media act like Marx's suicidal bourgeoisie: they are their own grave-diggers because their success sets the stage for their own supersession. The same logic can at times be found in Kittler and Ernst. Just as the reading practices of Kittler's Discourse Network 1800, with its instant transformation of letters into images, created a demand for cinematography, so the way in which the vowel alphabet analyses how sound waves are voiced, broken, checked, released and shaped when emanating from Siren lungs, anticipates the ways in which modern recording technology analyses the ways in which sound waves are stopped, broken and refracted when emanating from Siren islands. If Bradford's sudden vista of bygone temples (itself a product of filmic readings of ancient texts) serves to show the proximity between recursion and media-induced regression, we here have the exact opposite: recursions are enabled by media-induced anticipations. Krajewski is right:

recursions involve prolepsis and analepsis, but in ways that go far beyond the techno-algorithmic.

Granted, only a few decades separate Benjamin's Dadaism and Kittler's cinematographic reading practices from the technologies that appear to implement them fully, but in the case of the Siren-to-siren shortcut we are leapfrogging across millennia. Here, however, we come across a recursion of Hegelian splendour and magnitude that is related to the refunctionalization of the Greek alphabet. By way of a simple conversion of ordinal into cardinal, *alpha*, the first letter, also became the number 1; *beta*, the second letter, also became 2; and so on. The alphabet extended its signifying powers by recursively processing its own systemic properties. In time, the letters were also used as tones, with the result that one and the same sign system handled language, numbers and music. Kittler is less interested in the short-lived refunctionalization into tones; he prefers to focus on the more systematic refunctionalization into numbers, all the more so because the latter are used to indicate musical harmonies. In the Pythagorean tradition, however, the perfect harmony (expressed mathematically and musically) is that of the two Sirens singing. The answer to Tiberius' question *quid Sirenes cantare sint solitae*, then, is not only to quote Homer but to insist that the message is the medium itself. In Kittler's terminology, the Siren song is the first discourse on discourse channel conditions, insofar as the song performs its own notational and musical properties. But we should not completely bury the message under the medium, for according to Kittler the invitation expressed by the Sirens – 'Come hither Odysseus' – is an invitation to have sex. Odysseus accepts the invitation as eagerly as he later denies having done so. In the senior Kittlersphere, however, sex is a recursion of gods in humans, for it amounts to a human repetition of the act first performed by the gods. Sex is mimesis – no further philosophical elaboration of the term is necessary. To fuse Homer and Freud, what we call sex is a recursion of the *Urszene* of the gods.

We have, then, recursions through time and analogies through time and space that annihilate whatever temporal or conceptual distance may come into play. At one point, before philosophy and politics intervened, the Greeks had a multi-functional sign system that processed language, music and mathematics; now we have it again in the shape of binary code. How could we not be close to the Greeks? The fundamental property of the mathematical portion is the distinction between odd and even; our digital counterpart works with the one/zero binary. And in Kittler's heteronormative world this distinction reappears in the male/female opposition. To write is to sing is to calculate proportions and ratios is to practise mimesis of the gods is to pluck strings of a lyre is to fuck – and everything came together beautifully and recursively on a hot summer day in 1206 BCE off and on the Li Galli islands. *Rekursionen über Rekursionen* indeed. Kittler's later theory is – literally, metaphorically, numerically – making love to the Greeks.

Ernle Bradford, incidentally, never heard the Sirens again. A few years after the war, while tracking Odysseus' route down Italy's west coast towards Scylla and Charybdis (aka the Straits of Messina), he passed Li Galli without hearing anything. He did, however, furnish an explanation Kittler must have appreciated: he had his wife with him, and there is 'no record of the Sirens ever having sung to a ship that had a woman on board [. . .] They do not want anything from their own sex' (Bradford 133). Bradford's Sirens, like Kittler's, are resolutely heterosexual.

Conclusion: Recursive Reasons

Before we descend deeper into Suetonius mode, let us return to the main question. Why recursions? What does the concept allow German media theorists (and Kittler in particular) to do? Which implies the question: what dilemmas may this concept resolve? At the risk of further over-simplification I will conclude with a few observations that (maybe not recursively, but hopefully logically) follow from each other:

1 The most important sign Kittler ever deployed in his career is the slash between '1800' and '1900' in the title of *Discourse Networks*. It indicates breaks, caesuras, ruptures. In the footsteps of Foucault it signals the trademark affect against continuity so prominently on

display in early German *Medienwissenschaften*, which was a necessary stratagem to preclude the grand narratives of *Bildung, Geist*, dialectics, reason or enlightenment inf(l)ecting the humanities.

2 As has been discussed many times, Kittler further processed Foucault by critically refashioning *epistēmēs* as media-based discourse networks. On the one hand, the song remained the same. Both epistemic orders of speech and increasingly technologized networks for storing and distributing data can act as instances that determine how people think and speak; and they do it extremely well when they leave humans under the impression of autonomy. Humans do not gradually learn to make history; history gradually makes humans believe they do.

3 On the other hand, the 'grounding' of Foucault was liable to clash with the emphasis on discontinuity. Kittler was too conscientious a historian (in other words, too much a nineteenth-century creature) not to be aware of the links and transformations of technology, practice and knowledge that indicated connections through time. Or, to phrase the same problem from a different perspective: Kittler had grounded epistemic ruptures in medial changes, but what made the latter change?

4 One of Kittler's answers was war. As media technologies replaced each other in a game of war-driven one-upmanship, the medial *a priori* was collapsed into a martial *a priori*. There are several empirical and conceptual problems with this proposal (see Winthrop-Young 129–43), but one very basic difficulty is the fact that while war may function well as the motor of media evolution if you restrict yourself to the three modern centuries the younger Kittler focused on, it is pretty useless across the three millennia the older Kittler had in mind.

5 This is where recursion comes in. It is the 'only way' to write history because it is best equipped to structure Kittler's grand occidental narrative. First, as a step-by-step process that with each iteration calls itself, recursive history is very different from the questionable narratives of continuous, organic or dialectical growth. On the other hand, it does allow for sequences and connections through time. Recursive historiography, then, obeys the Foucauldian injunction on grand continuities while avoiding the dilemmas of exaggerated rupturism.[5] Second, it gestures towards a

self-enclosed, almost autopoietic process that precludes attempts to depict history as the playground of a master subject. However, while the martial Kittler of the 1980s subjected history to a self-recursive strategic escalation of military technologies (that subsequently were abused for entertainment purposes), Tiberius' hard-core Arcadian porn productions have little to do with war. It is instead a form of cultural technique, a term that has come to replace 'media' across a broad spectrum of German media and cultural studies because it goes beyond the strong artefactual bias that characterized Kittler's influential earlier work. To invoke Winkler's observation, Kittler's recursions function as expanded reproductions of cultural techniques. Third, recursive historiography allows for reappearances. More precisely, it provides a respectable framework for Kittler's attempts to find concrete examples of what Nietzsche called the eternal recurrence of the same: be it the attempt to dress up Jim Morrison and other rock stars as revenants of Pan and Dionysus or Tiberius' 'recursive' indulgence in nymphs and satyrs.

6 But the final point is the most important. Consider, in conclusion, how close Kittler's epic song of love and numbers is to Krajewski's recursive servant story. For Krajewski, the decisive methodological component was a movement back to a predefined point of return followed by a movement forward into the present – with the understanding that both the point of reversal and the present change as a result of the approach. And that is precisely what Kittler was aiming at across the seven projected volumes of *Musik und Mathematik*: to return to a different Greece (not the one defined by Socrates, Plato and Aristotle and the beginning of metaphysics), which, if it becomes our point of departure for a recursive trip back to the future, will result in a different present that unfolds and fulfils what is contained in the different beginning. As stated in the very beginning of the first volume, the stakes are high:

> We want to tell you about music and mathematics: the most beautiful things after love, the most difficult after faithfulness. We want to do it from the heart, because otherwise hearts remain sundered. [. . .] Either a new beginning succeeds, or that of Greece was in vain. (Kittler, *Eros* 12)

This is not – or not only – Kittler; it is Heidegger. Indeed, what separates the older Kittler from younger media theorists like Krajewski or Ernst is his allegiance to the older, outspoken Heidegger. Kittler is bringing numbers to the Black Forest – the very numbers that Heidegger disdained because he did not understand the other, different beginning of numbers in Greece. Ultimately, the function of recursion is to update and retrofit Heidegger's recursive *Seinsgeschichte* or history of Being (which is, as the older Kittler came to point out time and again, Foucault's history writ large). To understand recursions, to think in recursions, may be the only way to prepare ourselves for the recursive (re)approach of the gods in numbers, music and love.

Notes

1 'Für diese neue Art, Geschichte zu erschreiben, gibt es nur eine Weise, einen Namen: Rekursion.' Note Kittler's use of the upscale *erschreiben* as opposed to simple *schreiben* (to write). *Erschreiben*, usually accompanied by a dative reflexive pronoun, implies the acquisition of something by way of writing which one did not have before. One of the many *er*-verbs that dominate Kittler's later texts, it imbues the very act of writing with a certain creative agency.

2 *Verwindung* – one of Heidegger's fearsome untranslatables – is normally rendered as 'overcoming'. Overcoming, however, comes closer to *Überwindung* ('going beyond'). *Verwindung* involves transformation and/or (re)processing. In other words, it resembles recursion. This is one of the many instances in which Kittler uses Heidegger's idiolect to allude to formal algorithmic procedures in order to suggest a certain affinity that Heidegger himself was reluctant to recognize.

3 As opposed to K-1 (studied with Kittler in Freiburg from the late 1970s to the mid-1980s) and K-2 (Bochum from the mid-1980s to the early 1990s).

4 More to the point, Odysseus requests that Demodocus sing of the fall of Troy. For Kittler, this desire to get drawn back into his own exploits is further proof that Odysseus left the boat to join the Sirens, since this is precisely what they offer to him.

5 Ofak and von Hilgers subtitle their recursion collection *Faltungen des Wissens* ('Folds of Knowledge'). It could just as well have been called 'Folds of Time'. Recursions fold time and thus enable direct contact between points and events (and S/sirens) that are separated when history time is stretched out on a continuous line. In both cases there are obvious Deleuzian echoes. The focus on recursion is another example of German *Medienwissenschaften* technologically grounding and respecifying strands of French poststructuralism.

Works Cited

Benjamin, Walter. *Illuminations: Essays and Reflection*. Ed. Hannah Arendt. New York: Schocken, 1968.

Bradford, Ernle. *Ulysses Found*. London: Hodder and Stoughton, 1963.

Ernst, Wolfgang. 'Lokaltermin Sirenen oder Der Anfang eines gewissen Gesangs in Europa.' *Phonorama: Eine Kulturgeschichte der Stimme als Medium*. Ed. B. Felderer. Berlin: Matthes & Seitz, 2004. 257–66.

Ernst, Wolfgang. 'Der Appell der Medien: Wissensgeschichte und ihr Anderes.' *Rekursionen: Faltungen des Wissens*. Ed. Ana Ofak and Philipp von Hilgers. Munich: Fink, 2010. 177–97.

Ernst, Wolfgang. 'Media Archaeography: Method and Machine versus History and Narrative of Media.' *Media Archaeology: Approaches, Applcations and Implications*. Ed. Erkki Huhtamo and Jussi Parikka. Berkeley: University of California Press, 2011. 239–55.

von Hilgers, Philipp. 'Sirenen: Lösungen des Klangs vom Körper.' *Parasiten und Sirenen: Zwischenräume als Orte der materiellen Wissensproduktion*. Ed. Bernhard J. Dotzler and Henning Schmidgen. Bielefeld: Transcript, 2008. 195–218.

Homer. *The Odyssey*. Trans. Robert Fagles. New York: Viking, 1996.

Horkheimer, Max, and Theodor W. Adorno. *Dialectic of Enlightenment*. Trans. E. Jephcott. Stanford: Stanford University Press, 2002.

Kittler, Friedrich A. *Literature, Media, Information Systems: Essays*. Ed. John Johnston. Amsterdam: G+B Arts International, 1997.

Kittler, Friedrich A. *Gramophone, Film, Typewriter*. Trans. Geoffrey Winthrop-Young and Michael Wutz. Stanford: Stanford University Press, 1999.

Kittler, Friedrich A. *Short Cuts*. Frankfurt: Zweitausendundeins, 2002.

Kittler, Friedrich A. *Musik und Mathematik I: Hellas 1: Aphrodite*. Munich: Fink, 2006.

Kittler, Friedrich A. *Musik und Mathematik I: Hellas 2: Eros*. Munich: Fink, 2009.

Kittler, Friedrich A. *Optical Media*. Trans. Anthony Enns. Cambridge: Polity, 2010.

Krajewski, Markus. 'Ask Jeeves: Servants as Search Engines.' *Grey Room* 38 (2010): 6–19.

Krajewski, Markus. *Der Diener: Mediengeschichte einer Figur zwischen König und Klient*. Frankfurt: Fischer, 2010.

Ofak, Ana, and Philipp von Hilgers, eds. *Rekursionen: Faltungen des Wissens*. Munich: Fink, 2010.

Parikka, Jussi. 'Operative Media Archaeology: Wolfgang Ernst's Materialist Diagrammatics.' *Theory, Culture & Society* 28.5 (2011): 52–74.

Suetonius. *Volume I: Lives of the Caesars i–iv*. Trans. J. C. Rolfe. Cambridge, MA: Harvard University Press, 1998.

Svenbro, Jesper. *Phrasikleia: An Anthropology of Reading in Ancient Greece*. Ithaca, NY: Cornell University Press, 1993.

Winkler, Hartmut. 'Rekursion: Über Programmierbarkeit, Wiederholung, Verdichtung und Schema.' *c't Magazin* 9 (1999): 234–40.

Winthrop-Young, Geoffrey. *Kittler and the Media*. Cambridge: Polity, 2011.

5

Preparing the Arrival of the Gods

Friedrich A. Kittler

I will start with a simple double question from Jimi Hendrix's 'And the Gods Made Love', the first track on *Electric Ladyland*: what does 'Electric Ladyland' mean? And why should the gods make love? (Afghanistan, Iraq, do they not matter?)

These questions, I've neglected them so long. Being a child of the Second World War, I've written for many years on the feedback between media technology and warfare. England's great pop musicians of my age – to my knowledge – did much the same thing. When the Rolling Stones declared their sympathy for the devil, the Second World War was musically ever present: Mick Jagger sang of himself as a general commanding a tank during the blitzkrieg. And there was Roger Waters, singing about the Falklands War, when a mourning wife or girlfriend stood 'upon Southampton dock, with her handkerchief and her summer frock' to 'bravely wave the boys goodbye again' (Pink Floyd, 'Southampton Dock').

Recently, however, some sudden event or inspiration – Plato would even call it a god – has changed my mind. I decided to try the opposite. If you come to think about it, the opposite of war isn't just peace, war's uncanny aftermath. The opposite of war, by Jove, is love. This was already known to the earliest Greek philosophers who placed Aphrodite and Neikos, that is love and strife, high above all other gods and elements, be they heaven or earth, fire or water.

Speaking and writing on love, however, proves to be much more difficult than on war. The gods have left us and goddesses such as Aphrodite even more so. Even the nymphs, their humble companions (as T. S. Eliot has it), 'are departed' (33) from our meadows and forests, springs and lakes. No one, when drinking fresh water from a spring, would give its nymph a little flower, as was the custom for every girl in Homer. An economy of exponential growth, as Thomas Pynchon has denounced it, tries to destroy, maybe in vain, an economy of mutual gifts. Thus, not only the gods have left us, but also their traces on earth. The temples are in ruins and with them all the dimensions that Hölderlin recalled under the absolutely not Christian names of the salvation and the holy [*des Heils und des Heiligen*]. The task of thought, therefore, following Heidegger, consists these days in opening at least some spaces of the salvation which could prepare the holy which then in turn would make room for the arrival of the gods.

Fortunately, this task of ours is neither new nor unheard of. It has been done once before – namely at the beginning of Greek poetry. As Herodotus wrote long ago, it was from the poets Homer and Hesiod that the Greeks received the names and stories of their gods. As Wade-Gery, Cambridge's great classical scholar, wrote in the 1950s, it was for Homer's sake that a nameless Greek adapted the Phoenician consonantal alphabet to the Indo-European vowel system (11–15). That is why his twenty thousand hexameters have survived verbatim for almost three millennia. That is why you can read Greek, and only Greek, poetry without understanding a single word.

In doing so, Aphrodite may come back again. Because the greatest Greek poetess, Sappho from the island of Lesbos, has called her goddess to come, we too can call her.

Poíkilótron áthanat Áphrodíta
paí diós dolóploke líssomaí se
mé m'asaísi méd' oníaisi dámna,
pótnia, thúmon,[1]

Deathless Aphrodite of the spangled mind,
child of Zeus, who twists lures, I beg you
do not break with hard pains,
O lady, my heart,

but come here if ever before
you caught my voice far off
and listening left your father's
golden house and came,

yoking your car. And fine birds brought you,
quick sparrows over the black earth
whipping their wings down the sky
through midair –

they arrived. But you, O blessed one,
smiled in your deathless face
and asked what (now again) I have suffered and why
(now again) I'm calling out

and what I want to happen most of all
in my crazy heart. Whom should I persuade (now again)
to lead you back into her love? Who, O
Sappho, is wronging you?

For if she flees, soon she'll pursue.
If she refuses gifts, rather will she give them.
If she does not love, soon she will love
even unwilling.

Come to me now: loose me from hard
care and all my heart longs
to accomplish, accomplish. You
be my ally.

(Carson, *If Not, Winter* 1–5)

Sappho, it is said, wrote nine lyrical books on topics such as
love and marriage, gods and heroes. From all these songs this

hymn to Aphrodite is the only one to have survived complete. All others have been mutilated or even destroyed by fanatical Christian monks. That is why we can follow, in this instance only, the very flow of Sappho's invocation from beginning to end.

The poem starts by stating that the poetess suffers from something that only wily Aphrodite can cure, so the unhappy lover uses her poetic voice to call the goddess to come. This wish, however, immediately turns into a memory of things past. As the Canadian poet Anne Carson has brilliantly shown, the whole poem centres on Sappho's dialectal word '*deûte*', which paradoxically means 'now' and 'again' at the same time. To put it in other words: Sappho, for the first time in European history, calls Eros, the god of love, simultaneously bitter and sweet.[2] Aphrodite is bitter insofar as she is actually missed; she has been sweet insofar as she came from Zeus, her father – that is, from heaven itself – to the dark black earth of Lesbos. All this Sappho tells us in the simplest and most colloquial terms. Even the sparrows which pulled Aphrodite's golden chariot through the air are not the bloodless poetic metaphors they'll become for later poets. On the contrary, sparrows, hares and doves, given their famous fertility, stand for the sexual aspect of the goddess. Aphrodite is no deity in whom men and only men believe, but a presence and manifestation of nature as a whole. Here is a quotation from a great German classical scholar who, just after the Second World War, distinguished the Olympian gods from monotheistic religions as follows:

> The gods of the Greeks are a necessary part of the world, and this is reason enough why they should not be linked exclusively with national boundaries or privileged groups. How could there be any gods but those whose existence is self-evident, inherent in nature itself? Who, for instance, would gainsay that Aphrodite exists? Everybody knows that she is as active among all other peoples as she is among the Greeks; even the animals are subject to her rule. It would be downright absurd to maintain that one does not 'believe' in Aphrodite, the goddess of love. It is possible to neglect her, to pay no respect to her, as was done by the huntsman Hippolytus [in Euripides' play], but Aphrodite is present, and active, none the less. (Snell 25)

Precisely because poets, not priests, conceived the Olympian gods, Greek cult, ritual and myth are not religion at all. This crazy activity founded on faith or belief will only begin with the Romans and end up only today. Sappho, on the contrary, simply trusts in the power of her song. She bids the goddess to come again, now for a second time. She remembers how Aphrodite's own human voice once appeared against the background of many a sparrow's wings – just as music always emerges from a background of noise. She remembers Aphrodite laughing in the face of her own desperation. Simply because gods are immortal, they can witness human pain but not feel it. That is why Aphrodite, instead of sympathizing with desperate love, has the magical power to change the mind of the implied third, Sappho's beloved maiden, who, instead of fleeing her, will and must soon do the opposite. However, even before Aphrodite makes this explicit promise, she reminds Sappho of the fact that their whole dialogue is always already a repetition. So, when her words come to an end and Sappho, in the last stanza, finally takes over again, the number of encounters with the goddess amounts to three. Greek gods, just like music, seduce by sheer iteration. You can't even tell whether they are mortal or immortal. Whenever a human lover and a beloved human come together they turn into gods. They appear to each other more graceful, more beautiful; in short, more divine. And this is, as Nietzsche has strongly argued, no mere mutual illusion, but a biological fact to be observed in singing birds, peacocks and mortals alike. You simply cannot tell whether Sappho's last stanza is addressed to the goddess or the beloved. Its solemn cry '*Élthe moi kaí nun* – Come to me now' – applies to them both. Thus, it names the secret of love. 'My ally', Sappho's final name for Aphrodite, speaks of even more: lovers come together just like warriors.

As long as Greek poetry didn't turn into mere literature, that is, from Homer and Sappho until Sophocles, this 'come to me now' would never disappear from their epics, lyrics and tragedies. As long, however, as we silently read it on printed paper, its sound and music have always already vanished. Aristotle and his followers did everything to destroy the letters of Greek musical notation by supplying Attic script to Alexandria's museum. That is why, in order to recall Sappho's music, her actual environment, to our minds and ears, we should attend to another of her fragments:

> here to me from Krete to this holy temple
> where is your graceful grove
> of apple trees and altars smoking
> with frankincense.
>
> And in cold water makes a clear sound through
> apple branches and with roses the whole place
> is shadowed and down from radiant-shaking leaves
> sleep comes dropping.
>
> And in it a horse meadow has come into blossom
> with spring flowers and breezes
> like honey are blowing
> [. . .]
>
> In this place you Kypris taking up
> in gold cups delicately
> nectar mingled with festivities:
> pour.
>
> (Carson, *If Not, Winter* 7)

Here we can begin to understand Sappho's poetry in its sensual and magical environment. The place where she composes and sings to the sound of her seven-stringed lyre is a holy meadow surrounding one of Aphrodite's many houses. Because Greek temples are neither crowded with Christian believers nor emptied by post-Christian masses, they accommodate only a godlike statue and prescribe that mortals worship outside in the sunshine. In other words, when Sappho performs her song, young maidens will dance around her just like nymphs, following the length of each single syllable. Moreover, all this aphrodisiac play takes place among flowers, fragrances and gentle breezes whose equally sensual and verbal presence always already answers the call for Aphrodite. In other words, when sleep falls down like honey, two women spread on soft cushions will have enjoyed each other. No Greek was ever scandalized by the fact that Sappho's preference, at least before her happy marriage, was for lesbian brides rather than male bridegrooms. Marital – that is, genital – love, in order to succeed, presupposes the experience of all its polymorphic predecessors. This Pan-Hellenic freedom only died with Latin letters and literature, that is, after golden Aphrodite had sunk to the level of Caesar's bloody Venus. Horace and other Romans called the poetess a public whore. Byzantine monks destroyed her work and turned the goddess she had begged to appear into the obscene and satanic figure known as Lady Venus.

Under these disastrous conditions, what can be done in order to prepare what Nietzsche called the eternal return of the gods? Surprisingly, it is enough to listen. A simple piece of music points the way.

'Grantchester Meadows', written and composed by Roger Waters, came out in 1969. It was meant to bring Pink Floyd back to the Cambridge whence they came. It was meant to bring the sounds of yesterday into the London cityscape. And because its sounds are not just a human voice interwoven with an acoustic guitar, but the meadow's very river, lark and noise, Sappho's poetic landscape is suddenly back again. Under the conditions of high technology, many different sound tracks can be recorded, amplified and mixed together in order to combine the signifiers with their meaning, the music with its ambient noise. For the first time in history, the fundamental gap between nature and culture begins to disappear. Pop music can tell that we are body and soul, humans and singing birds at the same time. As in Helmholtz's phantastic theory of 'sound sensations', a kingfisher flashing to the water produces concentric little waves that always already resemble those of radio, television and vinyl long-playing records. Frequencies of whatever kind can be transformed, modulated and stored into each other. It is as if sound had become immortal.

Although Pink Floyd couldn't possibly know, 'Grantchester Meadows' has precisely this secret meaning. As the story goes, Alan Mathison Turing, when he laid down on its grass, conceived in 1935 the famous machine which later, on the other side of the river Cam, became his mathematical PhD thesis. And every desktop, laptop and mobile/cell phone that we use, in the final analysis, comes down to such a Turing machine, simply because the English mathematician proved the machine's capacity to imitate every other machine.

However, imitation, μίμησις in Greek, is the principle of love. When Jimi Hendrix cries out that the gods made love, the very secret of Electric Ladyland has been revealed. Because the gods are not lonely and unique, that is without wives, mortals may imitate them by mating. The Aristotelian formulation 'that the creator is such as the created [. . .] for man begets man' (14) is simply mistaken. As Frederick II, emperor of Germany as well as of Italy, wisely remarked, every being in nature needs two to beget. From the gods to our parents, from our parents to us and our children runs the great chain of life. The fury of Pope Gregory IX, when he read this statement, one can easily imagine.

For the early Greek poets, all this was evident, but it was to fall into monotheistic oblivion. Already in Plato's philosophy, there exists only one single god, who, moreover, is formally forbidden to change his shape and appearance. Thus, he can no longer approach young brides in the animal forms of a swan, an eagle or a bull. With Platonic idealism and Christian monotheism, the game of endless imitations has seemingly come to an end.

What, then, have been the necessary conditions to recreate, as for instance in Pink Floyd's lyrical meadows, the spirit of Greek music and poetry? In my ears, the answer is Wagner. In theory as well as in musical practice, Richard Wagner went back to tragedy as performed in classical Athens. Learning from Aeschylus and Sophocles, he rediscovered that tragedy, to quote Heraclitus, has to accomplish on its stage the big divide between masters and slaves, immortals and mortals, and, not to be forgotten, between the two genders. It is, in its essence, a harmony of war and love, daughter of Ares and Aphrodite.

Wagner's *Ring of the Nibelung* recalls exactly this story. It is the first serious music ever written in Europe that transgresses the limits of monotheism. The poet in Wagner has forgotten all his earlier Celtic or medieval plots. The musician in Wagner starts by composing father Rhine himself as that immemorial beginning when music and noise, art and nature are deeply interwoven. The river sings louder and louder, the strings play higher and higher until the instrumental foreplay materializes itself in the form of human voices. The Rhine's three daughters start with meaningless syllables that imperceptibly glide to words such as wave and cradle:

Weia! Waga!
Woge, du Welle,
walle zur Wiege!
Wagalaweia!
Wallala weiala weia!

(Wagner, *Das Rheingold* 6)

Thus, language emerges out of music, music out of noise. The big wave of oscillations encompasses in its flow both the singers and the instruments, the visible brides and the invisible orchestra pit beneath Bayreuth's stage. To reformulate it with Nietzsche's elegant formula: the birth of tragedy out of the spirit of music accomplishes itself.

At the same time, when the curtain rises and the light falls, Wagner enacts a new arrival of the gods. Twilight means both morning and evening, birth and death. Wotan, formerly a wholly nomadic god, gives orders to erect for himself and his feudal wife Fricka a fortified castle. Clearly, by doing so he imitates Napoleon at the very moment when the great French emperor marries into the old European nobility. Later, however, by abandoning all this family, the god returns to his revolutionary beginnings. Together with Erda/Earth herself, he engenders a clan of heroes and heroines all of whom imitate their father's or grandfather's necessarily incestuous love. On the other side, the dark side, of the gods, exactly the opposite happens: by engendering Hagen, his mortal revenger, Alberich perverts love itself to sex, power and money. Thus, in an endless play of rising and falling that lasts fourteen hours on Wagner's stage, the *Ring of the Nibelung* comes full circle. Immortals such as Wotan turn into mortals, heroes such as Siegfried into gods. When the castle and its divine owners are consumed by fire, when this fire is consumed by water, the physical elements of Greek thought come back into being and fighting. Under the mask of Rhine's daughters, the Sirens dear to Odysseus are shown to sing and flow again. As Thomas Pynchon will state in *Gravity's Rainbow*: 'How can flesh tumble and flow so, and never be any less beautiful?' (854). Or, as Jimi Hendrix has it in *Electric Ladyland*, when in 'Moon, Turn the Tides . . . Gently, Gently Away' the lovers sink down into Neptune's domain, to 'hear Atlantis, full of cheer' (The Jimi Hendrix Experience).

It is the same music, from Wagner to Hendrix, from Hendrix to Waters. At the same time, it is the same stage, be it musical drama or pop music's light show. Syd Barrett's 'Piper at the Gates of Dawn' resumes from the beginning what Wagner called the final 'Twilight of the Gods'. Here is Brünnhilde when she addresses her divine father in a monumental lullaby:

> *Weiss ich nun was dir frommt?*
> *Alles! Alles! Alles Weiss ich:*
> *Alles ward mir nun frei!*
> *Auch deine Raben hör' ich rauschen:*
> *mit bang ersehnter Botschaft*
> *send' ich die beiden nun heim.*
> *Ruhe! Ruhe, du Gott!*

> Know I now all thy need?
> All things, all things, all now know I.
> All to me is revealed.
> Wings of thy ravens wave around me;
> with tidings long desired,
> I send now thy messengers home.
> Rest thou, rest thou, o god!

> (Wagner, *Götterdämmerung* 83)

The German original makes it much clearer that noise and message fall as completely together as they do in Claude Shannon's mathematical theory of information. By waving their wings, Wotan's dark ravens find their way home to the sphere of eternal return. Death becomes sleep, and sleep rebirth. One of the most brilliant questions invented by Nietzsche tells us precisely this.

> What if some day or night a demon were to steal into your loneliest loneliness and say to you: 'This life as you now live it and have lived it you will have to live once again and innumerable times again; and

there will be nothing new in it, but every pain and every joy and every thought and sigh and everything unspeakably small or great in your life must return to you, all in the same succession and sequence – even this spider and this moonlight between the trees, and even this moment and I myself [. . .].' Would you not throw yourself down and gnash your teeth and curse the demon who spoke thus? Or have you once experienced a tremendous moment when you would have answered him: 'You are a god, and never have I heard anything more divine.' (194)

Nietzsche's question is clearly a riddle which answers itself: whoever guesses the demon's own name has solved it. By definition, Dionysus is the god who never ceases to return. In this coming and coming again consists his immortality. As long as we continue to invoke Homer, Sappho and Aphrodite, their fame, as Sappho prophesied, will endure.

'Speech has become, as it were, immortal.'[3] These were Edison's precise words when he presented, in 1877, his latest invention, the phonograph. From that year on, however, not only words have become immortal, but all kinds of music, sound and noise. The inventor himself made reproducible whatever can be recorded. On the banks of the Swanee River, for instance, Edison's phonograph immortalized not only the blues going under this name and the black people performing it, but also the steamboat's roaring machine, and the Swanee River's song. The Thames, as Kate Bush tells us, is 'a poet that never, ever ends'.

However, it was only when black music crossed the Atlantic Ocean, when hundreds of thousands of GIs landed in southern England and dozens of captured German tape recorders came to London's Abbey Road, that the Second World War turned into pop music. Invention and innovation are always a case of crossovers, be they cultural or technical. Neither jazz nor rock 'n' roll alone could have triggered Swinging London or street-fighting stars. It was only the feedback loop between European technology, classical harmonics and America's musical illiteracy that, in the Sixties, exploded between Marshall amps, lead guitars and microphone whispers. In order to write pop songs, no one is doomed to learn old Europe's five-line system in his boyhood, just as no one is forbidden to know it. Roger Waters may whisper as gently as he wishes, but the sounds of Grantchester's meadows will fill huge concert halls as well as microscopic sound tracks. This and only this distinguishes pop music from Wagner's musical drama. Whereas in serious music, composers, conductors and librettists usually remain hidden as persons and bodies, pop stars perform as a rule what in Wagner's case was a great exception: they write both the words and the music which they themselves play, record and execute. In other words, when the difference between Wagner and Wotan, mortal and god, disappears by implosion, the figure of a star is born. It was not in vain that Roger Waters addressed Syd Barrett, Pink Floyd's mad founder, with the invocation 'Shine on, you crazy diamond!'

Back in 1974, when Germany's football team won the title of world champions, the philosopher Martin Heidegger happened to take a train from Heidelberg back to Freiburg, our home town. He, just as I have, had spoken of Hegel, the Greeks and the gods. And since intercity trains at that time had restaurants of a quality unthinkable today, Germany's greatest thinker got a chance to make the acquaintance of Freiburg's theatre director. 'Why didn't we meet before?' was the director's urgent first question. 'Why don't you ever show up at dramatic performances I give?'

Heidegger's answer was simple: 'Because on your stage there are just actors that I'm not interested in seeing.'

> 'But, dear professor, I beg you: What else could we possibly do?'
> 'I'd rather see and hear not actors, but heroes and gods.'
> 'Impossible. Heroes don't exist and gods even less.'
> 'So, haven't you watched our recent world championship on TV? Although at home my wife and I don't have TV, I used to visit some nearby friends in order to watch. For me, the most obvious thing to remark was the fact that Franz Beckenbauer, and he alone in the German team, was never fouled or wounded. He's proven to be invincible and immortal. Now you can see, even amongst us, there are heroes and gods.'[4]

If Heidegger is right, the same logic applies equally well to pop stars. Otherwise there could never have arrived what, during the Sixties, the Americans called the British invasion. As mighty as Dionysus, young English voices and guitars broke into the standardized mass production of rock 'n' roll music. They swept away the old-fashioned divisions between singers and composers, between musicians and technicians, pop stars, heroes and gods. The price paid by the new-born stars has been immortalized in Jim Morrison's cry:

> Cancel my subscription to the resurrection!
> Send my credentials to the house of detention,
> I've got some friends inside.
>
> (The Doors, quoted in Sugarman 80)

Prophetic words, indeed, something like a self-fulfilling prophecy. Whoever cancels his or her subscription to the Christian faith gets a minor chance to become pop star, demon and god. Morrison's father, a highly decorated vice-admiral in the US navy, threw the sinner and son out of his Miami home. Morrison started to read the pagan poetry written by Nietzsche and Rimbaud, put it into lyrics, obscenities and music, and by doing all this created or, rather, opened The Doors, America's answer to the British invasion. From a girlfriend he learned to go without underwear, from Swinging London his lightshows.

Only two years later, the prophecy almost became true. The Doors and their lead singer toured Florida and, for the first time, performed in Morrison's home town. The seats in Miami's Dinner Key Auditorium had been removed in order to make place for more young people; the air inside was as hot as hell. Suddenly, without his band's foreknowledge, Morrison began to invoke the crowd:

> You're all a bunch of fuckin' idiots. You let people tell you what you're gonna do. Let people push you around. You love it, don't ya? Maybe you love gettin' your face shoved in shit . . . you're all a bunch of slaves. What are you going to do about it? What are you gonna do? [. . .] Hey, I'm not talkin' about revolution. I'm not talkin' about no demonstration. I'm talkin' about love your neighbour till it hurts. I'm talkin' about grab your friend. I'm talkin' about some love. Love, love,

love, love, love, love, love. Grab your friend . . . and love him. Come ooooaaaaann. Yeaaahhh! (Densmore 125)

These literal exhortations come from Morrison's drummer, who had to endure them and witness, immediately afterwards, the singer's jump into the audience. Certainly, the arrival of Dionysus among his followers has been greatly facilitated by cordless microphones and the like. The dancing got more and more frenetic, the dressing less and less correct. One day later, when the cleaning team entered the Miami auditorium, they discovered teenage clothes draped all over the place. After piling them up in one corner, the sum amounted to one and a half metres in height, three in diameter, as if the totally un-Greek habit of festival clothing had finally got its deserved punishment. The heap insofar as it was clothing consisted of sandals, gym shoes and moccasins, also of trousers, jeans and T-shirts, not to mention blouses, sweatshirts and skirts. As far as modern underwear came into play, Miami's cleaning team, as I've been told, discovered more slips and pants than bras. The relapse to transparent – and that means US-compliant – bra straps, which at least we men can bemoan, seems not to have been organized and implemented in 1969. Millions of petrodollars, the only common currency between three lonely gods, had yet to flow.

John Densmore, the drummer, when he learned of all this, just wondered how those Miami girls and boys had managed to get home from the concert. Without their slips and bras, so many of them had behaved like David Bowie's heroes: they were heroines just for one day, or one night. Only in late 1969 did Densmore arrive at a solution. The happening had received no mention at all in the local papers and television stations. Instead, Florida's bishop organized a teenage movement for moral decency. This anti-fan club supported by US senators and mayors declared with holy Christian oaths that they had witnessed on stage just one incredibly obscene event: Jim Morrison, the singer, had allegedly exhibited his underwear-free member and had even simulated oral sex with Robbie Krieger, the guitarist. The juvenile audience, meanwhile, was said to have withstood this sexual attack in all-American purity. Everybody remained in his or her clothes, not a single naked body was seen on the streets. Jim Morrison, the culprit, finally had to appear before a Miami jury that recommended six months' prison or detention. The judge, more lenient, sentenced him to pay five hundred dollars. The rest is silence.

Two years later, in 1971, Jim Morrison entered the underworld of his gods, Californian as well as Greek. Dionysus, following Heraclitus, and Hades are one and the same. On his grave in Paris, next to the poets he loved, in the graveyard of Père Lachaise, you'll read an uncanny inscription: 'Jim Morrison, poète, artiste et compositeur'. Precisely this is the trinity that They won't ever forgive us. Jahweh is jealous, Allah despotic, not to mention the father, the son and the (holy?) ghost. Washington, Tehran and Jerusalem. Everyone knows and no one, except our bygone heroes, has ever said it. As long as they reign, World War III, IV and so on will threaten us as doom or fate. Since the Latin word *fatum*, however, simply meant all that is said or sung, you should and could trust our rare poets. 'Nothing is real. Strawberry Fields forever' (The Beatles).

This is as far as I can go now. We have to speak in riddles and allusions. That the gods made love is called just a song. In the absence of Electric Ladyland, everything you love will be perverted. Nobody tells you any more that 'public', our common word for so-called democratic actions, trials, jurisdictions and so on, is derived from *pubes*, the Latin word for pubic hair. Think of gods and kids and pop stars, The Doors and Miami! America, as far as we know, doesn't allow us public Dionysian rites. Instead, after the lightshow, pop stars retire to their hotel rooms. And there, every groupie they fuck turns into a nymph. She has opened her cunt to the music. Every rock star is Dionysus, so that Aphrodite reigns again.

I will finish with Friedrich Hölderlin, Heidegger's long-gone poet, who declared that every cherry tree and every peach, every spring and swallow when they come to us from South or East, recall the ancient Greeks and Homer. Listen, love, to Hölderlin and me!

O Land des Homer!
Am purpurnen Kirschbaum oder wenn
Von dir gesandt im Weinberg mir

Die jungen Pfirsiche grünen,
Und die Schwalbe fernher kommt und vieles erzählend
An meinen Wänden ihr Haus baut, in
Den Tagen des Mais, auch unter den Sternen,
Gedenk' ich, o Ionia, dein!

Land of Homer!
By the scarlet cherry tree, or when
The young peaches you sent to me
Are still green in the vineyard,
And the swallow arrives from afar and, bringing endless news,
Builds her house in my walls, in
Maytime, and under stars,
Ionia, I think of you!

(Hölderlin 206–7)

Notes

This chapter was originally presented as a keynote lecture at the conference *Media Matters: Friedrich Kittler and Technoculture* held at Tate Modern, London, in 2008. The chapter is published in German as 'Das Nahen der Götter vorbereiten', in: Friedrich A. Kittler, *Das Nahen der Götter vorbereiten*. With a preface by Hans Ulrich Gumbrecht. Wilhelm Fink Verlag, Paderborn 2011, p. 10–29.

1 Editorial note: The Greek text of Sappho's fragments can be found in Eva-Maria Voigt, ed. *Sappho et Alcaeus: Fragmenta*. Amsterdam: Polak & Van Gennep, 1971. We have chosen to remain faithful to Kittler's transcription of the Greek, even though it does not employ the usual English transcription system used elsewhere in *Kittler Now*.

2 Editorial note: Kittler is here referring to Sappho's fragment 130 and Anne Carson's discussion of it in *Eros the Bittersweet: An Essay*. Princeton: Princeton University Press, 1986.

3 Editorial note: The quotation is correctly attributed to a correspondent to the *Scientific American* journal and not to Edison. E. H. Johnson, 'A Wonderful Invention' (Letter to the Editor). *Scientific American* 37 (November 17, 1877): 304.

4 Editorial note: This is Kittler's gloss on the story presented in Petzet (210).

Works Cited

Aristotle. *Metaphysics Books Z and H*. Trans. David Bostock. Oxford: Clarendon Press, 1994.

Barrett, Syd. *The Piper at the Gates of Dawn*. Columbia/EMI, 1967.

Beatles, The. 'Strawberry Fields Forever.' *Sgt. Pepper's Lonely Hearts Club Band*. Parlophone, 1967.

Bush, Kate. 'Oh, England, my Lionheart.' *Lionheart*. EMI, 1978.

Carson, Anne. *Eros the Bittersweet: An Essay*. Princeton, NJ: Princeton University Press, 1986.

Carson, Anne. *If Not, Winter: Fragments of Sappho*. London: Virago, 2002.

Densmore, John. *Riders on the Storm: My Life with Jim Morrison and The Doors*. London: Bloomsbury, 1991.

Doors, The. 'When the Music's Over.' *Strange Days*. Elektra, 1967.

Eliot, T. S. 'The Waste Land.' *The Waste Land and Other Poems*. London: Faber, 1971.

Helmholtz, Hermann von. *On the Sensations of Tone as a Physiological Basis for the Theory of Music*. New York: Dover, 1954.

Hölderlin, Friedrich. 'Die Wanderung.' *Hyperion and Selected Poems*. Ed. Eric L. Santner. New York: Continuum, 1990.

Jimi Hendrix Experience, The. 'Moon, Turn the Tides ... Gently, Gently Away.' *Electric Ladyland*. Polydor, 1968.

Nietzsche, Friedrich. *The Gay Science*. Ed. Bernard Williams. Trans. Josefine Nauckhoff. Cambridge: Cambridge University Press, 2001.

Petzet, Heinrich W. *Encounters and Dialogues with Martin Heidegger, 1929–1976*. Trans. Parvis Emad and Kenneth Maly. Chicago: University of Chicago Press, 1993.

Pink Floyd. 'Grantchester Meadows.' *Ummagumma*. Harvest/EMI, 1969.

Pink Floyd. 'Southampton Dock.' *The Final Cut*. EMI/Harvest, 1983.

Pynchon, Thomas. *Gravity's Rainbow*. New York: Random House, 1973.

Rolling Stones, The. 'Sympathy for the Devil.' *Beggars Banquet*. Decca Records, 1968.

Snell, Bruno. *The Discovery of the Mind in Greek Philosophy and Literature*. New York: Dover, 1953.

Sugarman, Danny. *The Doors: Complete Lyrics*. London: Abacas, 2001.

Wade-Gery, H. T. *The Poet of the Iliad*. Cambridge: Cambridge University Press, 1952.

Wagner, Richard. 'Das Rheingold.' *Der Ring des Nibelungen: Ein Bühnenfestspiel für Drei Tage und Einen Vorabend*. London: Schott, 1876.

Wagner, Richard. 'Götterdämmerung.' *Der Ring des Nibelungen: Ein Bühnenfestspiel für Drei Tage und Einen Vorabend*. London: Schott, 1876.

Part II

'Our Writing Tools are also Working on our Thoughts'

6
Scilicet: *Kittler, Media and Madness*

Steven Connor

Speaking Your Mind

In an interview with John Armitage published in 2006, Kittler spoke of his stratagem for speaking his mind:

> [M]y work in literary criticism was not only a pretext but also a histori-
> cal necessity which, all the same, permitted me to talk about German
> poets whilst saying things I wanted to state in my own name but did
> not dare to articulate. You may ask why it was so difficult to say things
> in my own name. Well, apart from the fact that I am a shy person,
> it was very hard during that time in Germany to move beyond the
> study of dialectics and the self's relation to itself. Consequently, I had
> to cover up all I wanted to say with nice stories about young German
> poets. (18)

All of this was prompted by the irritated apprehension that 'in
Germany in the 1970s and 1980s, one had always to pretend that
what one wrote had been written down in some book one had
consulted' (Armitage 18). Deleuze has spoken in rather similar
terms about his earlier work, in which he says that he used other

philosophers as mouthpieces, or rather, surrogate parents, on whom he fathered his own conceptions, before beginning to be able to write *in propria persona* (6). So Kittler seems to be saying that, in order to escape from the necessity of pretending that everything he had to say was already written down somewhere, he found himself surrendering to, indeed engineering something like, the very exigency he sought to evade, by saying what he had to say only through surrogate forms that were indeed already written down.

A few moments later in the interview, Kittler explains that even the title of the book that appeared in English as *Discourse Networks 1800/1900* had a title in German that seems to allude to this condition of prescription, since it is a phrase taken from *Memoirs of My Nervous Illness*, the book in which Daniel Paul Schreber provides a detailed account of his delusional system. What in English is a 'discourse network' is in German an *Aufschreibesystem*, a 'writing-down system', and 'it was not the done thing', Kittler remarks 'to take the title of a tenure track book from the text of a madman' (Armitage 18). I have it in mind, or someone has it, possibly somewhere else, to try to draw out some of the implications and outcomes of the gramophonic madness that supplies Kittler with his governing concept of the inscription system or, as it might otherwise be rendered, the registering, recording or notation system. In order to keep in mind the question of the already-written-down, I will be using the phrase 'inscription system' to translate *Aufschreibesystem* in place of 'discourse network'.

The inscription system is first described some hundred pages into Schreber's text: '*Books or other notes* are kept in which for years have been *written-down* all my thoughts, all my phrases, all my necessaries, all the articles in my possession or around me, all persons with whom I come into contact, etc.' (123). Schreber believes that the rays which are assailing him, the nerves of God, as he believes they ultimately are, are being drawn to him by his unique power of attractiveness. Indeed, the physical and mental tortures of the rays are in fact designed to protect them from being wholly assimilated to or absorbed into his being, as they otherwise would be. He explains that one of the principal purposes of the inscription system is actually to enable the rays to immunize themselves against him:

It was believed that my store of thoughts could be exhausted by being written-down, so that eventually the time would come when new ideas could no longer appear in me; this of course is quite absurd, because human thinking is quite inexhaustible; for instance reading a book or a newspaper always stimulates new thoughts. This was the trick: as soon as an idea I had had before and which was (already) written down, recurred – such a recurrence is of course quite un-avoidable in the case of many thoughts, for instance the thought in the morning 'Now I will wash' or when playing the piano 'This is a beautiful passage', etc. – as soon as such a budding thought was spotted in me, the approaching rays were sent down with the phrase 'We have already got this', *scilicet* written-down; in a manner hard to describe the rays were thereby made unreceptive to the power of attraction of such a thought. (8)

Schreber reassures himself of the inexhaustibility of mind, and yet feels emptied out by the unavoidable necessity of repeating oneself, since every such repetition seems to be the occasion for or proof of a spoken word that has written itself down in advance. Schreber begins to feel himself to be nothing else but a playback mechanism.

Later on, he suggests that the inscription system may also be employed to test whether he is still alive and capable of mental activity:

People around me are made to say certain words by stimulating their nerves; as for instance madmen throw in a certain learned term (possibly in a foreign language) which they perhaps remember from the past; these come to my ears and simultaneously the words 'has been recorded' (*scilicet* into awareness or comprehension) are spoken into my nerves: for example a madman says without any connec-tion 'rationalism', or 'social democracy' and the voices say 'has been recorded', thereby attempting to find out whether the terms 'rational-ism' or 'social democracy' still have a meaning for me, in other words whether I have enough reason left to comprehend these words. (220)

Reason now just means the residue of whatever has not yet been taken down in evidence. Reason is whatever can succeed in being off the record.

A number of media technologies were closely associated at their beginnings with disability or sensory deficit – deafness in the case of Edison, blindness in the case of the typewriters which were marketed as forms of automatic writing for the blind. The phonograph offers itself as a supplement that will plug that gap in being that voice is, since it streams out so unstintingly and irrecoverably. The phonograph promises to restore the voice to itself, to allow it to cleave to, no longer be deaf to itself. But the phonograph is itself deaf to what it nevertheless hears or overhears, in that it is unable to discriminate between phonemic structure and phonetic phenomenon. With the phonograph, the voice is not just an event or overflow of being; it is an object for having. And yet, at least in Kittler's commentary, universal and simultaneous autoinscription leaves the voice more depleted and defective than ever before, since recording confiscates all its powers of original utterance.

Schreber's systematic account of his delusional system provides more than a symptomatic registration of the awareness of new recording technologies. It is at the heart of Kittler's understanding of the drastic shift from one system of inscription to another that took place following the development, from the 1870s onwards, of apparatuses that allowed the storage and manipulation, not just of words, but of sound and of moving image. We might note, without being able to do much more at this stage than merely note it, that Kittler focuses his account of the inscription system much more on technologies of storage and recall, the phonograph and the cinematograph, than on the technologies of transmission and dissemination, the telephone and radio, which developed coevally with them.

1800/1900

The phonograph, or gramophone, is at the centre of the transformations undergone between 1800 and 1900 because Kittler sees them as involving a radical deformation of the values associated with the voice, as the embodiment of life, spontaneous expressiveness, and the continuity of Man and Nature. In speaking, Man gives voice to and is given voice by Nature. In 1800, according to Kittler, voice is still conceived as Aristotle conceived it in his *De Anima*, the sound of that which has soul in it, with the difference that Aristotle's notion of soul extended to animated beings in general, and not just to the human animal. Quoting Herder's 'On the Origin of Language', Kittler declares that 'language in 1800 "was full of living sounds"' (*Discourse Networks* 43). In a sense, this might seem to mean that the *Aufschreibesystem* of 1800 is not, or not yet, an inscription system at all, in that all writing is held to conduce or aspire to the condition of voice. Perhaps a better rendering might be a 'notation system', since notation describes those encodings of music and dance the purpose of which is not so much to record as to allow the production of actions. In a similar way, writing at the beginning of the nineteenth century is subject to what Kittler calls 'auditory hallucination'; it is an oralized writing, which contrasts with the engraphed or conscripted speech that holds sway at the far end of the century. The mediator between voice and script in 1800 is handwriting, which seems to enact the seamless continuity of mind, hand and word, a continuity which is broken apart by the typewriter, which breaks language down into separate units. Kittler attaches great importance to the cursive forms of handwriting, arguing that '[t]he great metaphysical unities invented in the age of Goethe – the developmental process of *Bildung*, autobiography, world history – could be seen as a flow of the continuous and the organic simply because they were supported by flowing, cursive handwriting' (*Discourse Networks* 83). The curves of the pen caress the page, monitored attentively by the eye of the writer; the keys of the typewriter blindly impact and incise it.

Kittler offers us an analogy for Schreber's condition in Ernst von Wildenbruch, the Wilhelmine poet laureate, who was one of a number of poets who were persuaded to record their voices with the new phonograph. Indeed, he even wrote a poem for the occasion, the feeble rhyming of which, says Kittler, attests to the paralysing effect of the new apparatus: 'the voice can no longer be pure poetic breath that vanishes even as it is heard and leaves no trace. What once necessarily escaped becomes inescapable; the bodiless becomes material' (*Discourse Networks* 236). Kittler represents the move from orality to media as a move from spirit to matter: soul gives way to material marks, or neurological sparks. Voice, that had previously signified spirit, or the translatability of soul and body, becomes reduced to pure matter. Phonography, the writing of voice, may be regarded as a kind of phonotopy, or the spatializing of voice.

This is exemplified most clearly in the trope of auditory persistence, which animates a number of fantasies and romances. The principle behind these stories is articulated in a paragraph read by the demented inventor who is the protagonist of Florence McLandburgh's 'The Automaton Ear' (1876):

> As a particle of the atmosphere is never lost, so sound is never lost. A strain of music or a simple tone will vibrate in the air forever and ever, decreasing according to a fixed ratio. The diffusion of the agitation extends in all directions, like the waves in a pool, but the ear is unable to detect it beyond a certain point. It is well known that some individuals can distinguish sounds which to others under precisely similar circumstances are wholly lost. Thus the fault is not in the sound itself, but in our organ of hearing, and a tone once in existence is always in existence. (8)

The idea serves as the *donnée* for a number of technological fables and scientific romances of the late nineteenth and early twentieth centuries, one of which, Salomo Friedlaender's 'Goethe Speaks Into the Phonograph' (1916), Kittler reproduces in the 'Gramophone' chapter of *Gramophone, Film, Typewriter* (59–68). The vanishing of words and sounds is therefore henceforth to be understood simply as a diminishment of volume.

In order to retrieve the lost voices of the past it is no longer necessary to traverse time: one must simply reach down into matter and, through a conjoined process of amplification and of attunement, restore the lost sounds of the past. We are not forgetful of the past, merely deaf to it, and so we need, not a time machine, but a hearing aid, like the ear-trumpet that the inventor in McLandburgh's 'The Automaton Ear' purchases and modifies. Phonography stockpiles sound and, inasmuch as the evanescence of sound figures the unstable flow of time itself, it can be said to materialize time too. The late nineteenth-century Recording Angel in this respect anticipates Walter Benjamin's Angel of History, who, with his back towards the future, experiences the passage of the centuries only as the steady accumulation of the pile of rubble at his feet.

The most important feature of the gramophone for Kittler, the one that entitles it to be identified with the real rather than the imaginary or the symbolic of Lacan's schema, is that it hears passively or non-selectively. This brings about a shift from a focus on the signifieds, or meanings of texts, to their material signifiers: 'the gramophone empties out words, by bypassing their imaginary aspect (signified) for their real aspects (the physiology of the voice)' (*Discourse Networks* 246). The gramophone allows the registration of the unconscious or inaudible noise that always inhabits and accompanies the voice. Perhaps the most telling parts of Kittler's analysis concern not so much the ways in which the phonograph captured the voice as the ways in which it revealed the voice to be a carrier of, and itself always emerging out of, noise. After the phonograph, the voice was not so much the defeat of noise by signal as the product of a specific signal-to-noise ratio, for, Kittler tells us, 'the discourse network of 1900 places all discourse against the background of white noise' (*Discourse Networks* 288). Thus 'writing circa 1900 means being without voice' (285), and the swallowing up of the voice in noise means the dissolution of the subject. All the media devices of the late nineteenth century, combined with analytic constructions like those of Freud which mimic them, 'can track traces without a subject. A writing without the writer, then, records the impossible reality at the basis of all media: white noise, primal sound' (316). Writers and writing are 'accidental events in a noise that generates accidents and can thus never be overcome by its accidents' (184). Where Nietzsche's voice is lost in the hollow howlings of his last madness, Schreber finds that the only way to keep down the noise of the twaddle that fills his head is to shout it down with more noise, with bellowing, with empty rhymes, with piano-playing, with words the import of which he does not understand, all this 'responding to Flechsig's psychophysics with a psychophysical nonsense' (*Discourse Networks* 301).

Kittler is surely right to insist that one important effect of the new media of the late nineteenth century was to make noise unignorable. Understandably and tellingly, Kittler focuses on those points in discourse in which pure noise, pure nonsense, breaks through or overwhelms sense, soul, voice. But most of the time this does not happen. In fact, the gramophone does not abolish voice or murder soul – it merges with them, forming a new, mixed body. Noise is not simply set aside or filtered out, even when it is defined as that which must be so set aside or filtered out. Rather, it enters into signal, providing its most essential features – the grain of the voice, the timbre that defines the essence of some sound.

The materialization of voice and of moving image allows for two effects that had previously been available only in fantasy or dream, and are both important features of nonsense: the modification of speed and the playing of sounds backward. Schreber reports the first effect in terms that suggest a familiarity with phonographs and cinematographs, which were commonly cranked at non-natural speeds:

> No one who has not personally experienced these phenomena like I have can have any idea of the extent to which speech has slowed down. To say 'But naturally' is spoken B.b.b.u.u.u.t.t.t.n.n.n.a.a.a.t.t. t.u.u.u.r.r.r.a.a.a.l.l.l.y.y.y., or 'Why do you not then shit?' W.w.w.h. h.h.y.y.y.d.d.d.o.o.o. .. ..; and each requires perhaps thirty or sixty seconds to be completed. This would be bound to cause nervous impatience in every human being, not like myself more and more inventive in using methods of defense, as to make him jump out of his skin; a faint idea of the nervous unrest caused is perhaps the example of a Judge or teacher always listening to a mentally dull witness or a stuttering scholar, who despite all attempts cannot clearly get out what he is asked or wants to say. (202–3)

Reversibility emerges from the decomposition of the seemingly natural ongoingness of the stream of speech, which ordinarily can never turn back on itself without actually extending its stream onwards, into the vibrations which are its elementary form. A vibration may give rise to a powerfully propagating wave, but the particles which compose it actually go nowhere, merely shuttling back and forth in a very small compass (in the case of a longitudinal wave), up and down (in the case of a transverse wave) or in repeated small orbits (in the case of a compound wave such as one finds in the sea). The transcription system of 1900 effects this elementary decomposition, moving in close to every discourse as one might move in closer and closer to a newspaper or video screen, until all one sees is the clustering of the dots which compose it. This cures or destroys the ongoingness of time; it makes time reversible at the cost of pulverizing all meaning, which becomes typified by reduplications like *mama, papa* and *DADA* and chiasmi like *phonograph* and *gramophone*.

The most important and far-reaching effect of all this is that Man, who both is the giver of meaning in the previous system of inscription and has his meaning given to him by it, is evacuated: 'Once the technological differentiation of optics, acoustics and writing exploded the Gutenberg monopoly around 1880, the fabrication of so-called Man became possible. His essence escapes into apparatuses [. . .] So-called Man is split up into physiology and information technology' (*Gramophone* 16). The larger narrative of Kittler's history of media is the removal of Man from the circuit of media, which henceforth speak directly to each other, without the mediation of human users or agents – like the two gramophones which Kafka imagined speaking to each other in lieu of a lover's conversation: 'the individual falls in the crossfire between psychophysics and psychoanalysis; in its place is an empty point of intersection constituted by statistical generality and unconscious simplicity' (*Discourse Networks* 280).

Scilicet

Schreber is rather uncertain as regards the actual mechanism of his inscription system:

> I cannot say with certainty who does the writing down. As I cannot imagine God's omnipotence lacks all intelligence, I presume that the writing-down is done by creatures given human shape on distant celestial bodies after the manner of the fleeting-improvised-men, but

lacking all intelligence; their hands are led automatically, as it were, by passing rays for the purpose of making them write-down, so that later rays can again look at what has been written. (123)

One of the most grotesque, but surprisingly common séance-room stunts was the materialization of an ectoplasmic mouth, throat or larynx. The more technically minded would have appreciated the explanation frequently given by spirit controls that this was a necessary mediating structure to allow otherwise bodiless spirits to make vocal sounds. In this case, an intermediary object is formed in order to allow a certain bodily action to take place. In Schreber's account, something different occurs. Here he imagines a transcription system whose means are brought about simultaneously with the action it performs. Like the 'fleeting-improvised-men' whom he believed were summoned up out of nowhere and nothing, the agents and means of transcription are nonce-formations. Here the message is, or magically conjures, the medium.

The inscription system of 1900 might seem to be identified with universal mediation; we are, after all, accustomed to think of Friedrich Kittler as a media theorist. But we can say that there are in fact two phases to this mediation. The first is the development of the capacity to capture, store and retrieve voices. The second is the development of something like the principle of spontaneous self-capture. The first is a reality; the second, needless to say, is a fantasy, though a powerfully diffused one. In Schreber's delusion, potential becomes achieved and absolute fact. Being-able-to-be-recorded loops back in time to become the fact of already-having-been-recorded, of being on record in advance of its having arisen for the illusory first time. At this point, the capacity for universal mediation has become a kind of *immediation*, in which the condition of every utterance is that it instantly inscribes itself, without delay, deflection or reflection. This might then suggest a reversal of the apparently obvious contrast between the systems of 1800 and 1900. It might appear at first that the focus on signifieds rather than signifiers of 1800, and the centring principle of the mother's voice, would imply minimal mediation, with the voice everywhere immediately present. The system of 1900 would appear by contrast to surround and inundate the voice with mediations and surrogates. In fact, however, the system of 1800 would give a voice that was everywhere implied and dissimulated, in which everything is required to be translated back into a voice that lay always behind material appearances. In the system of 1900, by contrast, the mediation is so total and so immediate that originals mediate themselves instantaneously and in real time. Play is indistinguishable from universal, simultaneous playback.

Kittler offers in *Discourse Networks* a brilliant reading of Schreber's text as a kind of autoanalysis, seeing his impossible 'endopsychic perceptions of brain functions' (*Discourse Networks* 296) as 'a psychic information system that Freud takes at its word rather than as mania' (292). In this, he follows Freud himself, who claimed that his insights on paranoia were anticipated in Schreber's self-analysis. In a passage quoted by Kittler, Freud writes that '[i]t remains for the future to decide whether there is more delusion in my theory than I should like to admit, or whether there is more truth in Schreber's delusion than other people are as yet prepared to believe' (*Discourse Networks* 291). Kittler wants us firmly to make up our mind to believe the latter. It is a perfect and obedient enactment of the 'soul murder' practised by the new psychophysics that, for Kittler, is so closely bound up with the materialization of language – 'the patient dissects his own organs and notes their modifications while he is still alive, with a positivism that honors psychophysics' (*Discourse Networks* 294).

Under these conditions, it is the claim to genuine expressive authorship that is real delirium, while the embrace of the condition of anonymous hallucination 'achieves discursive reality' and '[a] delirium written down coincides with what sciences and media themselves were doing' (*Discourse Networks* 305). Schreber's text is read as an inspired defence through simulation of his violent reduction to psychophysical phenomenon by psychiatry: he 'makes delirium into literature where [. . .] in defense against the imbecility forced upon him he occasionally simulated the imbecile' (*Discourse Networks* 305). It does not seem possible for Freud to take Schreber entirely at his word, perhaps because of his unnerving proclivity to reduce himself to the words imprinted on his nerves. But where Freud sees Schreber's persecution as the enactment of unconscious fantasies of Schreber's father, with the figure of Schreber's doctor

Flechsig as a screen or mask for Schreber senior, Kittler treats Schreber's allegations about Flechsig literally: Schreber's God is Flechsig, the one who literally reduces Schreber's thoughts to nerve impulses, who refuses to Schreber the possibility of any rest or intermission, but demands from him a voice that can nevertheless only speak nonsense – for ours is, as Kittler affirms, 'the epoch of nonsense' (*Gramophone* 86). And yet Schreber does succeed in systematically inscribing the inscription system. As Kittler puts it, 'Schreber as Writer [*Schreber als Schreiber*] writes up what has written him off' (*Discourse Networks* 304). This writing, that is, that writing. Schreber uses the fact of exact, immediate equivalence to establish his own equivalence. The hinge word for him is a bookish term he favours throughout his text – *scilicet*, that is to say, 'that is to say', literally, 'it is permitted to know', or that which lets itself be known. We have met it twice already: 'the approaching rays were sent down with the phrase, "We have already got this", *scilicet* written-down'; 'these come to my ears and simultaneously the words "has been recorded" (*scilicet* into awareness or comprehension)' (Schreber, *Memoirs of My Nervous Illness* 128, 220).

It is not that Schreber has taken leave of his senses: it is that he is incapable of standing apart from them. On the one hand, Schreber experiences his mind and body as utterly out of his control, subject to spasmodic and unwilled 'miracles' of autonomous operation. On the other, he cannot allow his phantasmal body ever to slip below the threshold of awareness, cannot allow either mind or body to work on its own, and so must subject himself to endless self-monitoring and supervision. One may suspect that this automatism is simply the side-effect of this hypertrophied self-attention. It is not the unconscious which is the mainspring of Schreber's madness – it is the intolerance of any idea of the unconscious. What torments him most are not the thoughts that assail him but rather the irremissibility of thought itself, the denial of the capacity to think of nothing.

Kittler finds in Schreber's text much more than evidence for the system of transcription of 1900. Schreber's text conjoins with that of Freud and with those of other psychophysical explicators of the mind, so that 'the mental apparatus as described by the psychotic and psychoanalytic corpus [is] a single, highly complex information system' (*Discourse Networks* 293). Schreber's writing is not merely a discourse network or system of inscription on its own terms; it is a kind of autobiographical self-inscription by the system of inscription of 1900 itself: 'The paranoid machine operates like an integrated system of all the data-storage devices that revolutionized recording circa 1900' (*Discourse Networks* 299). Here, in finding the principle of the self-identity of the 1900 system of transcription made literal in Schreber's system, Kittler risks succumbing to Schreber's madness, which consists in mistaking mediation for mind itself.

It is not in the mediation of mind – the self-representation of mind in terms of mediatic forms and processes – that Schreber's madness consists. Rather, it is in what might be called his immediation – the mistaking of mind for media, the collapsing of mind into media, of a metaphorical relation into one of identity. Why is Schreber mad? Not because he is not himself, for it is actually the condition of sanity never fully to coincide with or consist of one's own identity, always to be other than or to the side of oneself. Schreber's madness lies in his dream of absolute self-identity, the identity of a self that attempts encyclopaedically to explicate itself, to command and set down the entire system of which it believes itself to consist. His madness is the literalization of the Delphic prescription *nosce te ipsum* ('know thyself'). It is the intolerance of exception, anomaly, of anything unconscious. Like Murphy's mind, in Beckett's *Murphy*, his system 'excludes nothing that it does not already contain' (107). Signal and noise are therefore no longer antagonists, but perfect mirrors of each other: nothing is meaningless, every bit of nonsense is charged with significance, noise *scilicet* signal, signal *scilicet* noise. The delusions of mechanoiacs like Schreber are not so much the signs of a dissolution of a Cartesian subjectivity by telematic media, or the effects of the irruptive riot of the unconscious, as the signs of a crisis of hyperconsciousness, a consciousness brought to crisis by the terrifying intensity of its fancied consciousness of itself.

This is to say that the problem of taking Schreber as the poet or analyst of the discourse network of 1900 is precisely that he is – utterly, epically and appallingly – mad. What is more, his may not even be symptomatic delusions, delusions that belong

authentically and expressively to the period in which they arise and
to which Kittler claims they give a systematic, mutilated kind of
voice. Certainly Schreber's delusions are richly anticipated in other
periods. Kittler tells us that the '[t]he sudden, direct link between
data-storage machines and individual cases liquidates the basic
concept of 1800: the ownership of discourses' (*Discourse Networks*
299). But in fact there is a paranoid schizophrenic writing in
around 1800 who represents his condition in ways that are so close
to Schreber's that one could only suspect plagiarism, were it not
for the astonishing sameness of report across many times and places
of psychotic delusions. Indeed, the first example of what Victor
Tausk has called the 'influencing machine', the systematic fantasy
of a mechanism that systematically controls the sufferer's own
thoughts and powers of imagination, arises in the case of James
Tilly Matthews, who is writing, and having his words transcribed
by his doctor, James Haslam, in the very heart of Kittler's 1800
dispensation (Haslam; Jay). Similarly systematic delusions were set
out in 1838 by John Perceval and from 1852 onwards by Friedrich
Krauß, both of whom depend upon contemporary and proleptic
ideas of media machinery (Perceval, *A Narrative of the Treatment,
Perceval's Narrative*; Krauß).

Kittler frequently quotes with approval McLuhan's principle
that the content of one medium is always the form of the medium
it supersedes – thus, radio broadcasts theatre and live concerts, TV
transmits films. But his epochal, all-or-nothing view of the ages of
media makes his analysis less attuned to anachronisms, ambivalences
or historical syncopations than it might be. This is all the more odd
since, as he himself observes, his very method depends upon such
chimera-like consortings of new and old, given the overwhelming
use of literature to register the impact and meaning of new technological forms like phonography, film and radio – 'What writers
astonished by gramophones, films and typewriters – the first technological media – committed to paper between 1880 and 1920
amounts, therefore, to a ghostly image of our present as future'
(*Gramophone* xl). However, more recently, Kittler spoke in favour
of a Serresian notion of what he called 'recursive history', in which
the same forms and ideas recur repeatedly at different moments
in time, but with different emphases and effects – one example of

this being the siren, which begins life as the name of seductive sea nymph in Greek myth, develops into a more monstrous form in the medieval imagination, and is then adopted in 1819 as the name of an alarm signal that functions equally well in and out of water (Armitage 33; Kittler, *Eros*).

Perhaps the most striking thing about Kittler's analysis of the discourse network of 1900 is what it is said to replace. The discourse network of 1800 is centred on the universal principle of what might be called oralized writing. This is to say that it is built not on a specific material form and its effects, but rather upon what Kittler himself suggests is a constructed but consensual hallucination, namely the capacity for a kind of 'earsight' or 'hearsight' that allows one to mistake writing for voice, to imagine that writing is everywhere suffused with the most intimate and expressive accents of the voice. When Kittler comes on to describing the effects of the inscription system of 1900, he seems to forget this, for now it is the voice as such that seems to have been subject to capture. Indeed, the voice as such, the Lacanian 'real' of the voice, in the purely sonorous phenomenon of vocalization, drives away the fantasy of the voice as the marker of the human, as the vehicle and warrant of soul. In fact, however, one might wonder whether, if the voice as such was only ever formed of fantasy, it is really subject to such absolute obliteration and dispersal. We might expect to find instead the formation of other kinds of vocal phantasm. Indeed, the very notion of the pure materiality of the voice may be regarded as a particular product of a work of fantasy, rather than simple or given reality. Machinery cannot be said to have replaced dream-work, since machines are in large part formed of dreamwork. The mechanical magic of the phonograph does not so much capture and denature the voice as release a kind of magical mechanism. We have not passed out of imaginary relations into the real, as Kittler maintains, since that real is now more than ever itself a phantasmal precipitate. The real is always the *nom de plume*, or, better, perhaps, the *nom de stilo*, of the imaginary. But this then suddenly makes the choice of Schreber as the amanuensis of the inscription system fully appropriate after all.

I have suggested that Kittler's conception of the inscription system of 1900 is both impelled and impounded by the imprint it bears of Schreber's systematic fantasy of a universal system. Schreber's madness is not the madness of a rampant and irruptive unconscious, but rather that of a psychototalitarian hyperconsciousness, convinced that he is entirely responsible for himself, capable of coinciding with or precisely doubling himself, letting himself be known in his entirety. But seeing Schreber's system at the inceptive heart of Kittler's system also allows us to construe the argument not as a laying bare of a violent reality – the soul-murder of media technology – but as the illumination of a series of complex fantasies about the commingling of soul, mind and mechanism. Such a perspective might also help account for the irresistible sense one gets from a table of correspondences between the inscription systems of 1800 and 1900, such as the one I drew up earlier, that Kittler is in fact an historical writer principally in the sense that he projects into a historical form the terms of a conceptual opposition between voice and writing that has been an engine of philosophical argument at least since Plato. Read as a historian of the dreamwork whereby systems of inscription are themselves inscribed, Kittler would be offering an account not wholly and solely of what media do, but also of what we do to media, and what we do to what media do to us. In this account, man would no longer be abolished or displaced by media. He would be where he has always been: in the middle of things, as the mediator of mediations.

Works Cited

Armitage, John. 'From Discourse Networks to Cultural Mathematics: An Interview with Friedrich A. Kittler.' *Theory, Culture & Society* 23.7–8 (2006): 17–38.

Beckett, Samuel. *Murphy*. New York: Grove, 1957.

Deleuze, Gilles. *Negotiations: 1971–1990*. Trans. Martin Joughin. New York: Routledge, 1995.

Haslam, John. *Illustrations of Madness*. Ed. Roy Porter. London and New York: Routledge, 1988.

Jay, Mike. *The Air-Loom Gang: The Strange and True Story of James Tilly*

Matthews and His Visionary Madness. London and New York: Bantam Books, 2004.

Kittler, Friedrich A. *Discourse Networks 1800/1900*. Trans. Michael Metteer with Chris Cullens. Stanford: Stanford University Press, 1990.

Kittler, Friedrich A. *Gramophone, Film, Typewriter*. Trans. Geoffrey Winthrop-Young and Michael Wutz. Stanford: Stanford University Press, 1999.

Kittler, Friedrich A. *Musik und Mathematik I: Hellas 2: Eros*. Munich: Fink, 2009.

Krauß, Friedrich. *Nothschrei eines Magnetisch-Vergifteten (1852) und Nothgedrungene Fortsetzung meines Nothschrei (1867): Selbstschilderungen eines Geisteskranken*. Ed. H. Ahlenstiel and J. E. Meyer. Göttingen: Bayer-Leverkusen, 1967.

McLandburgh, Florence. 'The Automaton Ear.' *The Automaton Ear and Other Sketches*. Chicago: Jansen, McClurg, 1876.

Perceval, John. *A Narrative of the Treatment Experienced by a Gentleman, During a State of Mental Derangement: Designed to Explain the Causes and the Nature of Insanity, and to Expose the Injudicious Conduct Pursued Towards Many Sufferers Under That Calamity*. London: Effingham Wilson, 1838.

Perceval, John. *Perceval's Narrative: A Patient's Account of His Psychosis 1830–1832*. Ed. Gregory Bateson. Stanford: Stanford University Press, 1961.

Schreber, Daniel Paul. *Memoirs of My Nervous Illness*. Trans. Ida Macalpine and Robert A. Hunter. New York: New York Review of Books, 2000.

Tausk, Victor. 'On the Origin of the "Influencing Machine" in Schizophrenia.' Trans. Dorian Feigenbaum. *Sexuality, War and Schizophrenia: Collected Psychoanalytic Papers*. Ed. Paul Roazen. New Brunswick: Transaction, 1991. 185–219.

7

The Typewriter's Truth

Katherine Biers

In 1928, amid a roar of publicity, Ruth Snyder, a former telephone operator, typist and stenographer, was electrocuted at Sing Sing for murdering her husband. At the very instant of her death an attending journalist surreptitiously managed to snap a photograph using a camera strapped to his ankle. The following morning the *New York Daily News* splashed the image across its front page. Murky and terrifying, it shows a hazy but unmistakably female body strapped into the chair, wearing a mask and clad in a skirt, pumps and open-necked blouse. Above the photo is only one large word: 'Dead!'[1]

According to the poststructuralist media theory of Friedrich Kittler, the electrocution of a female clerical worker on the front page of the *Daily News* has a certain dark logic. In two landmark studies first published in English in 1990 and 1999, Kittler argued that the influx of women into the labour force as typists and office workers by 1900 led to a shift in the psychic register of experience with dire consequences for both sexes. The invention of mechanically reproduced writing and the access to paid professional work that it gave women, according to Kittler, destroyed '*the* woman' as an imaginary prop for the male ego by forcing men traumatically to confront real *women* – embodied, material and now jostling for space in the traditionally male preserve of the office. For as typewriters (a term initially used to indicate both the woman and the machine), women became suddenly legible as material objects, as if their bodies were of a piece with the recording devices they operated. From this point of view, Snyder's very public punishment, and the widespread horror and fascination it engendered, were a fitting end not so much for a murderer as for a female media professional. Once she entered the workforce, the ideal woman became just another body.

Snyder's path to the electric chair *was* inextricably linked to her career in new media and to the visibility and independence it brought. The archetypal 'new woman', Ruth Brown had gone to work at the age of 13, from a background of modest means, as a telephone operator at the New York Telephone Company. In 1914, working at one of a series of office jobs, she accidentally dialled a very wrong number – that of Albert Snyder, the art editor of *Motor Boating*. After talking on the phone for a week she went to work for him, and the two eventually married. According to the press who hounded her, Ruth Snyder committed her crime not because of mental and physical abuse, as she claimed, but because of voracious sexual desire that drove her to rebel against her new life as a Long Island housewife and return to her old one as a Manhattan typist-on-the-town. Probably decisive in the decision to execute were widespread press characterizations of Snyder as a cold and calculating proto-noirish 'Bloody Blonde' who dressed in typical 'flapper' fashion and frequented speakeasies – and of her lover, Judd Gray (who committed the crime), as an unwitting dupe. Perhaps the unassuming Gray seemed to so many to be the antithesis of the murderous adulteress because he worked at the outdated job of corset salesman.[2]

But did media 'determine' Ruth Snyder's 'situation', as Kittler might have it? On one level, the argument that clerical work radically changed women's psychic and cultural status ignores the fact that typing for a living was often narratively constructed in popular fiction as just another path to domestic bliss. Snyder's phone dates with Albert and eventual marriage to him fulfilled a widespread cultural narrative by which the secretary catches the eye of the boss and is thereby liberated from the drudgery of office work.[3] On another level, Kittler's notion of a sudden shift in women's status from imaginary to real downplays the contingency of women's arrival in the office and the richly productive ambiguities of their new position. Clerical work becomes instead a site of traumatic rupture, where the foreclosed materiality of both the machine and the female body become suddenly and unmistakably legible to an anguished and fascinated male gaze. Kittler's account thus in many ways reproduces the deterministic logic that justified the 'Bloody Blonde's' execution, by suggesting that typing transported the 'new woman' directly from ideal prop for the male ego to attractive floozy in the (office) chair. It is as if Ruth Snyder's chance phone call in 1914 could have been answered by no one other than her doomed husband-to-be.

In what follows, I examine two different cultural responses to the Ruth Snyder trial and the tabloid coverage it engendered – the classic noir film *Double Indemnity* (1944), directed by Billy Wilder, and the expressionist play *Machinal* (1928), by Sophie Treadwell – in order to complicate Kittler's account by emphasizing how ambiguous, and hence how interpretatively and narratively productive, women's place within the discourse network of 1900 actually was. Both Kittler's *Discourse Networks 1800/1900* and his *Gramophone, Film, Typewriter* rely predominantly on male textual sources to argue that new media technologies shifted the symbolic position of women, gender and gender difference circa 1900. By contrast, I examine the time-based media of film and feminist theatre to argue that the female office worker's interpretative resources necessarily serve to uncouple the technological and epistemic orders in Kittler's analysis. In their different strategies for representing (or attempting *not* to represent) Snyder's progress from mechanized office work to the electric chair, both *Double Indemnity* and *Machinal* put pressure on too easy assumptions about women's place in the shifting media *epistēmē*. They therefore allow us to see that there are some significant drawbacks to understanding typing, with Kittler, simply as the order of things.

The Madness of the Female Typist

Kittler's work owes a significant theoretical debt to poststructural-ist historian Michel Foucault, and in particular to the 'archaeology of knowledge' Foucault elaborated in his earlier works.[4] Drawing on Foucault in *Discourse Networks*, Kittler argued that, in Germany circa 1900, an abrupt change took place in the conditions of knowledge about the nature of the human in fields such as philoso-phy, experimental psychology and education. The cause, however, was not a break in the *epistēmē* – Foucault's name for the uncon-scious rules governing the production of truth claims in a given era – but in the displacement of handwriting and print by the invention of new media technologies, especially the typewriter, film and the gramophone. The rules for the production of true statements about the human in a given *epistēmē*, Kittler argues, are in fact established by the material and technological capacities of the communications 'networks' available for transmitting those statements.

Discourse Networks is notable among Kittler's writing for its pro-vocative implication that a particular set of truth claims about gender made by the practitioners of one German human science – psychoanalysis – were founded upon the *a priori* of new media technologies. Via Freud's case of Judge Schreber, and Lacan's work more broadly (particularly his 'return to Freud' starting in the 1930s), Kittler shows that the insights of psychoanalysis into gender and sexuality would not have been possible without the typewriter. For it was only after its invention that Freud and Lacan were able to formulate their key insight that gender is a sign that gains its meaning from other signs, rather than an essential aspect of human identity.[5] The typewriter's role in turning gender into a semiotic system, according to Kittler, lay in its capacity to disrupt the imaginary and unbroken circuit of meaning and intention previously imagined to inhere in handwriting, whose pedagogy was inseparable from the production of gender difference in 1800s Germany.[6] Within this earlier epistemic field, the male subject was a privileged interpreter, via writing, of a transcendent meaning housed in script and guaranteed by the imaginary plenitude and

wholeness of the mother's voice. With the invention of the typewriter in the late nineteenth century, this fantasy of 'the woman' as
totality was shattered; the typist, unlike the magically murmuring
mother's mouth or the smoothly gliding male pen, visibly selects
and combines letters one by one to form words and sentences
according to linguistic rules. Her material labour thereby exposes
writing as a differential system of exchange governed by the third
term of language, rather than a medium of translation from soul to
soul. Just as writing ceases to be a transparent mark of the soul, so
too do the signs of gender cease to point definitively to an essence
of male or female. Women are thereby liberated from their role as
aggrandizing mirrors for the male ego. After the typewriter, 'the
woman', in Lacan's famous formulation, ceases to exist (*Discourse
Networks* 347–69). And the 'new' woman – Ruth Snyder and
thousands like her – enters the office.

Kittler leaves largely unexamined the question of women's own
interpretations of the dramatic new place they came to occupy
within the late nineteenth-century discourse network. Given his
broader view with regard to the utterances of history's outcasts,
this omission is telling, for, with Foucault, Kittler tends to credit
the speech of those deemed abnormal or pathological by the limits
of a given *epistēmē* with insight into their plight. We might conclude that Kittler neglects the paranoia of female secretaries, for
example – in contrast to the 'endopsychic' observations of Freud's
paranoid patient Schreber – because of the mobility and freedom
that typewriting and secretarial work afforded to so many women
(*Discourse Networks* 291). Perhaps women, circa 1900, count for
Kittler as history's winners. They are incapable of madness – and
therefore of insight – because, unlike their male counterparts, they
are the happy beneficiaries of the new organization of knowledge.

Yet there is a more profound reason that the paranoid female
secretary does not figure in Kittler's account, which is that her
interpretations would dislocate typing itself from the order of
things. For if the operator of the all-determining typewriter can
intuit even something of its truth, then, as both Billy Wilder and
Sophie Treadwell suggest, typing for a living isn't all it's cracked
up to be.[7]

The Media Technological Order and the Persistence of Interpretation

Double Indemnity and *Machinal*, both of which can be read as responses to the trial and execution of Ruth Snyder, bear out the force of Kittler's critique. Each testifies to the ways in which the preconditions of truth or the real were indeed closely linked to the body of the typist and hence to the *a priori* of the typewriter circa 1900. But both also work within the constraints of dramatic forms governed by the forward arrow of time. *Double Indemnity*, true to its subject – insurance – strives to downplay those constraints at the thematic level, by means of a suspenseful narrative voiceover that directs us to equate crime and female desire, and at the formal level, by effacing the traces of its historical source material. *Machinal*, engaging more directly with Snyder's story in a feminist vein, heightens our awareness of time thematically and formally, using sonic elements to suggest that crime emerges gradually and unpredictably out of an irreducible confusion of motives, both psychic and environmental. Considering both in relation to Kittler's analysis results in a less impoverished notion of the interpretative resources to be found in women's psychic experiences than his provocative revision of Foucault would lead us to believe.

Double Indemnity tells the story of an insurance salesman, Walter Neff, who conspires with a wealthy housewife, Phyllis Dietrichson, to murder her husband and cash in on an insurance policy (as did the real Judd Gray and Ruth Snyder). The film follows Neff's attempts to outwit his boss, the claims adjuster Keyes, by meticulously planning the murder and staging an alibi. But the story is told via Neff's retrospective narration of events to Keyes on the latter's office Dictaphone, a confession that indicates the ultimate failure of the scheme from the outset. This denouement looms over the story with a particular portentousness because Neff makes his confession – which he describes as an 'office memorandum' – while visibly suffering from a bullet wound of unknown origin. Only at the very end do we learn that he has just been shot by the double-crossing Phyllis. *Double Indemnity* was adapted by Wilder and Raymond Chandler from the James M. Cain novel of the same name, which was itself an adaptation of the Snyder–Gray story; like Cain's novel, the film makes use of many of the narrative strategies and character types deployed by the tabloids in their coverage, including the portrait of the scheming housewife as a manipulative femme fatale, the dramatic recounting of a first-person confession, the recourse to psychological portraiture, and the highly fatalistic description of the lovers' progress towards the crime.[8] Insofar as the film would go on virtually to inaugurate the genre of film noir, the tabloid coverage of Snyder's trial arguably stands as an important and unacknowledged influence on the formation of the genre.

While the connections to the historical case of Ruth Snyder have been largely forgotten, *Double Indemnity* has received a significant amount of critical attention as a classic illustration of the Lacanian theory of desire and of the woman's problematic place in relationship to it. The film's juxtaposition of Neff's voiceover narration with shots of him dictating and dying alone in the office late at night makes explicit both his desperate desire to communicate and the ultimate impossibility of that communication, thereby granting 'Keyes', the object of Neff's address, a fantasmatic status (see Copjec). As his name, his cigars and his pet name for himself ('Poppa') all suggest, Keyes stands for Neff in the position of the father, occupying the place of the one who possesses the 'keys' of knowledge and certainty.[9] The flashbacks show Neff's refusal to accept this subordinate position in regard to the paternal law, as he simultaneously pursues insurance fraud and Phyllis, whose role as an aggrandizing mirror for Neff's ego signals her status as prohibited maternal object.[10] This mirror is shattered in the second-to-last scene when Neff sees another man leaving her house, revealing that her desire extends beyond him to an apparently limitless series of other men, each one of which she apparently plans to manipulate into killing off the one before.

From here, it is not difficult to discern the outlines of a more materially grounded reading of the film, one that would emphasize the constitutive role of technology in the Oedipal relationship between Neff, Keyes and Phyllis. The truth of Neff's desire for Phyllis, as a displacement of a desiring identification with Keyes, as Kittler would have us see, is dependent upon mechanical recording devices, particularly the dictation machine. On the one hand, the visual inscription of the bullet wound is framed in the film alongside the Dictaphone as Neff sits at the desk, suggesting that the latter functions as the unacknowledged condition by which the former becomes legible – ambivalently for the character, and more directly for the viewers.[11] On the other, the threat of Neff's subordination to Keyes is embodied in the film via Neff's relationship to office work, and in particular to clerical work. A turning point in the story comes when Keyes tries unsuccessfully to persuade Neff to give up the selling side of the insurance business and to come and work for him manning the actuarial tables in the claims department. Neff's resistance to the paternal law – his attempt to outwit Keyes and escape with Phyllis – is therefore inseparable from his resistance to becoming what is in essence a glorified typist.[12] The reason for his ambivalence is not hard to see, for the film places the only prominent female protagonist – the scheming Phyllis – in a structurally similar position to the Dictaphone. Both serve as the medium through which Neff 'addresses' Keyes. The prospect of Neff's becoming Keyes' typist is thus insistently linked by the film to his structural identification with the feminine, for, like the mother, woman and machine are visual and sonic mirrors. Their function is to offer an ultimately doomed and illusory assurance of the male protagonist's potency.

Finally, of course, the recording device is also the *a priori* of film itself. Neff's office memorandum-confession addresses not only the impossibility of his communion with Keyes, but also the impossibility of the spectator's own position of mastery over the events she witnesses on screen. It reminds us that the perception of depth and movement within the frame is enabled by the photograph's inscription on celluloid, and the afterimage's inscription on the retina. By framing the narrative as an intimate confession between men that is really an office memo to a recording device, *Double Indemnity* both thematizes the medial *a priori* of its own knowledge about gender and sexuality, and reflects on its own status as film in relation to other media.

In the context of the historical Ruth Snyder, however, it becomes clear that *Double Indemnity* owes a debt not to technologies of inscription in general, but to one particular incident of recording – that which signalled the denouement of Phyllis

Dietrichson's real-life counterpart. The original ending to the film, which was cut (and was not in Cain's novel), featured Neff walking into a gas chamber to face the ultimate punishment for his crime. According to the shooting script, the final frames focused on the face of Keyes, horrified at witnessing Neff's execution.[13] In placing the audience in the position of Neff, the final shot of the film would have created a disturbing frisson by disarticulating the spectators' point of view from an identification with the masterful Keyes and representing this shift as coming at the very price of life itself. But it also would have placed Neff and the audience in the position of the historical Snyder, and linked the unconscious moment of the film's own inscription to the one particular photograph that, in turn, captured *her* last moment. Wilder's motivation for the changed ending remains murky; however, it seems clear that the cut served a purpose beyond assuaging the worries of the censor.[14] For the ghost of Snyder's well-known death in the original ending would have exposed the larger substitution worked upon the Snyder story by the film's scheming writers and directors. Cain, Chandler and Wilder, after all, had colluded to make the hapless male lover, not the femme fatale, into a doomed office worker driven to kill (a history that better explains the reason for Neff's resistance to becoming Phyllis than does the film's unsubtle Oedipal schema). In short, the planned final scene would have revealed that the male protagonist's maddening – yet narratively and interpretatively productive – office job was initially that of a woman, perhaps even of *every* woman, rather than the brooding noir everyman.[15] *Double Indemnity* cuts its execution scene, in other words, for the same reasons that Kittler forgets about mad women typists: the presence of both would interfere with a masterful analysis of the semiotics of woman as both timeless psychic problem and recording machine.

It is precisely the terms of this analysis, and the semiotic exchangeability between woman and machine that it takes for granted, that Sophie Treadwell contests in her expressionist drama *Machinal*. In contrast to Wilder's foreclosed reference to Snyder at the end of *Double Indemnity*, *Machinal* (1928) was clearly inspired by the Snyder case of the previous year, and the play is nearly always discussed by critics as a challenge to the ways in which the tabloids represented

ordinary
psychosis

Snyder. *Machinal* consists of a series of 'episodes' that begin in an office ('To Business') and end with the main character's electrocution ('A Machine'), which, in pointed contrast to the *News* photo, takes place in total darkness. Along each step of the way, we are made witness to the lack of fit between the main character – who is simply called the 'Young Woman' – and the suffocating and imprisoning external world of office work and of marriage. Unlike *Double Indemnity*, *Machinal* openly affirms that office drudgery and the dangerous feminization it entails are women's lot, rather than men's. Snyder's crime, the play suggests, was a strike against the forced choice between the equally stultifying options of marriage and the domestic sphere and the sexualized and mechanized world of office work. As such, the madness of the female typist emerges in the play as intimately related to her correct assessment of the meaning behind the mechanical conditions of her labour.[16]

The play is most notable, however, for its innovative use of sound, which contests the representation of Snyder and her crime by more formal means. Each of the 'episodes' features characters who speak in highly mechanized, repetitive ways, and the transitions between episodes are made by sound, mostly those of machines. Read in relation both to the changing meanings of the typist's body and to the *News* photograph, Treadwell's decision to contextualize the Young Woman's electrocution as the end point of a series of explicitly sonic 'episodes' reveals that her target is not chiefly Snyder's guilt but the mechanistic causality that characterized portrayals of her act in the press. Via sound, *Machinal* reinserts the category of temporality and contingency into the story of the 'Bloody Blonde', and, by extension, into the narrative and characterological elements of noir being forged by the tabloids, and soon to be codified by *Double Indemnity*'s final cut.[17] In so doing, the play disarticulates the psychic and the mechanical registers of the Young Woman's experience, turning theatrical spectatorship into a mode of immersive interpretation. Treadwell invites the audience to listen in with her on the Young Woman's utterances, seeking an answer to why she committed her crime in ways that – like Freud at his best – are attuned to the chanciness and partiality of interpretation, and the resonance and interference with which it must always contend.[18]

The play's opening 'episode' is set in the office where the Young Woman works, signalling Treadwell's conviction that the story of how Snyder ended up dying at Sing Sing begins with the conditions of her labour. Before the Young Woman arrives, we encounter the adding and filing clerks, a telephone girl, a stenographer and the boss – 'George H. Jones', soon to be the protagonist's husband and victim – all of whom speak, as Treadwell puts it in the stage directions, 'in the monotonous voice of [their] monotonous thoughts' (2). Speech is governed by sonic patterns such as alliteration and repetition, rather than the intentions or intonations of individual characters. Cue the Adding Clerk, Jones and the female Stenographer:

> JONES. I just wanted her to take a letter.
> STENOGRAPHER. I'll take the letter.
> JONES. One thing at a time and that done well.
> ADDING CLERK (*yessing*). Done well.
> STENOGRAPHER. I'll finish it later.
> JONES. Hew to the line.
> ADDING CLERK. Hew to the line.
> STENOGRAPHER. Then I'll hurry.
> JONES. Haste makes waste.
> ADDING CLERK. Waste.
> STENOGRAPHER. But if you're in a hurry.
> JONES. I'm never in a hurry – That's how I get ahead! (*Laughs. They all laugh.*) (Treadwell 4)

The exchange demonstrates the close connection between the advent of mechanized writing and the exposure of meaning in language as the product of a differential system of sounds and letters. Treadwell's Kittlerian insight is perhaps clearest in the description of the Stenographer's job – 'taking a letter' – as if her body were a pure surface of inscription for Jones' sexual and textual advances. It emerges as well in the passage just quoted in the boss's hackneyed sayings and in the Adding Clerk's responses, which consist simply of repeating the endings of those sayings. The absence of meaning and intention, Treadwell archly suggests, is no bar to a conversation taking place. Nor is it a bar to conflict between dominant and submissive males – arguably *Double Indemnity*'s central concern. In fact, it enhances that conflict. The pathetic clerk's subordinate position is made all the clearer by his own mechanical action of copying the boss's truisms, as if he, too, like the Stenographer, were no more than a surface for taking down the boss's letters. After typing, communication proceeds in the absence of subjects: it is as if the office machines, rather than the humans who supposedly operate them, have begun to converse.

Moreover, *Machinal*, here very much like *Double Indemnity*, shows that within the unsettling linguistic autonomy of the 1900 discourse network, woman is the symptom of man. The female Stenographer fails to convince Jones of her efficiency because Jones doesn't find her sexually interesting. Although, and more precisely *because*, anyone can perform the tasks required by the mechanical language game, only women suitable as props for a particular male ego need apply. The Stenographer's failure to be Jones' maternal-sexual imago – according to Treadwell's stage directions, she is to be played as the 'faded, efficient woman office worker. Drying, dried' (1) – makes her an outsider not only to the mechanical exchanges of letter-taking and love-making, but also to the relentlessly exteriorized texture of the drama. In *Machinal*, the degree of women's subordination to the letter of the male unconscious translates into the difference that character makes. The Stenographer emerges as a more fully fleshed-out dramatic character than the others because she does more than repeat the endings of the boss's borrowed words. She tries to convince him that she can do the Young Woman's job equally well, and without haste or waste, putting up a resistance to the rhythmic and sonic patterning that pervades the scene.

But Treadwell's portrait of the Telephone Girl – another of Ruth Snyder's jobs –suggests that the distinction between character and machine is determined by something other than the circuit of male desire. It is also shaped by the different *kinds* of office work open to women. Throughout the scene, the Telephone Girl takes calls to the office, chats covertly and reassuringly to a lover on the phone, and offers explanations and interpretations of the boss and the Young Woman's behaviour to her office mates. Unlike the Stenographer, the Telephone Girl does not aspire to the purely mechanized and degrading position of 'taking a letter', although, as the stage directions tell us, she *is* 'young, cheap and amorous' (Treadwell 1). Instead, she occupies a more distanced position from which she can grasp the truth of the scene as a whole, suggesting that the position of telephone operator might require a degree of interpretative acumen foreign to stenography.[19] Later in the play, the Telephone Girl's hermeneutic abilities come more fully, and fatalistically, to the fore as she sets up an illicit meeting between the Young Woman, now married, and her lover-to-be in a 'speakeasy'. By making the Telephone Girl the gatekeeper to this aptly named, illicit space, in which we also encounter a homosexual pickup and a couple fighting over an abortion, Treadwell suggests that herme-neutics persists in the underground world of sexual minorities, and of 'cheap and amorous' – aka non-reproductive – women. Even, perhaps, in the work of female modernist playwrights.[20]

The parallel characters of the Telephone Girl and the Stenographer, and the parallel 'episodes' of the Speakeasy and the Office, thus reveal a crucial difference between *Machinal* and *Double Indemnity*. While the latter figures mechanical reproduction as the traumatic truth behind gender difference – by continu-ally cutting back to Neff's wounded dictation as generative of his omniscient voiceover – the former depicts the relationship between the orders of typewriting and gender as one of adjust-ment and conflict between two parallel and sometimes conflicting systems of exchange, neither of which, therefore, can function as the symptom, or 'truth', of the other. The adjacency of the two orders in the play is conveyed most directly in Treadwell's strat-egy of exteriorizing the Young Woman's thoughts. Surprisingly, her internal monologue at the end of the Office episode proceeds according to the same associative, mechanical logic as the external-ized speech of the other characters. Just as they talk by repeating others' phrases, so too does her unconscious:

> YOUNG WOMAN (*thinking her thoughts aloud—to the subdued accompaniment of the office sounds and voices*). Marry me – wants to marry me – George H. Jones – George H. Jones and Company – Mrs. George H. Jones – Mrs. George H. Jones. Dear Madame – marry – do you take this man to be your wedded husband – I do – to love

honor and to love – kisses – no – I can't – [. . .] – no rest – must rest – no rest – must rest – no rest – late today – yesterday – before – late – subway – air – pressing – bodies pressing – bodies – trembling – air – stop – air – late – job – no job – fired – late – alarm clock – alarm clock – alarm clock – hurry – job – ma – nag – nag – nag – ma – hurry – job – no job [. . .]. (Treadwell 11)

At first glance, it seems as if the typewriter is shown here to be 'working on' the Young Woman's thoughts, to paraphrase Nietzsche, with a vengeance (Kittler, *Gramophone* 200). Treadwell's evident conception of the unconscious as a machine would seem to undermine the protagonist's desperate attempts to retain her humanity, and possibly also Treadwell's feminist critique as well. For the Young Woman's desire to escape to the freedom of her lover and the 'speakeasy' seems as if it could only have been produced by the typewriter. Just as George H. Jones repeats hackneyed, anonymous phrases, so too does the Young Woman's unconscious, via her imagined future marriage vows. And just as the Adding Clerk's responses to Jones are simple repetitions of his words, so are those of the Young Woman's inner monologue – it repeats fragments of speech from her dialogue with Jones as well as the Adding Clerk. Finally, this unsettling internal speech makes dramatic sense by pure sonic and associative patterning, like all of the exchanges in the office. We gain insight into her predicament in the passage just quoted from simple repetition of the boss's name and the alarm clock's ringing words; from words in chiasmic order ('ma – nag – nag – ma'); and from binary oppositions ('must rest – no rest – must rest – no rest').

Yet there is more to the Young Woman's desire for freedom than a deluded language machine misrecognizing itself, as Kittler might have it. First and most obviously this is because the Young Woman's mechanical internal world is presented in the play as offering a *resistance* to the world of work. The stage directions specify that the 'confusion of her own inner thoughts, emotions, desires, dreams *cuts her off from* any actual adjustment to the routine of work' (Treadwell 1; my emphasis). The resistance between inner and outer is further emphasized throughout the play by the fact that the Young Woman does not speak in the mechanical patter of those around her, but in halting, simple speech, or simply through the utterance of 'no'. Her nonconformity links her to the older Stenographer, whose speech indicates a depth of character that others lack. But the Young Woman also has something in common with the Telephone Girl, who despite her attractiveness and amorousness has no interest in 'taking a letter'. Finally, Treadwell adds in a particularly telling dramatic detail that seems deliberately aimed at disarticulating the female typewriter's truth from the order of mechanical reproduction as such: the Young Woman's typewriter is broken in the opening scene. In response to the Stenographer's query 'Why don't you get to work?', and the Adding Clerk's follow-on repetition-command, 'Work!', the Young Woman replies, 'Can't [. . .] My machine's out of order' (Treadwell 8–9). The broken machine suggests that the essential truth of the coming crime – unlike the case of the unfortunate Walter Neff – lies in its perpetrator's inability to work.

The Young Woman's inner monologues in the play retain a kernel of truth because Treadwell establishes the relationship between the unconscious and writing machines primarily through sound rather than plot, dialogue or visual symbol. The stage directions specify, for instance, that the utterance of the Young Woman's internal thoughts should have an '*accompaniment* of [. . .] office sounds and voices' (Treadwell 11; my emphasis). The effect is aptly illustrated in Episode 7 ('Domestic'), in which her decision to murder her husband is conveyed through a mix of soundscape and unconscious voiceover. As the Young Woman sits silently at home, next to her still-wisecracking boss/husband, we hear her lover's voice and unspecified 'voices' that sing or chant of freedom and suggest a murder weapon. The scene bears out Kittler's claim that literature in the discourse network of 1900 is a 'simulation of madness' (*Discourse Networks* 304–47). But Treadwell's recourse to sonic accompaniment onstage establishes a likeness between internal voice and external media order as a secondary product of a more fundamental relationship of resonance and interference between them. Both the typewriter and the unconscious are machines, in short, but Treadwell insists that they are *different* machines.[21]

The stakes of Treadwell's decision to foreground the sonic

dimension are clearest in the way she structures the transition from one episode to the next in *Machinal*. For it is here that she addresses the most pernicious aspect of Snyder's notoriety – the implication that she was inexorably 'driven' to her crime by desire. As *Double Indemnity* illustrates, the 'law' of women's overmastering libido can offer a reassuring foil against chance and contingency, even as, on another level, it exposes the arbitrariness of the psychoanalytic and media-technological order. Neff, Keyes and Phyllis refer throughout *Double Indemnity* to crimes motivated by desire, all the while using highly mechanistic terms. For Keyes, as if quoting from his actuarial tables, such crimes are always 'a one way trip on a trolley line, whose last stop is the cemetery'. Neff persists in thinking that his plan will carry him and Phyllis 'straight down the line' to freedom and escape from the feminized position of the dictating machine. This view is corroborated in his flashbacks, for he always seems to be the driving force behind their scheme (after the murder, inexplicably, he can start her car, while she has no luck). But, flashing back to the present and to Neff's wounded dictation to an absent Keyes, the film reveals that it is the doomed attempt to resist the trauma of sexual difference that in fact has the hero stuck behind a desk, travelling rapidly towards his date with destiny. In the revised ending, Neff dies almost in Keyes' arms as the technical specifications of sexual desire triumph over the insurance salesman's visions of manful escape from clerical work. Meanwhile the film deep-sixes its own alternative ending's indebtedness to the chancy photographic registration of history. The result is a triumph of film noir.

Treadwell's triumph, by contrast, lies in her sonic rather than visual exploration of her protagonist's desiring journey from office to electric chair, which suggests that the relationship between the episodes of her working life and that of many other young women's cannot be so easily narrativized. Between each of *Machinal*'s episodes, Treadwell calls for a blackout during the scene changes, accompanied by a sound bridge. For instance, in Episode 2 ('At Home'), we learn about the Young Woman's straitened financial circumstances, her parents' bad marriage, her mother's neediness, and her own fear of and ignorance about sex. During the transition to Episode 3 ('Honeymoon'), we hear an offstage radio crooning 'a sentimental mother song or popular home song', which transitions into the 'very faint' (Treadwell 20) sound of jazz. On the surface, the 'At Home' scene provides the 'motivation' for the Young Woman's marriage to George H. Jones in the inescapable fact of her poverty, a common trope of the typewriter romance, as well as her inability to separate from her mother, a common trope of psychoanalysis. But the transition from a sentimental mother's song to jazz, which will accompany Jones' sexual overtures to the Young Woman on their honeymoon, refuses to endorse either fully as a motive for the crime. As the croon on the radio merges into a syncopated rhythm, and sounds fill in the dark spaces between scenes without measuring them out with words, the audience hears, rather than sees, the beginning of Snyder's progress to the electric chair. Treadwell thereby challenges the notion of a linear progress from place to place, whether on Keyes' trolley, or in between the abstract subject positions of Kittler's and *Double Indemnity*'s media-technological order. Instead, Treadwell suggests, the crime emerged gradually, in ways that could not have been known or represented ahead of time, even by the most meticulous claims adjuster, film director or media critic.

Perhaps Treadwell's most significant challenge to the trolley-ride of unconscious desire attributed to Snyder in real life and to Phyllis by the characters in *Double Indemnity* comes in the most significant transition of all – that between Episodes 8 ('The Law') and 9 ('A Machine'), which portray, respectively, the Young Woman's trial and execution. In providing a connection between these two moments in the Snyder saga, this scene change comments most directly on the 'causes' of her grisly end. Episode 8 follows some of the details of the real trial, including Synder's confession on the stand, and ends with the Young Woman collapsed and moaning after her fateful revelation. But the very final lines of the scene come from the reporters covering the trial, who, like the Young Woman's office mates, speak in the monotonous voices of their monotonous thoughts. These voices are identical with what they write:

FIRST REPORTER. Murderess confesses.
SECOND REPORTER. Paramour brings confession.
THIRD REPORTER. I did it! Woman cries! (Treadwell 76)

During the blackout, Treadwell then calls for us to hear 'a great burst of speed from the telegraphic instruments', which keep up 'a constant accompaniment to the WOMAN'S moans' (76). With this final sound bridge, leading to the execution scene, Treadwell challenges not only the claim that desire made Ruth Snyder do it, but also the equally deterministic notion that her demise can be credited to the symbolic order itself, as embodied in the representations of her and Judd that were circulated in the press. For the telegraphic instruments sound off in tandem with the Young Woman's moans, making it impossible to decide whether the material order outside or the psychic order inside rules over her fate. The media machines and the desiring machines are different, but they are not always so easy to distinguish. With this final cue to its audience of interpreters, the play emphasizes the continuing need to discern that difference, even with the advent of a media-technological order operated by women.

Notes

1 Ramey details the coverage of Ruth Snyder's trial and reprints the photograph.

2 For details of Snyder's life, see MacKellar. For details of the trial and trial coverage see also Kobler.

3 By the time of Snyder's trial, the 'typewriter girl' had been portrayed for several decades in works of popular fiction and drama as a hard-working labourer rescued by marriage on the doorstep of starvation. See Thurschwell, Shiach and Fleissner. On typewriter romances, see Rainey.

4 For an overview of Kittler's debts to Foucault, see Wellbery and Winthrop-Young. As Wellbery notes, Kittler's work draws on Lacan, Derrida and Foucault. I emphasize the debts to Foucault in order to put pressure on the problem of technological determinism in Kittler's work.

5 Kittler finds the most direct connection between the typewriter and knowledge production in the writings of Nietzsche, but he also strongly suggests the importance of the typewriter to Freud and Lacan

by analysing the importance of transposition to Freud's method of dream interpretation. 'All of Freud's case histories', Kittler notes, 'demonstrate that the romanticism of the soul has yielded to the materialism of written signs' (*Discourse Networks* 283).

6 In a remarkable analysis, Kittler (*Discourse Networks* 25–70) shows that the Prussian state directive that mothers should teach their children phonetics and spelling at home provided the material conditions for the flourishing of philosophical and literary critical hermeneutics circa 1800.

7 If the mad typist can interpret the typewriter, in other words, there must be some space in between orders of knowledge and their technological determinants, for the mad are alienated from the discourse network. For Foucault and Kittler both, their speech marks an opening to an outside because it occupies the border between sense and nonsense, which is continually shifting. On the suffering body as a privileged locus of speech in Kittler and Foucault, see Wellbery (xv).

8 Critical writing about *Double Indemnity* has almost completely neglected its ties to the Ruth Snyder trial, although, as Pelizzon and West have shown, Cain was profoundly influenced by the tabloids. For further details, see West and Pelizzon ('Multiple Indemnity') and Ramey.

9 This is a position that subjects in language must always implicitly address, according to Lacan, even though it is by definition empty.

10 Manon has argued that Neff fetishizes Phyllis as the disavowed signifier of his own lack.

11 More specifically, the wound is visible just before Neff begins his dictation, but as he raises the speaking tube to his mouth, his hand then blocks it from our view.

12 Auerbach has argued that the film should be understood as a reflection on the alienating effects of corporate labour, rather than on psychic alienation as such.

13 The film was released instead with an ending featuring Neff dying in a doorway of his gunshot wound, with Keyes by his side. For further details on the censored original ending, along with some intriguing publicity stills showing Neff in the death chamber, see Naremore.

14 West and Pelizzon ('Multiple Indemnity' 211) note that censorship was the likely explanation; however, Wilder later described the exci-

sion as unnecessary and the scene as one of the two best he'd ever shot.

15 Given the influence of *Double Indemnity* on the genre, it is not going too far to say that the historical event of Ruth Snyder's photograph serves as the unacknowledged medial *a priori* for film noir's persistent thematic coupling of femininity and recording. As West and Pelizzon ('Snap Me Deadly') note, noir films are disproportionately obsessed with depicting photography, particularly the domestic photo and the glamour portrait.

16 See Koritz on the relationship between *Machinal* and other contemporaneous dramas exploring the cultural meaning of work. For an analysis of the ways in which the play engages with Snyder's trial and media frenzy, see Jones and Strand. For a discussion of the distinctly American tradition of expressionism of which Treadwell was a part, see Walker.

17 Treadwell's strategy is clear in her use of the term 'episode', rather than act, which signals in Brechtian fashion the open-endedness she hoped to inject back into each step in Snyder's progress.

18 Treadwell was no stranger herself to the life of an impoverished typist on the town, or to the nervous illness she depicts in the Young Woman. On similarities between her life and that of her character, see Walker (211).

19 As Jennifer Fleissner and Pamela Thurschwell have noted, not all female clerical workers were treated like mechanized bodies – secretaries, for instance, needed a degree of insight into the information they processed that often placed them in frustratingly compromised positions.

20 The Telephone Girl's ability to cognize the whole and to assemble characters in dramatic situations in dimly lit rooms makes her something of a stand-in for Treadwell herself. Ignoring the performative contradiction with regard to his own interpretations, Kittler often claims that mechanical media, particularly the phonograph, banished interpretation altogether. As he notes, '[r]ecord grooves dig the grave of the author' (*Gramophone* 83).

21 Treadwell also uses sound in this way to figure the Young Woman's treatment by her boss as a violation of bodily boundaries. Like Nietzsche's Ariadne, as analysed by Kittler (*Discourse Networks* 198), throughout the play she is continually seeking to cover her ears.

Works Cited

Auerbach, Jonathan. *Dark Borders: Film Noir and American Citizenship.* Durham, NC: Duke University Press, 2011.

Copjec, Joan. 'The Phenomenal Nonphenomenal: Private Space in Film Noir.' *Shades of Noir.* Ed. Joan Copjec. London: Verso, 1993. 167–99.

Double Indemnity. Dir. Billy Wilder. Paramount, 1944. Film.

Fleissner, Jennifer. 'Dictation Anxiety: The Stenographer's Stake in *Dracula.' Literary Secretaries/Secretarial Culture.* Ed. Leah Price and Pamela Thurschwell. Farnham: Ashgate, 2005. 63–90.

Jones, Jennifer. *Medea's Daughters: Forming and Performing the Woman Who Kills.* Columbus: Ohio State University Press, 2003.

Kittler, Friedrich A. *Discourse Networks 1800/1900.* Trans. Michael Metteer with Chris Cullens. Stanford: Stanford University Press, 1990.

Kittler, Friedrich A. *Gramophone, Film, Typewriter.* Trans. Geoffrey Winthrop-Young and Michael Wutz. Stanford: Stanford University Press, 1999.

Kobler, John. *The Trial of Ruth Snyder and Judd Gray, Edited with a History of the Case.* New York: Doubleday, 1938.

Koritz, Amy. *Culture Makers: Urban Performance and Literature in the 1920s.* Urbana: University of Illinois Press, 2009.

MacKellar, Landis. *The 'Double Indemnity' Murder: Ruth Snyder, Judd Gray, and New York's Crime of the Century.* Syracuse: Syracuse University Press, 1996.

Manon, Hugh. 'Some Like It Cold.' *Cinema Journal* 44.4 (2005): 18–43.

Naremore, James. *More Than Night: Film Noir in its Contexts.* Berkeley: University of California Press, 1998.

Rainey, Lawrence. 'Pretty Typewriters, Melodramatic Modernity: Edna, Belle, and Estelle.' *Modernism/Modernity* 16.1 (2009): 105–22.

Ramey, Jesse. 'The Bloody Blonde and the Marble Woman: Gender and Power in the Case of Ruth Snyder.' *Journal of Social History* 37.3 (2004): 625–50.

Shiach, Morag. *Modernism, Labour and Selfhood in British Literature and Culture, 1890–1930.* Cambridge: Cambridge University Press, 2004.

Strand, Ginger. 'Treadwell's Neologism.' *Theater Journal* 44.2 (1992): 155–68.

Thurschwell, Pamela. 'Supple Minds and Automatic Hands: Secretarial

Agency in Early Twentieth-Century Literature.' *Forum for Modern Language Studies* 37.2 (2001): 155–68.

Treadwell, Sophie. *Machinal*. London: Nick Herne Books and Royal National Theatre, 1993.

Walker, Julia. *Expressionism and Modernism in the American Theatre: Bodies, Voices, Words*. Cambridge: Cambridge University Press, 2005.

Wellbery, David E. Foreword. *Discourse Networks 1800/1900*. By Friedrich A. Kittler. Stanford: Stanford University Press, 1990. vii–xxxiii.

West, Nancy, and Penelope Pelizzon. 'Snap Me Deadly: Reading the Still Photograph in Film Noir.' *American Studies* 43.2 (2002): 73–101.

West, Nancy, and Penelope Pelizzon. 'Multiple Indemnity: Film Noir, James M. Cain and Adaptations of a Tabloid Case.' *Narrative* 13.3 (2005): 211–37.

Winthrop-Young, Geoffrey. 'Silicon Sociology, or, Two Kings on Hegel's Throne? Kittler, Luhmann, and the Posthuman Merger of German Media Theory.' *Yale Journal of Criticism* 13.2 (2000): 391–420.

8

Films in Books/Books in Film:
Fahrenheit 451 *and the Media Wars*

Gill Partington

Four minutes and forty-seven seconds into the film *Fahrenheit 451* sits a strange, striking and distinctly Kittlerian intersection of media technologies. A troop of uniformed men are ransacking an apartment in a search for contraband books. Having rifled through cabinets and furniture with some success, they turn their attention to the TV set and, prising back the screen, uncover the largest hoard of all: a stack of books secreted where the jumble of wires and circuits should be. This is an image worth pausing over. Its immediate effect is incongruity – something on which the film in general trades. In this opening sequence, viewers' expectations are confounded by the slightly absurd mismatch between the seriousness of the search on the one hand, its tension ramped up relentlessly by Bernard Herrmann's Hitchcockian musical score, and on the other hand the innocuousness of its object. It isn't weapons, political dissidents or secret files that the sinister-looking storm troopers are after, but a pile of dog-eared paperbacks. In this future dystopia full of paradoxical reversals, reading is illegal and the job of these 'firemen' is not to put out fires but to burn books.

But the image of a television stuffed with books is prescient as well as incongruous. It undermines our assumptions about media and the relationship between them. The real 'content' of any medium is always another distinct medium, according to Marshall McLuhan. New media technologies incorporate and synthesize the capabilities of older ones, so that 'the content of the book is speech, and the content of the movie is the novel' (McLuhan 305). But this perversely literal manifestation of his words has a troubling logic that leads us away from McLuhan and in the direction of an altogether different approach to media. The motif seems to under-cut McLuhan's developmental trajectory for a start; these books inhabit the space that should be taken up by the technological machinery of the TV, and instead of being effortlessly subsumed into a newer media, they threaten to disrupt its workings. But beyond this, in its absurdity and 'out of placeness', the concept of books inside the TV carries a strange and even dreamlike quality. It could almost function *as* a dream symbol, in fact. The spectacle of actual novels behind an actual screen doesn't so much illustrate McLuhan's well-known dictum of media theory as refract and distort its logic into a visual pun, much as Freud describes dreams as condensing waking thoughts into apparently nonsensical images.[1] This moment of haunted media is one in which technologies cut across and into one another in unexpected ways, and media theory collides with psychoanalysis and the Freudian uncanny. It is precisely at such dense junctures of technologies, theories and subjectivities that the work of Friedrich Kittler positions itself.

If the discovery of a library inside a TV provides an oblique, unconventional and Kittlerian entry point into a discussion of media interrelations, in the context of *Fahrenheit 451* these interre-lations are themselves particularly intriguing. Ray Bradbury's 1953 science fiction novel, a cautionary tale of a future in which reading is criminalized, is a piously humanist defence of Literature and literary values. The film adaptation, released thirteen years later by New Wave auteur Francois Truffaut, does not alter Bradbury's narrative significantly (the film has a novel as its 'content', in other words), but exists in considerable tension with it. If Bradbury's novel is a paean to Literature, then Truffaut's film seems to have a quite different, opposing subtext, in which reading is defamiliar-ized and the book is an alien object, at odds with the world of the screen. This chapter explores the antagonisms between book and film as played out across the two versions of *Fahrenheit 451*. In the first instance, I will argue that this fraught relationship between media is to do with the conflict between text and film staged by the central narrative itself, a conflict which ensures Truffaut's remediation of the novel has a paradox built into it from the start. The plot and themes mean that there are problematic issues surrounding the representation of one medium (the printed book) in another (the celluloid film). Second, however, I set out to show that these issues can productively be seen in terms of what Kittler has described as the 'competition between media' (*Gramophone* 153), a competition that arises as a result of the twentieth-century divergence of media channels into the written, the visual and the auditory.

For Kittler, writing is a serial storage medium, one that for centuries enjoyed a monopoly. In the era of German Romanticism (which forms the starting point of his work; see *Discourse Networks*), writing faced no competition, so there was effectively 'no concept of medium' (*Gramophone* 6) at all. For readers in this pre-technological 'discourse network', text was more than mere text. It was able to merge with the inner voice, since literacy was culturally constructed as a kind of 'imaginary orality'. Writing could thus lay claim to a particular kind of magic, conjuring up the sound and even images that no technology could yet store: 'words quivered with sensuality and memory. It was the passion of all reading to hallucinate meaning between lines and letters; the visible and audible world of Romantic poetics' (*Gramophone* 10). The act of reading enabled an imagined dematerialization of the page surface, so that writing enjoyed a very special privilege: it could, in effect, make itself disappear. Readers could forget they were reading and the book 'would forget being a book' (*Discourse Networks* 53). At the close of the nineteenth century, however, when the advent of the typewriter closely coincided with the invention of other technologies able to store sound and moving pictures, media began to develop specialized functions. As Winthrop-Young and Wutz suggest, a 'differentiation of data streams' (xxv) occurs which transforms the book's place in the media ecology. Writing now becomes technologized; but just as importantly, as merely one media channel among others its monopoly is now lost. Film technology, able for the first time in history to record and project moving images, usurps the magic of writing, and 'feature films take over all of the fantastic or the imaginary, which for a century has gone by the name of Literature' (*Gramophone* 154). The printed page, newly demoted, emerges anew as a two-dimensional, inscribed surface, generating meaning through the pure differentiation of typewritten symbols rather than the transcendent voice of poetry. No longer the ultimate expression of inwardness or spirit, writing becomes visible simply as a series of mechanical marks on a material page.

This new milieu – 'Discourse Network 1900' – thus introduces an antagonistic relationship between media, one which Kittler frames in characteristically martial terms: 'The real wars are not fought for people or fatherlands, but take place between different media, information technologies, data flows' (*Gramophone* xli). Occupying distinct registers and roles, media now have no option but to cultivate their own specificity. Writing, post-1900, writes about itself, about the materiality and opacity of signs. It writes, so to speak, about what it can do and other media cannot. In the words of the modernist poet Stéphane Mallarmé: 'one does not make poetry with ideas, but with words' (quoted in Kittler, *Discourse Networks* 184). Cinema, likewise, participates in the media turf wars of the twentieth century, cultivating its own language, utilizing illusions and devices, conjuring doppelgängers and manipulating the flow of time through camera trickery. 'Books (since Moses and Mohammed) have been writing writing, films are filming filming [. . .] [M]edia have always been advertising themselves', states Kittler (*Gramophone* 155). In what follows, I show how both iterations of *Fahrenheit 451* – Bradbury's text and Truffaut's film – may be seen as what Kittler calls 'discourses on discourse channel conditions' ('The God of Ears', this volume 10). Such (meta)discourses are 'messages about their own medium' (Winthrop-Young 4), but they are also, in this case, messages about the complex interrelations of media, about books in films and films in books.

Ray Bradbury's novel was first published less than a decade after the Second World War, and the spectre of Nazi-orchestrated book-burnings clearly hovers in the background, along with incipient post-war anxieties about threats to liberty and free speech, from McCarthyism on the one hand and communism on the other.[2] Easily packaged as both a cold-war-friendly message about

individual liberty and a humanist polemic about the value of
reading, it was quickly established as a fixture of the American
High School Literature curriculum, and brandished over subsequent decades as a mobile and adaptable emblem of the dangers
of censorship and cultural vandalism more broadly. Yet, on closer
reading, the novel is less concerned with 'book-burning' itself
than with another threat: the corrosive effects of mass media. The
novel's protagonist, Montag, may be a fireman whose job is to find
and destroy illegal literature, but it is clear that the disappearance of
books is only partly to do with state control, and mainly to do with
the triumph of debased, popular cultural forms. Captain Beatty,
Montag's superior, explains:

> [T]he public, knowing what it wanted, spinning happily, let the comic
> books survive. And the three-dimensional sex magazines, of course.
> There you have it, Montag. It didn't come from the Government
> down. There was no dictum, no declaration, no censorship, to start
> with, no! Technology, mass exploitation, and minority pressure
> carried the trick, thank God. (61)

Even before they were banned, books were rejected by a gullible
public seduced by the tawdry and superficial allure of subliterary visual forms. Beatty's point is embodied by Montag's wife,
Linda. Surrounded by wall-sized TV screens pumping out inane
entertainment shows, she is not only uninterested in books, but
confused and frightened by them. She is also unable, when ques-
tioned, to recall any concrete details about the programmes she
watches. This post-literary, amnesiac society has been brought
about not by the will of the state, but by the creeping influence
of the screen. The novel therefore delivers the familiar refrain of
cultural conservatism: that popular culture (and in particular television) will rot your brain. If Bradbury's novel is a polemic, then its
main target actually seems to be popular, primarily visual media,
and the threat they present to literary values.[3]

   Truffaut's film carries a subtext that exists in considerable tension
with this polemic, despite implementing only slight changes to
Bradbury's narrative. Whereas in Bradbury's dystopia only certain
(canonical, literary) books are banned, Truffaut's film depicts a

world in which the printed word has been outlawed completely. From the distinctive spoken-voice opening credit sequence to Montag's pictorial bedtime reading and the blank facsimiles of books he uses in training exercises, this is a world strangely devoid of text, a fact which makes writing seem all the more alien when it does appear. Laura Carroll argues that we are 'pre-sensitised for the scarifying impression of print [. . .] by a staggering demonstration of what it means to be deprived of it', and that the film's close-up shots of burning pages force us to race in order to take in the text almost in the same instant as it is devoured by flames, manipulating and intensifying our desire to read. This may be true, but we are also curiously estranged from text, and forced to see it through fresh eyes. Montag, having taken an illicit copy of *David Copperfield* from its hiding place, begins reading to himself, aloud and awkwardly. The scene has been viewed as an expression of Truffaut's supposed 'reverence for books': Montag's white bathrobe, reminiscent of a monk's habit, could perhaps suggest sacred ritual (Allen 116). However, this is to ignore the distinctive way that the act of reading and the book itself are filmed, not to mention the idiosyncrasies of Montag's unpractised technique. Apparently unsure where the book starts, he begins reading not with page one but with the paratextual publication information and title page. The camera foregrounds his physical interaction with the book, gradually closing in not only on the text, but on his moving finger as he traces it beneath the lines. The page eventually fills the whole screen, but the familiarity of the page surface and this most recognizable of texts, when presented in extreme close-up, is made to seem unfamiliar. The camera movements, ostensibly mimicking the movement of the eye by jerking back and forward across the page, make reading seem unnatural, effortful rather than absorptive, immersive or enjoyable.

And if the act of reading, seen through the eye of the camera, is rendered strange, then so too is the book in general. In Bradbury's novel, images of 'flapping, pigeon-winged books' serve to anthropomorphize them, but also often to lend them a fragile, otherworldly and unmistakably seraphic quality: 'A book alighted, almost obediently, like a white pigeon, in his hands, wings fluttering. In the dim, wavering light a page hung open and it was like a snowy feather, the words delicately painted thereon' (*Fahrenheit* 42). In contrast to Bradbury's weightless and ethereal books, however, Truffaut's film presents us with volumes that *have* volume. They seem continually earthbound, falling and weighty. The initial book search culminates in a sack of books being thrown from a balcony, splitting open as it hits the ground and spilling its contents in slow motion on the tarmac below. On another occasion, a news report from one of the ubiquitous wall screens itemizes the destruction of illegal books by weight: '2750 pounds of conventional editions, 85 pounds of first editions. 17 pounds of manuscripts'.

Over and over, it is the mass and materiality of books, their dimensions and bulk, their 'thingness', that the film foregrounds. 'I don't want these things in the house' declares Linda, Montag's wife, while he in the course of his work describes them simply as a 'rectangular object'. In a demonstration exercise about how to find such objects, he employs other, similar objects to stand in for them: book-simulacra with entirely blank pages, or else rectangular blocks of wood. Books play a central role in the film, yet aside from Montag's encounter with *David Copperfield*, they are hardly ever depicted in the process of being read. Instead, they feature in ways that draw attention to the space they take up, their physical presence, and, of course, their physical destruction, itemized neatly by Laura Carroll:

> Books are hidden, revealed, furtively, or openly handled, fingered, torn, burned. People throw books out of windows, at heads, secrete them in pockets; they slot them into toasters and roll them inside vases; they hoard them inside dummy TV sets, heaters, clocks, laundry baskets, light fittings, cocktail cabinets, and scoop whole shelves of them to the floor.

In Bradbury's novel, books are of course objects, too, but are most often referred to in terms of their contents: Whitman, Thoreau, Faulkner, Shakespeare. The authors' names designate a body of work, a set of texts perhaps, but not a mound of paper. In such canonical lists, it is not books as physical things, but the category of Literature in the abstract that is being evoked. In the film, such abstractions are replaced, inevitably, by the visual reality of specific editions. And Truffaut's choice of these editions is telling. Where the prop men reportedly collected beautifully bound hardback books for use in the film, the director objected that these were too elegant and promptly replaced them with a much more eclectic set of used books, mostly paperbacks in recognizable cheap editions, many appearing noticeably worn or tatty (Bluestone).

The discovery of an entire hidden library in the attic of a house provides the film's central bibliophobic set piece. Here we see not neat rows of orderly leather spines but messy, teetering piles of books organized according to no discernible system. Cramped and dark, its space difficult to read, this library bears little resemblance to any idealized space of bookish knowledge and enlightenment. The claustrophobic effect is in stark contrast to the uncluttered, spare and blandly futuristic look of the film in general. Panning across the crowded shelves and tables, the camera reveals an indiscriminate array of genres and languages, in all shapes and sizes – pages creased and dirty even before they are thrown onto the pyre. The highbrow mingles with crime fiction, metallurgy primers, children's books, comic strips and snooker manuals in a bizarre mix which bears little relation to the neat canonical list of literary greats presented in Bradbury's novel. Truffaut pans across and cuts between Proust's *Swann's Way*, Charlie Chaplin's autobiography, Adolf Hitler's *Mein Kampf*, a book of Salvador Dali's paintings, *Cahiers du Cinéma* (a publication in which Truffaut himself regularly featured) and *MAD* magazine. The 'uncomprehending mechanical gaze of the camera' (Carroll) cuts from title to title, registering no qualitative difference between them.

Removed from their shelves and thrown (once again from a height) into the hallway, where they cover the floor in a jumbled mess, these texts then take on the appearance of waste and detritus rather than a collection of individual books. The camera observes in close-up, in almost pornographic detail, as they are first hosed with kerosene and then set alight. Such sustained and detailed book-burning scenes makes Truffaut's film something of an anomaly in post-war cinema. Book pyres undoubtedly make compelling viewing but are rather too thrilling to watch, given that their strong association with Nazism renders them such an uncomfortable and ethically difficult subject and has even, according to

Matthew Fishburn (167), rendered them something of a post-war cinematic taboo. Truffaut exhibits no such qualms about voyeurism, however. His lovingly framed montage sequences of curling and blackening pages, some of the most arresting scenes in the film, create a cumulatively hypnotic effect: 'The lingering close-ups of burning books have a depth and colour that makes them the emotional highlight' (Fishburn 163). There is an ambivalence, to say the least, between the film's ostensible anti-censorship message, and its sheer enjoyment of book-destruction.

But 'why should cinema, after all, deplore the disappearance of books?', ask Denis Hollier and Alyson Waters (Hollier and Waters 16). The death of paper is clearly not film's problem, and so, they suggest, 'Truffaut is led, by the logic of his medium, to something diametrically opposed to the humanist cult of the books associated with Bradbury's novel' (16). The idea leads us back to Kittler's concept of warring media channels, which seems a promising way to frame this cinematic antagonism towards the book. From the outset, the film renders the book strange, transforming this most familiar and benign of objects into something dangerous, illegal and, above all, alien. We are forced to read the world through 'the language of film', in which books are figured in terms of mass, weight and waste rather than textual content (Whalen). They have a disquieting material presence, emanating from unexpected hiding places and proliferating in disorderly piles. They appear where they do not belong, out of place and also out of time, haunting TV sets and inhabiting darkened gothic attics in this otherwise brightly lit and anodyne science fictional future. Truffaut positions the book as an odd, uncanny, anachronistic and occasionally abject thing, and there is no doubt which side his film is on in the war of media. Little wonder that his firemen travel to book-burnings not on an actual fire engine but – in a serendipitous piece of prop provision – on a converted and painted film truck.

To explore this fully, however, we need to revisit briefly Kittler's concept of media, understanding how it is inflected by psychoanalytic theory. The splitting of media channels circa 1900 is something he reads not only in technological but in Lacanian terms, since for Lacan, entry into subjectivity involves a potentially analogous splitting of the psyche. The symbolic order – the realm of language, system and signification – becomes separated from the imaginary order, the realm of desire and dream. For Kittler, these 'methodological distinctions of modern psychoanalysis clearly coincide with the distinctions of media technology' (*Gramophone* 16). Such symmetries make sense because the psychological and the technological, self and media, are always closely bound together. In the words of Nietzsche, which Kittler uses more than once, 'our writing tools are also working on our thoughts' (quoted in *Gramophone* 220). And so, since it is '[o]nly in the competition between media [that] the symbolic and the imaginary bifurcate' (*Gramophone* 153), Kittler proceeds to map the media channels of discourse 1900 onto Lacan's psychic registers. The symbolic order, with its logic of structure and differentiation, he links to the typewritten technology of the written word. Film, meanwhile, corresponds to the imaginary realm. For Lacan, the imaginary realm is so called because it centres on a misrecognition of the self's wholeness – a delusion necessary in order to sustain the fantasy of a unified, coherent subject. In this sense the self is something of a psychic illusion, and, as Kittler points out, it operates according to the same logic of optical trickery as film, which conjures an illusion of wholeness and continuity from the celluloid reel's succession of disjointed still images. The third part of Lacan's triad, the real, is something Kittler maps onto early sound recording technology, which stored not only words but also the raw, unfiltered noise which could not be incorporated into any symbolic system.

Approaching Truffaut's film in these terms may explain not only its distinctive treatment of books, but also its other idiosyncrasies. *Fahrenheit 451* was a departure for the director on several levels, as his first in colour, his only film in English, and certainly his only dalliance with science fiction. It remains a curio in his oeuvre, and one which many considered a failure. Truffaut's breezy New Wave aesthetic, transferred to unfamiliar territory both geographi-cally and in terms of genre, left many critics bemused. Those attempting to find humanity and believable relationships in the film were frustrated. It was condemned as 'unconvincing', while some of its technical tricks were bizarre or clumsy, and the acting performances – particularly that of Oskar Werner as Montag – were stiff and robotic (see Whalen). But perhaps such criticisms miss the

point. The film may lack 'humanity', but its central subject may
not be humanity at all, but rather technology. Just like his later
self-referential work *Day for Night, Fahrenheit 451* films filming
itself, employing tricks and devices unique to film. Repeatedly, it
exploits the technical ability to manipulate and reverse the flow of
time (the firemen slide up rather than down the pole at the station,
while Montag, donning his fireproof suit, is actually taking it off
in reverse). It also conjures up doppelgängers in the form of Julie
Christie's peculiar dual role as both Montag's zombie wife Linda
and mysterious, subversive neighbour Clarisse. Such devices show
Truffaut revelling in a distinctively filmic, visual language, but
they also seem to hint at a very Kittlerian correlation between
media and the unconscious. The film's creaky effects, as well as its
curious doubles and its wooden acting, are best understood not as
a failure to achieve naturalism, but as examples of a distinctively
unreal, uncanny quality, evident in images such as a miniature
book retrieved from the pocket of an infant, the solipsistic and
sensual self-caressing of passengers on a train, and most bizarrely
of all, one of the firemen appearing briefly in drag as a teacher.
Truffaut's film often summons up not the 'real' world, whatever
that might be, but a dreamlike, fantasy realm, lending weight to
Kittler's claim that 'dreams are films and vice versa' (*Gramophone*
159). And, to pursue this logic of juxtaposing the technological
and the psychoanalytic, it may be that in staging a conflict between
media, the film also produces an uncomfortable meeting of psychic
orders. If dreams are indeed films, and vice versa, then the object
of the book, when it appears on screen, functions as a troubling
intrusion of the symbolic order into the film's imaginary realm.
It makes sense that the flat, hard surface of the printed page, seen
through the gaze of the camera, seems out of place, or belongs to
another sphere of being.

Truffaut's film wages war on the printed word, then, but is the
antagonism mutual? It would certainly appear so from the novel's
impassioned defence of books, and its polemic against the seductive dangers of the visual. The typewriter, according to Kittler, is a
technology 'whose basic action [. . .] consists of strikes and triggers
[and] proceeds in automated and discrete steps, as does ammuni-
tions transport in a revolver or a machine-gun' (*Gramophone* 191).

And in Bradbury's case, this 'discursive machine-gun' (*Gramophone* 191) – firing relentlessly as he hammered out his novel in just nine days – seems to have the cinema screen firmly in its sights. Yet before positioning the two versions of *Fahrenheit 451* in a neatly symmetrical relationship of enmity, we first have to confront a potential obstacle. When Kittler discusses the competition between film and writing, it seems that he has in mind only a specific kind of writing. Since 1900, he argues, literature has aspired to the condition of 'unfilmability', experimenting with its own specific media channel. Mallarmé is Kittler's exemplar of this trait. However, writing that does not correspond to this model of modernist formal experimentation is designated as the 'entertainment novel', a category which, it seems, is more properly seen as a subset of film (*Gramophone* 174). The distinction, as Winthrop-Young argues, is a stark one between 'intramedial autism [and] intermedial serfdom' (63).[4] One form of writing positions itself in opposition to film, while the other is already a form of 'screenplay', merely awaiting its transition into visual images. Faced with this choice, it is obvious that the label of entertainment writer must be applied to Ray Bradbury, whose work keenly anticipates rather than resists adaptation into film. A writer for whom the boundary between film and print was porous, he described himself as a 'hybrid author', producing no fewer than thirteen screenplays from his own work, adapting four of his novels *from* screenplays, and overseeing seventy-six TV adaptations of his work, including the long-running series *Ray Bradbury Theatre* (Touponce 7). *Fahrenheit 451* is a novel written by a jobbing screenwriter in little more than a week, on a typewriter hired for a dime per half-hour. In Kittler's terms, this was evidently a 'typewritten screenplay' (*Optical Media* 179) even before it was adapted by Truffaut into a movie script. It seems that it could have little or nothing to say about the media channel of writing, since it actually speaks the language of film.

However, while it is certainly true that as a novel *Fahrenheit 451* is implicated in the world of visual media, its attitude towards the screen, and technological media in general, is in reality highly ambivalent. It refuses Kittler's distinction between resistance to, or collusion with, film, and instead develops a complex, if contradictory critique of the intermedial condition of print in the

mid–twentieth century. Through the mouthpiece of chief fireman
Beatty, the novel describes the changing nature of the book, and
its relationship with technological media:

> Picture it. Nineteenth–century man with his horses, dogs, carts, slow
> motion. Then, in the twentieth century, speed up your camera. Books
> cut shorter. Condensations, Digests. Tabloids. Everything boils down
> to the gag, the snap ending. (Bradbury, *Fahrenheit* 58)

Beatty's history lesson is delivered, significantly, using the language
of visual media. It is the accelerated, visual sensibilities of film that
are responsible for the disappearance of Literature, which demands
too much time and thought to be consistent with the demands of
modern life. In this speeded–up age, culture has been transformed
and traduced by the pace of twentieth–century media and the
shortening of attention spans. Print may survive in some form,
but literary reading, associated with humanity, emotional depth
and the endurance of memory, cannot survive when the book
is subsumed into an all–pervasive multimedia environment. The
transformation of the book in this twentieth–century technological world has other implications too. Beatty describes the changes
wrought by the advent of motion pictures, radio and television:

> Things began to have *mass* [. . .] [a]nd because they had mass, they
> became simpler [. . .] Once, books appealed to a few people, here,
> there, everywhere. They could afford to be different. The world was
> roomy. But then the world got full of eyes and elbows and mouths.
> Double, triple, quadruple population. Films and radios, magazines,
> books levelled down to a sort of paste pudding norm, do you follow
> me? (*Fahrenheit* 58)

In actual fact, this logic is rather difficult to follow. On one level
it appears to be a rather garbled account of the emergence of 'mass
media' or 'mass communications', terms conventionally used to
designate technologies capable of reaching large numbers of people
more or less simultaneously. Beatty seems to describe a quantitative change in the audience, as well as a change in its nature which
would tally with this reading. Yet there is a strange slippage in the

use of the term 'mass', which is not actually used to refer to this large-scale audience (the masses), as we might expect, but instead is a property of media itself. Things begin to 'have mass', making them problematic in an increasingly crowded world, and somehow leading to the simplification and uniformity of cultural products. Mass media are media that have a *physical* mass – that take up space.

As a media historian, Beatty shares a surprising amount of common ground with Kittler. He describes here writing's incorporation into the technological ecology of media. Like Kittler's, this is a narrative about writing's fall from grace – its transition from universal alpha medium to mere material or 'mass'. Moreover, this sense of the book's materiality is given a certain set of implications by the strange term 'paste pudding', and by the analogous images of 'vanilla tapioca' and 'dishwater' used elsewhere by Beatty (*Fahrenheit* 61). Such terms convey a visceral disgust at the blandness and uniformity of writing in the technological era. They are clearly at odds with the imagery of flight used elsewhere to describe books. Illegal, canonical literature is vaguely seraphic, it seems, whereas permitted, popular types of printed entertainment are mere sludge. But there is something else at work in this persistent mushy imagery that is worth teasing out. The term 'paste' is only a semantic step or two away from another, far more loaded term: 'pulp'. And pulp literature – that lowly, derided milieu of print ephemera – was where Bradbury enjoyed something of a celebrity status. Dubbed 'the poet of the pulps' by *Time* magazine, he spent his early career writing prolifically for such popular SF titles as *Amazing Stories, Thrilling Wonder Stories* and *Weird Tales. Fahrenheit 451* had itself been published in an early, shorter form as 'The Fireman' in Horace Gold's magazine *Galaxy* (Mogen 17). The invitation by Ballantine to extend the story into his first full-length novel was a crucial juncture in Bradbury's career. Leaving behind the cheap, disposable SF magazines with their lurid covers and publishing instead in the relative permanence of book form was a step up on the cultural ladder.[5] Seen in this context, the novel's visceral disgust at the sordid nature and sludgy 'mass' of popular, subliterary forms acquires a new dimension. It seems to be a rejection of the commercial and all-too-material world of pulp publishing, from which the novel emerges but attempts to distance itself. To use Kittler's phrase again, it is a discourse 'on discourse channel conditions'; it is a report on the status of popular print in the mid-twentieth century, with its inescapable materiality and ephemerality, its promiscuously intermedial relationship with film and the visual, and perhaps even its imminent technological obsolescence.

It is perhaps unsurprising, then, that while it emerges from this 'paste pudding' world of pulp materiality, *Fahrenheit 451* eulogizes a different kind of literary world altogether. It is suffused with a conservative nostalgia for the direct antithesis of its own commercial, media-saturated environment. Montag, the fireman turned bibliophile, reads Matthew Arnold's 'Dover Beach' to his horrified wife and her friends, and the choice of text is by no means an arbitrary one. Bradbury's novel, like Arnold's poem, is a lament for vanished certainties, presenting an Arnoldian view of 'Culture' – as 'the best which has been thought and said' (Arnold 6). Only the written word, conceived as part of this ennobling vision of high culture, promises to restore coherence and even spiritual meaning to life. The kind of reading the novel idealizes is that which belongs to Kittler's discourse network of 1800, prior to the advent of technological media, when 'to read was to raise and cultivate a soul, to internalise the fundamental order of nature and culture' (Winthrop-Young 63). *Fahrenheit 451* longs for the return of the pre-technological, transcendent poetic word, and of an oralized mode of reading epitomized for Kittler by German Romanticism, when text is more than just text, when words change into 'optical-acoustic hallucinations' (*Gramophone* 167), and the book could forget about being a book. In short, this is a novel that dreams of its own disappearance.

This disappearance is, in a way, precisely what it tries to enact. It closes with Montag, a wanted criminal, on the run from the authorities. Fleeing the city, he encounters and joins a group of itinerant dissidents dedicated to the preservation of Literature through its destruction. Each commits a book to memory and then burns it. This denouement has often prompted bemusement, since it seems to run counter to the novel's defence of the book. Fishburn states that 'if the novel is a fable which suggests nothing can ever be lost, it is also one in which books are redundant' (163).

True, except that it isn't books themselves that are of primary concern but rather their contents, which are safer preserved in an oral tradition than in print. 'Better to keep it in the old heads, where no one can see it or suspect it' (Bradbury, *Fahrenheit* 146), as Montag's new compatriots tell him. Books and literature become separated at this point, therefore. Books are mere matter, subject to decay and destruction, whereas their content is immortal. Or, at least, content of a certain kind, since it is only the high-water marks of bookish culture and knowledge that these wandering bookmen are memorizing: Thoreau, Swift, Plato, Darwin and Bertrand Russell. Here, the literary is allied with the philosophical and scientific discourse to constitute an unmistakably virile, masculine canon of writing, in the context of which there is a strong suggestion that burning books is purifying rather than destructive. What rises, phoenix-like, from the ashes of this cleansing fire is words and ideas in their pure form.

Burning is an apotheosis that frees writing from its material receptacle because, in the world of this novel, print can be a problematic thing. On the one hand it can carry Plato or Shakespeare, and on the other hand give rise to 'three-dimensional sex magazines' and other horrors. Books are corruptible, sullied by their incorporation into the paste, sludge and 'mass' of popular culture. Better to dispense with them altogether in an act of cultural purgation. If book-burning is the hallmark of dystopia, it is historically also never far from utopia either, and from a desire to erase the past and start again (Fishburn 10–15). To reinforce the point, the city Montag has escaped is promptly annihilated, and as this technological Sodom and Gomorrah burns in the distance it seems that the slate has been wiped clean, leaving only the enduring wisdom of the canon transformed into human memory and voice. In Bradbury's novel, writing does indeed enter into the competition between media, but it must triumph in the only way it can. It does away not only with its technological rival, the screen, but with the book too. Only in this way, paradoxically, can it restore literature to its pre-technological status as universal medium. Through getting rid of the book itself, the novel stages a nostalgic return to an 'originary orality', recovering 'a transcendent inner voice superior and anterior to [. . .] written language' (Winthrop-Young and

Wutz, xxv). Once again, the book can forget about being a book, and text becomes interiorized, dematerializing into pure voice.

A pyrrhic victory for writing, then. But Truffaut gets his revenge on the written word, and the media wars have a different outcome in the film adaptation even if the closing episode is essentially the same. The notion of Literature without books in one sense allows the film to resolve the tensions inherent in visually representing the printed page. In counterpoint to the claustrophobic and cramped shelves shown earlier, this library of 'book-people' wander backwards and forwards in the gently falling snow, absorbed in memorizing and reciting their own text. The contrast with Montag's earlier laboured reading lesson could not be greater. And so, like the novel before it, the film dispels the base materiality of books in favour of the voice. But there are some crucial differences. The film gleefully dismantles the literary hierarchies that Bradbury's monastic community strives so earnestly to preserve. Much like the earlier chaotic jumble of books, this human library mixes high and low. Stendhal, Sartre and Dickens mingle with Poe and even, in a wry twist, Bradbury himself. But also, represented visually, these human tomes are made to seem more than a little strange. If their murmured recitations are in contrast to effortful reading, they are also weirdly solipsistic figures, wandering like sleepwalkers, oblivious to one another; murmured and disconnected snippets of different books and different languages becoming audible as they pass in front of the camera. The human library doesn't so much hold out the promise of an organic cultural community as threaten to dissolve into a meaningless Babel. This is not so much a nostalgic return to 'imaginary orality' as a surreal parody of it. Because, of course, there is a deep irony in staging such a return to a pre-technological, oralized mode of reading via the technological medium of film, and this irony is one Truffaut seems to enjoy. The joke is on the book. If, as Kittler argues, film has stolen writing's auditory and visual magic, the only way this magic can now be invoked is through film, not writing. Bradbury's novel can only *write* about writing's dematerialization, whereas the film can truly perform a disappearing act on the book. Truffaut has the last laugh: the book might yearn to forget being a book, but the only place this can take place is on the screen.

Notes

1 In chapter 6 of *The Interpretation of Dreams*, Freud gives the term 'rebus', or puzzle, to such dream symbols which work through the logic of puns and wordplay, and must be decoded in order to reveal the dream's 'latent' meanings.

2 Bradbury made explicit the influence of the Nazi autos-da-fé, with obvious echoes of Heinrich Heine: 'When Hitler burned a book I felt it as keenly . . . as the burning of a human. For in the long sum of history they are one and the same flesh' ('At What Temperature' 19).

3 Roger Luckhurst locates the novel in the context of a more general hostility towards mass culture in the 1950s, but notes the contradiction inherent in using a popular genre – science fiction – as a vehicle for such conservative sentiments (118–19).

4 One of the more recurrent criticisms of Kittler is the crudeness of this distinction, and an unwillingness to engage with popular fiction on any meaningful level. See, for example, Luckhurst's comment that Kittler 'steadfastly ignores' science fiction (29).

5 As if to illustrate this point, a limited run first edition of *Fahrenheit 451* was produced in asbestos covers. While the fireproof binding obviously works as a tongue-in-cheek punchline to the novel, it also meant that Bradbury's publications took a slightly comical leap from the ephemeral to the indestructible. The novel's move out of the realms of the popular and the lowbrow was only partial; it was serialized in early issues of *Playboy* magazine.

Works Cited

Allen, Don. *Finally Truffaut*. London: Secker and Warburg, 1985.

Arnold, Matthew. *Culture and Anarchy*. Cambridge: Cambridge University Press, 1960.

Bluestone, George. 'The Fire and the Future.' *Film Quarterly* 24 (1967): 3–10.

Bradbury, Ray. 'At What Temperature do Books Burn?' *Writer* July (1967): 19–20.

Bradbury, Ray. *Fahrenheit 451*. London: Corgi, 1973.

Carroll, Laura. *Fahrenheit 451*. Web. http://www.sensesofcinema. com/2005/cteq/fahrenheit_451/#6

Fahrenheit 451. Dir. Francois Truffaut. Universal Pictures, 1966. Film.

Fishburn, Matthew. *Burning Books*. Basingstoke: Palgrave Macmillan, 2008.

Freud, Sigmund. *The Interpretation of Dreams*. Trans. A. A. Brill. 3rd edn. New York: Macmillan, 1913.

Hollier, Denis, and Alyson Waters. 'The Death of Paper: A Radio Play.' *October* 78 (1996): 3–20.

Kittler, Friedrich A. *Discourse Networks 1800/1900*. Trans. Michael Meteer with Chris Cullens. Stanford: Stanford University Press, 1990.

Kittler, Friedrich A. *Gramophone, Film, Typewriter*. Trans. Geoffrey Winthrop-Young and Michael Wutz. Stanford: Stanford University Press, 1999.

Kittler, Friedrich A. *Optical Media: Berlin Lectures 1999*. Trans. Anthony Enns. Cambridge: Polity, 2009.

Luckhurst, Roger. *Science Fiction*. Cambridge: Polity, 2005.

McLuhan, Marshall. *Understanding Media: The Extensions of Man*. Cambridge, MA: MIT Press, 1994.

Mogen, David. *Ray Bradbury*. Boston: Twayne, 1987.

Touponce, William F. 'Introduction: Situating Ray Bradbury in the "Reign of Adaptations".' *New Ray Bradbury Review* 1 (2008): 7–10.

Whalen, Tom. 'The Consequences of Passivity: Re-Evaluating Truffaut's *Fahrenheit 451*.' *Literature/Film Quarterly* 35 (2008): 181–90.

Winthrop-Young, Geoffrey. *Kittler and the Media*. Cambridge: Polity, 2010.

Winthrop-Young, Geoffrey and Michael Wutz. Translators' Introduction. *Gramophone, Film, Typewriter*. By Friedrich A. Kittler. Stanford: Stanford University Press, 1999. xi–xxxviii.

Part III
Turingzeit

Computer does not have
being as a object — does not mediate being —
reduces being to a form of
mediation i.e. thought.

Obsession = mediation
compulsion = media

9

If the Cinema Is an Ontology, the Computer Is an Ethic

Alexander R. Galloway

T. J. Clark observed once, with the simple voice of experience, that in Courbet the entire world is one of proximity; the paintable is that thing, that space, that can be transformed into a Second Empire drawing room. This is Stanley Cavell's assessment too when, in *The World Viewed*, following Michael Fried's 1967 essay 'Art and Objecthood', he likens painting to a certain desire for presentness. Painting assembles a space. But it is always a proximal space, a bounded space of textures and things brought around, not too close exactly, but certainly unconcealed and arrayed for handling. Painting is not Cavell's primary concern in *The World Viewed*, it is cinema after all, but painting offers a road down which one might travel to ascertain a certain quality shared by painting, photography, film and a number of other art forms. It is the desire that the world be brought near to us.

A desire to be brought near – such a desire is most certainly at the very base of human life. Indeed the relative nearness and farness of things may account for all manner of action, from love to hate, from the joy of communion to the perils of exile. But that is not all, for in art it concerns a specific, not a general, iteration of this desire for nearness. The phenomenon is most acute in photography, and thereby, for Cavell, in cinema (for him, a photography derivative);

as he puts it: the world of the image is present to us, but we were never present to it. So it is nearness with a catch. The viewer does not attend the filming of the 'profilmic event', to use the parlance of cinema studies. Thus it is a desire to be brought near, but one already afflicted with a specific neurosis, that of the rejection of the self. With each attempt to array the world in proximal relation to us, we must at the same time make ourselves disappear. With each step forward in Cavell's world, one becomes that much more inert. Every step done is a step undone.

In Plato there is a magical ring, the Ring of Gyges, that grants invisibility to the wearer and thus potential immunity from moral consequence. In effect, the cinema forces us to don the Ring of Gyges, making the self an invisible half-participant in the world.[1] The self becomes a viewing self, and the world becomes a world viewed. This is, in a nutshell, the cinematic condition for Cavell, and I guess I agree with him. The penalties and rewards are clear: to be 'cinematically' present to the world, to experience the pleasure of the movies, one must be a masochist. That is to say, to be in a relation of presence with the world cinematically, one must subject the self to the ultimate in pain and humiliation, which is nothing short of complete erasure. It has been said that the cinema is the most phenomenological of media. But whether this is a phenomenology or the absolute impossibility of one is not entirely clear.

'A painting *is* a world; a photograph is *of* a world' (24), wrote Cavell. What can one say then of the cinema? Or the computer? Paraphrasing Cavell's definition of cinema, one might say, with considerably less panache than he, that the cinema automatically projects worlds (in series). So might it be *for* a world? The computer, then, is simply *on* a world, as it tends to rise in separation from some referent, modelling and supplementing it. But enough phrase-making: the crucial thing is to determine the nature of the machine.

The object of the computer is not a man, nor is it this or that human face or body. In this sense it breaks with those arts (painting, photography, cinema) that fixate upon the embodied human form – the face, but not always; the hand, but not always – and its proximal relation to a world, if not as their immediate subject matter then at least as the absolute horizon of their various aesthetic investments. The computer has not this same obsession. It aims not for man as an object. The reason is simple: because the computer is this object in and of itself.

This is why we do not cry at websites like we cry at the movies. It is why there is no 'faciality' with the computer, why there is no concept of a celebrity star system (except ourselves), no characters or story (except our own), no notion of recognition and reversal, as Aristotle said of poetry. If the cinema screen always directs towards, the computer screen always directs away. If at the movies you tilt your head back, with a computer you tilt in.

But, you say, there is more affect than ever today, is there not? The net is nothing if not the grand parade of personality profiles, wants and needs, projected egos, 'second' selves and 'second' lives. This is true. The waning of affect comes at the moment of its absolute rationalization. At the moment when something is perfected, it is dead. This is the condition of affect today online, and it is why the object of the computer is not a man: because its data is one.

Might one go so far as to make the ultimate leap, then, and assert the following: that the computer is an anti-Ring of Gyges? The set-up is reversed. The wearer of the ring is free to roam around in plain sight, while the world, invisible, retreats in absolute alterity. The world no longer indicates to us what it is. We indicate ourselves to it, and in the process the world materializes in our image.

Again the penalties and rewards are clear: to be 'informatically' present to the world, to experience the pleasure of the computer, one must be a sadist.[2] That is to say, in contrast to the cinema, in order to be in a relation with the world informatically, one must erase the world, subjecting it to various forms of manipulation, preemption, modelling and synthetic transformation. The computer takes our own superlative power over worlds as the condition of possibility for the creation of worlds. Our intense investment in worlds – our acute fact finding, our scanning and data mining, our spidering and extracting – is the precondition for how worlds are revealed. The promise is not one of revealing something as it is, but one of simulating a thing so effectively that 'what it is' becomes less and less necessary to speak about, not because it is gone for good, but because we have perfected a language *for* it. As it is in the work of Alain Badiou: there are only bodies and languages.[3]

It is necessary, then, to distinguish two grand domains which are, like fighting siblings, so much more different from one another strictly by virtue of being so intimately conjoined. *Media* and *mediation*; one might speak casually about one or the other without realizing the fundamental difference dividing them. It would not be necessary to accentuate the difference if others had not already mixed them up so awkwardly, or as is often the case failed to understand the subtlety in the first place. In reality these two systems are violently unconnected.

Consider the famous pronouncement from Friedrich Kittler that all technical media either store things, transmit things or process things (*Optical Media* 26).[4] At the risk of sounding too juvenile, one may observe that this definition of media is particularly media–centric! By which is meant that Kittler first posits the existence of specific media technologies, say the camera obscura or the magic lantern, and then shows how they may or may not be furnished with special characteristics (sending, saving or calculating). Technical media exist in various forms, and they do *x, y* or *z*. His is a revelatory story of objects and the qualities they carry. His is, in short, a hermeneutics of media devices as they appear after being pulled from the pit of history.

It leads to some delightful places, in particular the central thesis of the first section of his *Optical Media* lectures, in which he places the camera obscura and the magic lantern at the centre of the history of all optical media. The camera obscura has a special relationship to linear perspective, the so–called 'self–depiction of nature', and hence to the Renaissance figures Filippo Brunelleschi and Leon Battista Alberti. Because of this, it typifies for Kittler what Heidegger later would call 'the age of the world picture': '[B]eing first constituted itself in the form of a representation (*Vorstellung*) in European modernity. Representational thinking delivered being as an object for a subject [. . .] [I]t can be said, following Heidegger's line of thought, that linear perspective and the *camera obscura* were precisely the media of this representation' (Kittler, *Optical Media* 75). As a device for automatically recording images, the camera obscura functioned as a first–order simulation. It allowed reality to appear on a wall. By contrast, as a device for automatically reproducing or transmitting images, the magic lantern functioned as a second-order simulation. It allowed smaller images to appear larger on a wall. (The progression from first order to second order is appealing, and it sets Kittler up for a nice denouement: the film projector adopts the second-order quality of the magic lantern while adding a new digital simulation along the axis of time; television departs from the image entirely and instead goes for the symbolic space of language in which things are arranged in pixels and grids; and the computer annihilates the imaginary entirely, reverting back to that oldest of age-old media, writing.) Putting small, portable images up on a wall as large images, the essential task of the magic lantern, Kittler associates with Descartes's *cogito ergo sum*, wherein 'the representation of the subject is re-presented to the subject once again as such' (Kittler, *Optical Media* 75). Descartes's insistence in the *Meditations* that the philosopher must blot out the sun and sky and ball up his ears with wax illustrates for Kittler a particular model of mediation. Only the Cartesian self does what the magic lantern had already demonstrated: projects a representation, the thinking mind, back inward towards a previous representation, the self, and therefore (for Descartes at least) shores up the metaphysical relation. So what Heidegger saw as a spark in early modern European man, his ability to cognize the world as a reflection, Descartes bent back into the folds of a baroque philosophy in which man reflects not on the primary data of nature but on the image of man himself. Copernicus, it seems, was wrong.

Yet at the same time Kittler's fixation on the media-centric nature of media puts him temporarily on some dangerous ground. For instance, this foolishness that 'philosophy [. . .] has been necessarily unable to conceive of media as media', owing chiefly to the lack of imagination in a certain Aristotle, whose 'ontology deals only with things, their matter and form, but not with relations between things in time and space. The very concept of a (physical) medium (*tò metaxú*) is relegated to his theory of sensorial perception (*aisthesis*)' (Kittler, 'Towards an Ontology of Media' 23–4). The insinuation here is bright and clear, so why not state it unequivocally: Western philosophy since the Greeks has had no theory of mediation.[5]

Of course it is foolish to think that the Greeks had no theory of mediation. Certain philosophers may have had certain negative views regarding hypomnesis. Yet the Greeks indubitably had an intimate understanding of the physicality of transmission and message sending: Hermes. They differentiated between mediation as immanence and mediation as expression: Iris versus Hermes. They understood the mediation of poetry via the Muses and their *technē*. They understood the mediation of bodies through the 'middle loving' Aphrodite. They even understood swarming and networked presence (in the incontinent mediating forms of the Eumenides, who pursued Orestes in order to 'process' him at the *procès* of Athena). Thus one need only look a little bit further to shed the commonplace, consumer-electronics view of media, and instead graduate into a deeper history of media as modes of mediation, a task that with a bit of luck will be accomplished presently *vespere et mane*.

Luckily Kittler backs down slightly from such an extreme claim. He explains that, while Aristotle might exclude media from his theory of matter and form, he doesn't act likewise in his discussion of human perception:

> Aristotle, however, speaks of two elements, namely air and water, as of two 'betweens'. In other words, he is the first to turn a common Greek preposition – *metaxú*, between – into a philosophical noun or concept: *tò metaxú*, the medium. 'In the middle' of absence and presence, farness and nearness, being and soul, there exists no nothing any more, but a mediatic relation. *Es gibt Medien*, we could say. (Kittler, 'Towards an Ontology of Media' 26)

Hence even if Aristotle does not discuss mediation when he talks about hylomorphism and ontology, he nevertheless inaugurates philosophy's centuries-long relationship to media via a discussion of the human senses. The missing interlocutor here is of course Bernard Stiegler, who has perhaps more clearly than anyone since Heidegger framed the intimate co-construction of technology and being.[6]

With all this out in the light of day, we are in a position to identify more clearly the conservatism of Kittler, who on this point finds a confrère in Marshall McLuhan. By 'conservative' I mean the claim that *technē* is object and only object. For Kittler and McLuhan alike, media mean hypomnesis. Both define media via the externalization of man into objects. Once starting down this road, one ends up sooner or later talking about things like augmentation, prosthesis and supplementarity, all of which presume an elemental relationship between a body, deemed original or pure, and a device, deemed accessory and impure. Hence a fundamentally conservative dichotomy is inaugurated – which, to be clear, was in Plato before it was in Aristotle – between the good and balanced human specimen and the dead junk of the hypomnemata. Contrast this with an alternative philosophical tradition that views *technē* as technique, art, *habitus*, ethos or lived practice. Such an alternative tradition is what was alluded to previously, through the contrast between media (as objects) and practices of mediation (as middles). (In fact it is ironic that Kittler relies so much on Heidegger, as Heidegger was one of the philosophers who best understood both aspects of *technē*.)

But we are not entirely finished on this score. For Kittler harbours as well a deep-seated interest in another yearning of philosophy, one which is as ancient as it is powerful. It is the desire to reduce the many to the one. In *Optical Media*, during his discussion of film, Kittler stresses the way in which Étienne-Jules Marey was committed to a single camera, thereby reducing many devices to a single apparatus: 'By holding tight to the unifying, linearising power of writing paper, Marey always only needed one single piece of equipment, while Muybridge had to position 12 different cameras. The task, therefore, was *to dispose of 11 cameras* and still be able to supply serial photographs. In the process, Colt's good old revolver was once again honoured, as it had also reduced the need for six pistols down to one' (Kittler, *Optical Media* 159; my emphasis). Later, in his discussion of television, he says something similar: 'In contrast to film, therefore, the problem of television from the very beginning was how to make a single channel dimension from two image dimensions, and how to make a single time variable from convertible surfaces' (208). And again later in the albeit short discussion of computers: '[C]omputers represent the successful reduction of all dimensions to zero' (227). (Given what will be said in another essay addressed to the fundamental 'parallelity' of the image, it will be possible to demonstrate that the computer is never the product of a reduction from two to one, or from the multiple to the zero, but in fact the reverse, for the computer belongs to that long aesthetic tradition that derives all of its energy from a fission of the one dividing into the multiple.[7]) The reduction of the many to the one is symptomatic not only of a latent politics lurking within the Kittlerian corpus, but also, more simply, of the aforementioned prioritization of the object over the middle. A philosophy of mediation will tend to proliferate multiplicity; a philosophy of media will tend to agglomerate difference into reified objects. Perhaps this is why Kittler, although notable among his generation for an intrepid willingness to write on computers, never fully theorized digital media as much as he did other media technologies and platforms, for where is the object of distributed network located, where is a rhizome, where is software? Alas for Kittler there is no software.

That said, Kittler certainly understands how computers come down on the question of the optical. Many scholars today continue to classify the computer as another instalment in the long march of visual culture. As Kittler points out, such a position is, of course, totally wrong. Following the example of television, which began a retreat away from optical media and a return to the symbolic in the form of signal codification, the computer consummates the retreat from the realm of the imaginary to the purely symbolic realm of writing. 'In contrast to film, television was already no longer optics', he writes. 'Digital image processing thus ultimately represents the liquidation of this last remainder of the imaginary. The reason is simple: computers, as they have existed since World War II, are not designed for image-processing at all' (Kittler, *Optical Media* 226).

So for Kittler all technical media either store things, transmit things or process things. But what if one were to take the ultimate step and pose the question of media in reverse? What if we refuse to embark from the premise of 'technical media' and instead begins from the perspective of their supposed predicates: storing, transmitting and processing? With the verbal nouns at the helm, a new set of possibilities appears. These are not media per se; we have entered the realm of modes of mediation. The mode of storage appears instantly within its own illumination; the mode of transmitting returns from a far-off place; the mode of processing wells up like a flood of pure energy.

Such is the urging of Gilles Deleuze, who in the essay 'What Is a *Dispositif?*' suggests that one should not focus so much on devices or apparatuses as such, but more on the physical systems of power they mobilize, that is, more on curves of visibility and lines of force. 'These apparatuses, then, are composed of the following elements: lines of visibility and enunciation, lines of force, lines of subjectification, lines of splitting, breakage, fracture, all of which criss-cross and mingle together, some lines reproducing or giving rise to others, by means of variations or even changes in the way they are grouped' (162). When Kittler elevates apparatuses over modes of mediation, he forfeits an interest in techniques in favour of an interest in objects. A middle – a compromise, a translation, a corruption, a revelation, a certainty, an infuriation, a touch, a flux – is not a medium, by virtue of its not being a technical media device.

What is the computer, then, as a mode of mediation? Cavell – and he is not the only one, simply the most convenient – speaks of the possibility of a medium. The possibility of a medium stands in intimate relation to what a medium is, that is to say, the definition of whatever medium is in question. Thus when one asks 'What is the possibility of video?' one is in the same breath asking 'What is the definition of video?' Yet the computer occupies an uneasy position in relation to both definition and possibility, for in many cases the very words that people use to address the question of the computer are those selfsame words 'definition' and 'possibility'. One hears stories about computers being 'definitional' machines: not only does computer code operate through the definitions of states and state changes, but computers themselves are those special machines that nominalize the world, that define and model its behaviour using variables and functions. Likewise one hears stories about computers being 'possibility' machines: they operate not through vague estimations of practice, but through hard, machinic possibilities of truth or falsehood, openness or closedness, on or off. So I suggest that these terms 'definition' and 'possibility' might do more harm than good if our aim is to understand the machine and how it works. How can one determine the possibility of new media if new media are nothing but possibility machines? How can one define them if they are already cast from the mould of definition?

To adopt shorthand, one might summarize this state of affairs by asserting that the computer has hitherto been understood in terms of metaphysics. That is to say, when people speak about the computer as an 'essencing machine' what they really mean is that computers simulate ontologies: they define horizons of possibility. This is the terrain of metaphysics. These sorts of definitions can be found in Lev Manovich, Janet Murray, and all across the discourse on new media today. The notion is that one must define the medium with reference to a specific 'language' or set of essential formal qualities, which then, following the metaphysical logic, manifest in the world a number of instances or effects. (One of the shortcomings of this approach, which I will not delve into very deeply here, is the problem of essentialism, that is to say, the notion that new media objects are *a priori* a certain way, and it is merely the job of the critic to examine them, and extract the universal laws or languages that constitute their proper functioning in the world; my elders in the anti-essentialist critical tradition – from Homi Bhabha to Donna Haraway and beyond – have rightly pointed out how this leads eventually to a number of political and theoretical problems, the least of which being that it forecloses on contingency and historicity, two things that turn out to be indeed quite desirable.[8])

This is all well and good. However, the story becomes more complicated once one acknowledges that the computer is dramatically unlike other media. Instead of facilitating the metaphysical arrangement, the computer does something quite different: it *simulates* the metaphysical arrangement. In short, the computer does not remediate other physical media; it remediates metaphysics itself (and hence should be more correctly labelled a metaphysical medium). I shall refrain from saying it remediates mediation itself, but the temptation exists. The metaphysical 'medium' of essences and instances is fundamentally dead today. And because it is dead, the medium of essences and instances re-emerges in a new mediatic form, the computer. Informatic machines do not *participate* in the worldly logic of essences and instances; they simulate it. For example, on the one hand principles like disposability and planned obsolescence seem to occlude age-old metaphysical problems about the persistence of essential identity in the form of universals or transcendents. Quite frankly, the metaphysical questions are simply not the interesting ones to ask in the face of all this junk. But on the other hand, within the logic of the machine one sees little more than an effigy and an undead persistence of these same metaphysical principles. A thing always reaches perfection in death.

But what of this notion of remediating metaphysics itself? The remediation argument (handed down from McLuhan and his followers, including Kittler) is so full of holes that it is probably best to toss it away wholesale. But if any hope may be found for the theory, it is in the 'itself'. Television does not simply remediate film; it remediates film *itself.* The important issue is not that this or that film is scanned and broadcast as the 'content' of television (this being one version of McLuhan's remediation argument). The important issue is that television incorporates film itself; that is, it incorporates the entire cinematic condition.

But as soon as the remediation theory is given any legs at all, one realizes rather quickly a number of problems with the hypothesis that one medium could be a content for another, historically or otherwise. Kittler's amazing discussion of time axis manipulation in recorded sound is instructive on this point.[9] Recorded sound may remediate performed music. But what is being remediated when a musician plays magnetic tape backward and hears for the first time a true sonic reversal (not simply the reversal of phonemes)? Or consider the computer. A computer might remediate text and image. But what about a computer crash? What is being remediated at that moment? It can't be text or image any more, for they are not subject to crashes of this variety. So is a computer crash an example of non-media? In short, the remediation hypothesis leads very quickly to a feedback loop in which much of what we consider to be media is in fact reclassified as non-media, thereby putting into question the suitability of the original hypothesis.

Or to attack the issue from another direction: McLuhan's law of remediation is first and foremost a way of classifying, segregating and managing different zones of the universe of sense, such that it becomes possible to speak about something called 'media'.

To give a specific example of the remediation of metaphysics itself one might reference object-oriented programming – the metaphysico–Platonic logic here is awe-inspiring – and the way in which classes (forms) define objects (instantiated things): classes are programmer-defined templates, usually static, that state in abstract terms how objects define data types and process data; objects are instances of classes, created in the image of a class, and persist for finite amounts of time and eventually are destroyed. On the one hand an idea, on the other a body. On the one hand an essence, on the other an instance. On the one hand the ontological, on the other the ontical.

The cinema so captured the twentieth-century imagination that it is common to assume that other media are also at root cinematic. And since the cinema is, in general, an ontology (in particular it is a phenomenology), it seems logical to assume that other media are ontological in the same way. The computer, however, is not *of* an ontological condition; it is *on* that condition. It does not facilitate or make reference to an arrangement of being, but remediates the very conditions of being itself. If one may be so crude: the medium of the computer is being. But we should take this in an entirely unglamorous way. It is not to say that the computer is the ontological actor par excellence, that it marks the way for some cyborg Dasein of the future. No, the point is that the computer has so degraded the ontological plane that it may reduce and simulate it using the simple principles of logical relation. Being is its object, not its experience. And if being is merely its object, one ought to look elsewhere to try to understand its experience.

If cinema is, in general, an ontology, the computer is, in general, an ethic. The computer instantiates a practice, not a presence. Perhaps a useful way to understand the difference between the two is to draw a distinction between a language and a calculus. A language operates at the level of description and reference. To encode the world: this is the primary goal of language. (Of course one might also speak about the autonomous space of language, in for example textuality, as a space of interconnection and deferral of meaning, and so on. But let's not get off track.) A calculus, on the other hand, operates at the level of computation and process. To do something to the world, or to simulate doing something to the world: this is the primary goal of a calculus. With a calculus, one speaks of a system of reasoning, an executable machine that can work through a problem, step by step. The difference between the two, in one aspect, is that a calculus implies a method, whereas a language does not.

But to say that the computer is in general an ethic is not to suggest that computers are necessarily ethic*al*. I make a distinction between an ethic, which describes general principles for practice, and the realm of the ethical, which defines such general principles for practice within the context of a specifically human relationship to moral conceptions of the good. Note therefore that mine is not a personification of the machine, but rather an anti-anthropocentrism of the realm of practice. And I will always defend the unpopular notion that, in the end, machines really have no need for humans at all (just in the same way that the real has no need for us, but we have a horrifying need for it). Yet in actual fact the machine does have an anthropocentric relation, and this is where one might speak to the question of a computer ethic. As an ethic, the computer takes our action in the world as such as the condition of the world's expression. So in saying 'practice', one is really indicating a relationship of command. The machine is an ethic because it is premised on the notion that objects are subject to definition and manipulation according to a set of principles for action. The matter at hand is not that of coming to know a world, but rather that of how specific, abstract definitions are executed to form a world.

To restate the argument: the computer has hitherto been defined ontologically; but this approach (using the ontological concepts of possibility and definition) is dubious because the computer itself is already a matter of possibility and definition; thus if the computer might better be understood in terms of a practice or a set of executions or actions in relation to a world, the proper branch of philosophy that one should turn to is ethics, not ontology or metaphysics; as an ethics, the computer takes our execution of the world as the condition of the world's expression.

Where does this end up? First, beyond the response to Kittler contained here, one must address the response to Lev Manovich implicit in the claims just made. The main difficulty with a book like *The Language of New Media*, for all its strength, is not simply that it participates in the various squabbles over this or that formal detail. Are games fundamentally about play or about narrative? What has greater semiotic priority: code or interface? In the end these territorial skirmishes are not all that interesting. The main difficulty is the simple premise of the book: that new media may be defined via reference to a foundational set of formal qualities, and that these qualities form a coherent language that may be identified across all sorts of new media objects, and above all that the qualities may be read, and may be interpreted. This is what was called, many years ago, structuralism. To be clear, it is not so much that these sorts of books are misguided (and not so much to pick on Manovich, for there are scores of other texts that do similar work; his is simply one of the earliest and most accomplished examples), but that their conclusions are unappetizing. This is the crux of the matter: they contain no injunction. The problem is not formal definition – for after all I am willing to participate in such a project, suggesting for example that with informatic machines we must fundamentally come to terms with the problem of action. The sticking point is that, in this instance, the use of formalism as a method does not ultimately conform most faithfully to the object at hand. That is, if the computer *were* a formal medium, then perhaps our analysis of it could be formal too. But my position is that the computer is not such a medium. So in a certain sense, Manovich is, shall we say, slightly avant-garde, performing an 'intervention', while my call is much more conservative. If the language (of new media) is really an executable language and not simply a natural one, then would it not make sense for one's critical appraisal to be in step with that same notion of executability? So when I say these books' conclusions are unappetizing I mean it in the most mundane sense: that the discourse on 'excitable' machines does not, to put it bluntly, excite me. In other words, if computers must be understood in terms of an ethics (those who wish instead to call it a politics should do so), then the discourse produced about them must also fulfil various ethical and political expectations. Else what is the good?

Notes

1 Cavell's reflections on this are worth reproducing at adequate length: 'How do movies reproduce the world magically? Not by literally presenting us with the world, but by permitting us to view it unseen. This is not a wish for power over creation (as Pygmalion's was), but a wish not to need power, not to have to bear its burdens. It is, in this sense, the reverse of the myth of Faust. And the wish for invisibility is old enough. Gods have profited from it, and Plato tells it in Book II of the *Republic* as the Myth of the Ring of Gyges. In viewing films, the sense of invisibility is an expression of modern privacy or anonymity. It is as though the world's projection explains our forms of unknownness and of our inability to know. The explanation is not so much that the world is passing us by, as that we are displaced from our natural habitation within it, placed at a distance from it. The screen overcomes our fixed distance; it makes displacement appear as our natural condition' (40–1).

2 Much more could be said on the question of whether sadism is in fact a suitable opposite for masochism and how and why they might be paired in the first place. For example, the necessary narcissism of the masochist, the fact that all trauma must ultimately find both its cause and its solution in the self, also finds an opposite in the 'split mind' of the schizophrenic, for whom the fragmentation of the self connects to elements both external and internal, but also enigmatically *within*, or orthogonal to, the subject.

3 In Badiou this is both a simple claim about being and a lament of the highest order. The existence of 'only' bodies and languages indicates a triumph of a specific political regime, democratic materialism, for which Badiou has zero affection. In a trick of language Badiou reveals the secret: bodies and languages are what *are*, but there are also things that *are not*: truths (4).

4 He expresses this in many ways in many places, but this is one convenient spot.

5 This position has been endorsed recently by John Guillory. Guillory's thorough investigation, driven largely by the *Oxford English Dictionary* entries on media and related terms, nevertheless, after a brief consideration of Aristotle, discounts the classical and medieval periods entirely. 'The philological record informs us that the substantive noun *medium*

was rarely connected with matters of communication before the later nineteenth century' (321). Guillory stresses 'a lacuna' of 'several centuries', leading to a 'long silence in Western thought on the question of medium' (321, 324).

6 See, in particular, Stiegler.

7 Note the spectacular finale to Kittler's essay on the ontology of media: '"There will arrive the day when holy Troy has been destroyed", was one of Hector's famous sayings in Homer's *Iliad*. We cannot predict but gloomingly foresee the night of this fire. Perhaps a rosy new dawn will arise and realize the dream most dear to solid state physicians: computers based on parallel and tiny quantum states instead of on big and serial silicon connections. Then I, or rather my successors, shall withdraw this paper' ('Towards an Ontology of Media' 30). One can respond, respectfully albeit slightly hubristically, that the day has already come. Kittler thinks in terms of seriality. Yet despite the fluttering Turing tape of endless length, one must remember that the computer is a device born of parallelity, not seriality.

8 Another thorny shortcoming of the formalist approach is that it is often very difficult to find solid accord between one's formal checklist and the object at hand. I recount a 2008 lecture as an example. Speaking on 'Software Studies', Warren Sack gave the following list of formal characteristics in defining what computer programs are (or to be more specific, how code differs from other forms of writing): (1) programs deploy the *imperative* (and sometimes the conditional) mode; (2) they are *autonomous*, meaning they can be executed; (3) they are *impersonal*, meaning they eschew pronouns like 'I', 'me' or 'you'; (4) programs are below the level of the naked eye and hence *infinitesimal*; (5) they are *illegible*, as in the inability of humans to read compiled code; (6) and they are *instantaneous*. Now, I don't disagree with these observations, and in fact believe in the utility of many of them. However, as definitional qualities, they all seem rather flimsy. As an exercise I will cite valid counter-examples for each so-called characteristic: (1) code comments exist in programs, yet are not imperative; (2) computer programs frequently crash, putting their pure autonomy in doubt; (3) programs may not use personal pronouns, but variables and variable declaration are at the heart of most programs, meaning they are quite fundamentally oriented around the identification and addressing of objects and entities; (4) consider the example of the computer punch

card, which is a program that exists at the human level of visibility; (5) open source code formats – HTML, even – defy the principle of illegibility; (6) phenomena such as network lag routinely inhibit online games, making their non-instantaneous reality painfully evident. This is not to single out Sack, simply to demonstrate that formalist checklists are often extremely hard to ratify given the complexity of the subject matter.

9 See for example Kittler, *Gramophone* (34–6).

Works Cited

Badiou, Alain. *Logics of Worlds: Being and Event, 2.* Trans. Alberto Toscano. London: Continuum, 2009.

Cavell, Stanley. *The World Viewed: Reflections on the Ontology of Film.* Cambridge, MA: Harvard University Press, 1979.

Deleuze, Gilles. 'What Is a *Dispositif?*' *Michel Foucault, Philosopher: Essays.* Ed. and trans. Timothy J. Armstrong. New York: Routledge, 1992. 159–66.

Fried, Michael. 'Art and Objecthood.' *Artforum* 5 (1967): 12–23.

Guillory, John. 'Genesis of the Media Concept.' *Critical Inquiry* 36 (2010): 321–62.

Kittler, Friedrich A. *Gramophone, Film, Typewriter.* Trans. Geoffrey Winthrop-Young and Michael Wutz. Stanford: Stanford University Press, 1999.

Kittler, Friedrich A. 'Towards an Ontology of Media.' *Theory, Culture & Society* 26.2–3 (2009): 23–31.

Kittler, Friedrich A. *Optical Media: Berlin Lectures 1999.* Trans. Anthony Enns. Cambridge: Polity, 2010.

Manovich, Lev. *The Language of New Media.* Cambridge, MA: MIT Press, 2001.

Murray, Janet. *Hamlet on the Holodeck: The Future of Narrative in Cyberspace.* Cambridge, MA: MIT Press, 1997.

Sack, Warren. 'Software Studies.' University of Amsterdam. 11 August 2008. Lecture.

Stiegler, Bernard. *Technics and Time, 1: The Fault of Epimetheus.* Trans. Richard Beardsworth and George Collins. Stanford: Stanford University Press, 1998.

10

Staring into the Sun

Caroline Bassett

'Quaint'

'Kittler'; in cultural studies, once called a 'quaint' discipline,[1] the name produces a sharp intake of breath, a flicker on the galvanic register of bodily unease, and it is known that the skin is faster than the word (Massumi 89). This nervous reaction is understandable perhaps. The claim that the '[m]edia determine our situation' made in *Gramophone, Film, Typewriter* (xxix), and brought into the present by the claim that 'code' now 'encodes the world' (Kittler, quoted in Fuller 45), sets a (technological) cat amongst (hermeneutic) pigeons.

Above all, this claim contests the position that culture (more or less linguistically defined) determines technology, so that in the end humans control their machines and by extension themselves and their world. Not only representation and language, but also human experience and human interpretation (meaning-making), are valorized in such approaches, which are, says Kittler, misguided. This has been so at least since the advent of technical media, and is even more the case today in conditions where the computer – the culmination and the end point of the media, terminating all medial distinctions and working only with data – increasingly orders our world with no reference to humans – and does so at speeds and times too fast for human perception. In 'Thinking Colours and/or Machines', Kittler thus argues for the rechristening of hopelessly 'language-bound' humanities as cultural studies, and the absorption of the latter, now more properly viewed as (only) 'a part of media theory' (40). The media-theoretical approach, deemed 'functional' rather than 'quaint', adopts different methods. It is not through considering dimensions of human perception or human experience, and not through natural language, which computers do not speak, that the essentials of what is now ordering our world can be grasped. Instead what is called for is a moment of 'implosion' (Winthrop-Young and Gane 6). To find the patterns of our culture, we should explore the innards of machines. It's there, in the patterning of the circuitry (or in Kittler's later work in the fundamental patterns of alphanumerical unities), that what should perhaps no longer be called cultural logics will be discerned – there that we might find our techno-social algorithm.

There are ways in which the rather brutal dismissal evident here elides differences, not least between the specifically literary project of certain areas of humanities – and it is within the realm of literary studies that Kittler directs his arguments, albeit in ways that avoid using conventional distinctions such as 'understanding', 'interpretation', 'meaning', 'referent' or 'representation' (Krämer 94) – and cultural studies traditions. Some of the latter have, after all, made it their business not to be 'language-bound' but rather to consider the multiple 'articulations' (material and symbolic) of the formations they have explored, and have themselves often been influenced by medium theory (of note here is the influence of McLuhan in everyday life studies, including those by Meyrowitz and Silverstone).

Kittler's sense of epochal change, the degree to which he is influenced by Foucault, explains this brutality somewhat. He has been named an 'heir to discourse analysis', and although he takes this on 'only in order to radically alter the inheritance' by providing a medial explanation for Foucault's moments of historical rupture (Krämer 97), for him, the rules have changed and adherence to an older order would be nothing but nostalgia. But he does recognize that making the break, from discourse analysis to crypto-analysis (see 'Media and Drugs'), is not easy. Kittler, indeed, is very clear about the difficulty of moving beyond modes of analysis that begin with the human experience – a difficulty which both might be said to produce the necessity for literary heroics (evidenced in Kittler's gladiatorial style) as a mode of critical engagement, and also powers his search for such endeavours in the real. Certainly the heroic activities of Gustav Fechner are key in the archaeology of film that Kittler sets out in *Gramophone, Film, Typewriter*.

Or perhaps these are 'staged' rather than 'set out': it might be the literary nature of Kittler's writing, the paradoxical detour through fictional stages, often undertaken with a mordant humour that is oddly unremarked upon, that enable a mode of engagement with – rather than either total defiance of, or utter capitulation to – his position. And one way in which Kittler, despite his absolutism, does open up some grounds for such engagements is that, through the tense of his work, he gives us some time. The future anterior orientation he adopts (not uncommon in highly essentialist writing around techno-culture) essentially allows further discussion about what would otherwise be, certainly in relation to the writing on computerization, a terminal debate. Thus, we are at once already *in* the future where technology determines and also not quite there, and therefore this future can still be contemplated – it is the not quite yet inevitable, or is perhaps, in medial terms, unevenly inevitable: some media streams are more advanced than others, some anomalies persist. And may be exploited.

Perhaps because of this, Kittler's thinking already (increasingly) intrudes, from time to time, unannounced and only partially materialized, 'like the grin, without the cat', into other streams of techno-cultural analysis, and in doing so opens up new perspectives. Eschewing continuity and gradualism, mocking the tendency to elide the distinction between the image of technology and technology in its material operation that plagues cultural studies' attempts to grapple with material effects (with how technologies are determinant), and the problem the latter faces in exploring media technologies that extend beyond the embodied limits of human sense perception, Kittler perhaps can provide a shock treatment. And a shock treatment cultural studies needs. In this chapter this idea is explored, or perhaps this shock is administered, through a consideration of the newly mobilized image, in particular in relation to networked media and the personalized address.

In or At the Movies: Film

We are 'not yet' in the movies, 'maybe not quite yet. You'd better enjoy it while you can. Someday, when the film is fast enough, the equipment pocket size and burdenless and selling at people's prices, the lights and the booms no longer necessary, *then* . . . then'. (Pynchon 614, quoted in Kittler, 'Media and Drugs' 169)

Gustav Theodor Fechner was the father of psychophysics and of the afterimage – a visual phenomenon which he discovered at the cost of temporary blindness, staring straight into the sun and observing the peculiar reversed-out ghosts that danced before his eyes. What Fechner saw signalled the persistence of vision, allowing what was cut (in the real) to be rejoined (in the imaginary) – the principle of cinema, and also that of Lacanian psychoanalysis, with its focus on the mirror stage (see *Gramophone, Film, Typewriter*). Kittler notes that Fechner's experiments with light, alongside others involving 'artificial noise', were specifically designed to counter the perceived sense that the world is meaningful only as it is interpreted; that is, they were designed to confront hermeneutics ('Thinking Colours' 40).

Today the cinema is, if not gone, then coming to an end (Kittler, 'Media and Drugs' 31). The 'machines capable of storing and therefore separating sounds, sights, and writing' (Kittler, *Gramophone* xl), respectively gramophone, film, typewriter, each of which maps to a specific place in the Lacanian register (real, imaginary, symbolic) and form our sensory registers, are about to be terminated. *Gramophone, Film, Typewriter* is a genealogy of the media (of modernist media essentially) that gains its shape from this awareness of what is now ending – this is why it is also a history of the present. In new technical circumstances, what is sound, image or word will become/becomes a matter only of surface effect, essentially an interface – the 'psychophysical connection', which turned what was cut into the imaginary, is replaced by forms of calculation working on data. The computer (neither human, nor human tool), which has no use for old divisions, for instance those that divided visual from auditory data streams or those that tended to produce a hierarchy of the senses, completes a trajectory in which it determines 'reality'. This is a forbidding destination, as many (see Hansen) have noted. Moreover, we are often said by Kittler to have reached it. And yet, there are still places where data streams remain relatively differentiated, or where this mode of differentiation might still be *arranged*, and where the new perhaps still confronts, rather than subsumes, the old. So even today the fate of individual media, and of specific data streams, might still matter.

In my arrangement, we are going to the cinema but we are taking our mobile/cell phones; as a preamble, first it might be noted that there are parallels to be drawn between the development of visual telephony today and sound cinema in the 1920s. In both, different sense data streams had an uneven inauguration. The picture is to the mobile/cell phone as sound was to cinema, in that it came late, and was for some time only partially integrated into the mobile device's established routines, operating serially. One consequence of this is the prioritization of the sonic over the visual in the study of mobile media, notably in ethnographically inspired cultural-theoretical work exploring intimate forms of listening (see Bull). It is partly with a view to dis-intimatizing mobile media that it is useful to 'persist' the division of the senses that each medium began with, but with the twist that, in the case of the mobile/cell phone, it is not that the pictures are added, but rather, that sound is taken away. But now let us take the mobile screen to the cinema . . .

. . . specifically to an evening in a multiplex cinema, Brighton, England, some time ago. Then (as now) Orange, one of the UK's largest mobile network operators, offered cinema-goers free tickets every Wednesday. Tickets are claimed by SMS, thus proclaiming Orange Wednesday cinema audiences as also mobile/cell phone users. That evening, the audience was largely made up of teenagers, long avid text messengers (and latterly heavy mobile camera users), and also of course users of voice telephony; but in the cinema, their mobile/cell phones were muted, so that the encounter between old and new media that took place was confined to the image alone. Or rather to two images, as they appeared on two very different types of screen in the auditorium: the first an integral part of the famously immobilizing cinematic apparatus, the second portable; the first prioritizing narrative and spectacle, the second communication and interaction. As the programme began the big screen came to life, projecting advertisements, trailers and injunctions against 'noisy' mobile/cell phone use. This is the traditional cinema screen, the screen space produced in/as a vacuum 'which dreams readily fill' (Leirens, quoted in Metz 10). These dreams, it is said, are produced through techniques of alignment, of camera and projector with silenced audience – the engineered forms of identification with life on screen in which screen theory has often dealt – and also perhaps through the alignment of screen narrative with a certain cued narrative expectation. Thus Christian Metz argued that cinematic signification 'renders explicit what had first been experienced as [. . .] perception', assuming 'by virtue of an implicit or prior stage, something like a phenomenology of its subject' (17). In other words the cinematic apparatus, viewed as a narrative machine, here becomes something that enables an already existing narrative (Bassett, *Arc* 16). Metz, a pioneer of apparatus theory (after all, a form of medium theory), wondered why the investigation of cinema as technical media became an investigation of the symbolic content of individual films, noting that 'in the days when the cinema was a novel and astonishing thing and its very existence seemed problematical, the literature of cinematography tended to be theoretical and fundamental [. . .] today we tend to smile at this attitude; at any rate we believe [. . .] that the criticism of individual films states all there is to be said about film in general' (1). Metz turned to narrative, but his early cinematic dreams were profoundly technological. Perhaps they were, as Kittler put it about early film in general – dreams of cinema itself (*Gramophone* 168): medium dreams.

The cinema screen thus demands attention and arranges it, but many in the Orange Wednesday audience continued to attend to the small screens in their hands, rather than paying attention, so that, as the film approached and final texts were sent, the auditorium lit up. This firefly audience, with their light-shedding mobile/cell phones, countered the discipline of the big screen apparatus and its injunction to silence, which is also an injunction to watch, escaping the cinematic form of incarceration by thumbing themselves a lift, hitching their way out by way of their own screens; meet the tribes of the thumbs, early users, so labelled and somewhat notorious at the time.

In the cinema that evening, one screen faced many others. Two apparatuses intersected and the confrontation between these two kinds of screens, the larger bidding to marshal the audience from the front, the other dispersed through the auditorium, was one in which, for a moment, each side seemed well-matched. There may, already, however, even then, have been more mobile screen 'real estate' in this auditorium than cinema screen space. The distinction between being *in* the movies rather than *at* them, drawn by Pynchon's aforementioned character, may still be extant, but the trajectory towards interactive and immersed engagement (the subject of the phone message is, by virtue of the address, the user who becomes a participant in the tale) is also very clear. One kind of story-telling, traditional cinema with its peculiar fusion of motion chopped up 'in the real' and 'fusion and flow' in the imaginary (Kittler, 'Media and Drugs' 117), is ending – and with it perhaps a certain way of prioritizing the visual and the forms of narrative it might dictate (what is seen to be heard) too. The Kittler Grin, that dis-embodied commentary function, is quoting Goethe: 'no more listeners for tales: all are involved now' (Kittler, 'Media and Drugs' 159).

The question arising then concerns the form that 'involvement' in technical media might take, how it might be organized. At the cinema something striking was the lit-up quality of these teenagers, apparently made pure medium by their mobile prostheses, and appearing – certainly in contrast with the corralled form of viewing activity the screen was calling them to order to experience – to be individually engaged, freely extended into their own personal virtual worlds. Ethnographic work on mobile devices, focusing tightly on user experience (how the technology's effects are understood through the users' embodied experiences), have often found that mobile devices are experienced by their users as escape pods, offered and understood as devices (tools) enabling their owner increasingly to evade not only other screens (old technology and its controlling apparatus) but control in general. This offer/promise is bound up with engineered intimacy, for instance increasing 'fit' or tactile feedback between hand and device (see Cooley). It is as it becomes more personalized, more intimate with the user, that these media are increasingly understood as a personal tool for routing around; once again, for getting out of control.

Conceiving of mobile media as intimate media in its turn encourages a reading based on prosthesis or extension. McLuhan, of course, explored reorganization of the human sensorium wrought by mass communication systems – this is what makes him famous/notorious as a technological determinist. However, he also understood those systems as extensions of man, specifically as extensions of the nervous system, entailing a form of fusion that might be said to re-embody technology as well as to dis-embody the human somewhat, but that might write the human into the developing system.

Recourse to Kittler suggests a different way of reading these developments. Following Kittler's logic of implosion, the demand is to not consider the interface (the human–machine relation as it might be imagined or conceived of in the symbolic), but rather to look into the machine in order to get 'a technologically informed grip on that which grips you' (Winthrop-Young and Gane 6), or in other words to understand cultural technologies and their determinations. This approach produces a different perspective, enabling mobile technologies to be explored outside of the intimate relation.

Viewed in this way mobile/cell phones might still be understood as particularly shaped extensions, but also become visible as themselves extensions of an information network that is dispersed, highly hierarchical, and in large part (at many levels or protocols), radically uninformed by the human form. These machines are not intimate, neither are they to be conceptualized as tools, a term that, as Kittler himself notes, can rarely be used to consider technical media functions.

Techniques of implosion, deployed to reverse out intimacy and the peculiarly intense focus on the human it implies, thus function to designate the mobile device as network element. For Kittler, such exercises in implosion 'will not result in any human command over inhuman media or notation systems, but [. . .] will at least free us of the ongoing delusion that we can establish such mastery' (Winthrop-Young and Gane 6). The *degree* of personal control offered to the user of the mobile device, apparently so much greater than that offered to the incarcerated viewer in the traditional cinema screen, is thus here revealed to be a chimera; although of course the *question* of control within a world increasingly mediated by code remains central. In further pursuit of what increased involvement might imply in this un–intimate media-centric view of the world, we might leave the cinema and follow the mobile/cell phone, now equipped with a camera, outside.

An Arm's-Length Observation

not palaces but open laboratories

(Zielinski 276)[2]

Philippe Kahn, an expert in real-world computer distribution, also invented the camera phone to transport images. Kahn defined camera phones as 'end-to-end solutions for picture messaging', a technical definition that describes a process through which data is selected (cut out), saved (storage) and put in motion (sending). The fact of putting the image in motion suggests camera phones can be understood to be post-cinematic as well as post-photographic, but what travels 'end-to-end' of course is digital data, so that the emphasis of inquiry might properly shift from a basis in cinematography to one based on considerations of cultural technologies (Winthrop-Young and Gane 8), and once again an implosive view might be adopted. As a starting point here, it is striking that Kahn's definition does not stipulate a human at either end of the system he describes/invents.

On summer evenings, visitors to Brighton beach use their mobile cameras to take pictures, even when the glare makes it too bright to see anything on their screens. The cameras are held at arm's length and simply passed in front of the scene. When sunset is dramatic this happens over and over again. Groups arrive and take pictures, and everyone takes the same picture, each arm rising 'automatically' to the same place, provoked by the same stimuli ('I came down to catch the light'). Click to take. Click to send. A certain synchrony emerges, the sonic completing the image, perhaps, or being completed within it (Chion), but this completion would only be countenanced in relation to human perception. The key here is that once again, at the outset of a new era of media technology, there is a moment of staring into the sun. This time, however, nobody is looking, nobody's nerves are shot. There are no heroics. This time the stare is instrumentally distanced, which also means that this time-conscious registration is not undercut by the psychophysics of the afterimage – so there is, strictly speaking, no cinema either. Instead, conscious registration is replaced by the proxy 'eye' of the mobile device, which 'persists' what is no longer 'our' vision (but which might remain our 'view', as I'll explore later) by capturing it and sending it on, as data.

The body, apparently, has left the circuit. It might even be said that the device now does our looking 'for us' – unless, that is, it is looking for itself? As a proposition or a thought experiment this is worth pursuing. If it has the disadvantage of incipient anthropomorphism (threatening the attribution of a particular kind of volition), it has the advantage of displacing the human-centric focus that habitually attaches to personal devices, and of moving to a place where, at least in theory, features including local (but hidden) CMOS architectures, the extent and inhuman scale of the dispersed network (which cannot be visualized), the depth and hierarchies of the layered systems that produce transport across the web, all of which are impossible to process at a human scale, can be discerned. Or perhaps it is better to say that we can thereby reorganize our view of computational operations, always necessarily to some extent imaginary, given the limitations or incompatibilities of natural and computational language (see Hansen; Fuller). As Kittler himself put it, in an oddly anthropomorphically slanted comment in 'Thinking Colours and/or Machines', which might also indicate this paradoxical difficulty, 'we being language bound and computers not being, they can understand things we cannot about their calculations/their automation' (40).

In this upside-down world where the camera is presumed to be doing the looking, or rather to be acquiring the data, for itself, the role of the human is almost extinguished, but a swap perhaps could be envisaged; now that mobile cameras are taking pictures, humans could take on the role of being mobile. They always have provided portability to the system. In this secondary dromedary-ology, humans are thus reduced to fleshy carrying pouches, (Mac) Accessories after the fact, perhaps. A different way of seeing this again is, however, not to work with the mobile camera (where that device-based anthropomorphism familiar in a thousand childhood stories is easier to sustain), but to consider the thoroughly and more obviously inhuman network which resists configuration in human form, even in the imaginary. In a model in which the *network* takes the picture for itself, the human might slot in, might once again be viewed as a purely physical local transport system; but now it is the peripheral device (and the mobile camera its local link into the network), which selects and acquires (uploads) data, for the network, according to certain rules.

Kittler, of course, is not arguing that humans do not use com-municational technologies – but he *is* arguing that humans are, in profound ways, exterior to those technologies' operations and calculations, now generalized as techno-cultural logics – and this is one reason why his work is inimical to much work deploying Latourian actor networks, where agents of all kinds, including humans, are given a stake in what becomes a system.

This leaves no room for questions of meaning – as would be expected given Kittler's reliance on first-wave information theory in his formulation of technical media and their operations. But this also means there is no place in his approach to make a distinc-tion between one picture and another, the camera's, the human's, the network's, *except* in terms of data. The specificity of the data being captured in this case cannot be considered, except in relation perhaps to whether it *is* successfully captured or not. But what is being 'end-to-ended' here? Something that conforms to a particu-lar category, and not one that makes sense without considering what it means. It is that which humans would tag, or frame, as 'a good sunset'. These are the certain rules already referred to. And at this point, whoever or whatever takes the picture, the question of the human re-enters the system.

At issue here is not who/what clicked the camera 'shutter' (that is, whether we remain within the thought experiment or back out of it) but rather the question of framing – and here I want to invoke Mark Hansen's insistence on the role of embodiment in technical media systems, which he argues cannot be understood without considering questions of semantics – and it is this that forms the basis of his critique of Kittler.[3] Hansen's 2002 consideration of framing, read as something that holds (or perhaps *delegates*, to draw on Bruno Latour) earlier practices of embodied activity, is used to find a way to let meaning, for Hansen comprehensible only as an embodied process, operate at a distance. If the camera couldn't/didn't frame the view – since it only recognized as a view what had already been framed as such (which of course is why it was 'recognized' as a view by the many humans who came to take it in), then who/what did? Hansen's line of argument leads us to the conclusion that humans did. Moreover, the argument can then be taken further: if the data collected isn't a 'view' (since this category arises from embodied experience) but is simply 'data', what does its progress as information through the system from end to end constitute, or in other words – those Kittler would like to avoid – how is its passage meaningfully understood?

If the intimate perspective explored in the first example in the cinema produces a tool-based view that tends to constrain how a media technology is conceived in relation to its extent, its capacity and even how its 'outline' (its 'body' or imaginary anatomy) is understood, and thus demonstrates the distortions arising through human-centric perspectives which Kittler's theory may 'correct', here the perils of inverting this approach entirely become apparent. Stripping the user out of an exploration of the technological process of mobile camera use, refusing to countenance the body as (also) a medium, and therefore as engaged in the process – the latter a move that, in Hansen's hands, enables the exclusion of questions of meaning from questions of information to be addressed – builds a model of media operations in which a significant component is absent, and threatens to produce not an operational but an abstract model.

Paradoxically, however, even whilst contesting, at the level of theorization, Kittler's view that media determine our situation, it can also be recognized that, in various spheres, this way of thinking has increasing cultural resonance, is producing actions that respond to the situation, more or less as Kittler lays it out. Thus, although camera phone systems are not entirely automated messaging systems (not yet, and if we follow Hansen's line not ever), cultures begin to operate as if they were, which is to say that they begin to incorporate assumptions arising around the presumption of automated vision into everyday practices and other cultural productions. This might be evidenced in a certain self-suspicion, in the way we begin to lean on the mobile camera, not only as personal view-taker, but also as a view-finder. A few years ago this would have been counter-intuitive; Adobe's Photoshop and other image-manipulation programs like it, emerging in the last decades of the twentieth century, were supposed to produce an increasingly sceptical attitude towards the photographic image and about the 'veracity' (understood differently in a series of contexts and registers) of what it imaged. Today the issue perhaps is that automation means that increasingly it is the evidence of our own eyes that is not trusted. This could be traced out by exploring shifts in the conventions of fictional realism (see Bassett, 'Digital Media'), but here it is simpler to note that in the case of the cameras on the beach, it is precisely the distancing operation undertaken, the camera held at arm's length from the body, that suggests that the image might offer an un-spun record of the event, a real and immediate record of what was 'really there', untouched by the human, and (therefore) making claims to be offering a particular version of the 'truth'. In so far as reliable witnessing is now understood to be electronic, we are, as Kittler noted, already, even if still only partially, in an era beyond the differentiation of the data stream into categories previously aligned with the human sensorium – each, historically, having a certain perceived relation to truth – the well-known example of this being the residual authority of 'auditing' accounts. In this sense perhaps we are no longer able to find a view that is entirely our own. The cultural consequences of this are very evident in relation to CCTV, which with networked mobile cameras produces what is essentially a witness proliferation programme. Moreover, while these cameras declare themselves to be 'personal', what happens to visual culture, through these kinds of activities, is a form of depersonalization: there are billions of camera phones; a myriad angles, a myriad clicks, many users, a surplus; endless sunsets. This people-ported system has its correlative in mounted (and less mobile) CCTV systems, which operate with parallel data collection and data processing principles (although less well). Everything is recorded. The last question I would like to address is whether any of it is live.

Wish You Were Here?

Concert audiences, again holding their mobile/cell phones at arm's length, but this time high above their heads, once again let their mobile cameras, this time set on video, operate. Not stopping to cut, and ignoring the storage mechanism at the heart of data capture that institutes the break with the real, and that produces mediation, they are in a sense not sending images or even storing an experience for later, but rather opening a channel to distant others, to show them, to send them, their 'good time'; wishing you were here.

Sybille Krämer notes that for Kittler '[d]ata processing becomes the process by which temporal order becomes moveable and reversible in the very experience of space' (94). This manipulation, for Kittler founded on escaping syntactic structures (those of conventional narrative, perhaps, which may easily be understood precisely as an ordering of experience in time, as Paul Ricoeur's work would tell us), extends, of course, only as far as mediation itself can – and is in this sense still incomplete. Here the imperatives of 'liveness' which demand at least the appearance of dis-intermediation, in order to guarantee immediacy, block the degree to which this reordering may be convincingly undertaken – although it is also precisely this capacity for reordering that enables what is offered as 'live' transmission. The reverse salient here, the retarded data

stream that stalls the kinds of necessary combinations and reorgani-
zations that would enable a completed form of 'liveness', which
might be the apogee of time axis manipulability to be recon-
structed, is here, of course, neither sonic nor visual, but concerns
tactility.

Touch, demanding embodiment, intervenes, so that, so far at
least, technologically determined presence, absence or space/time
control is not experienced as leading towards simultaneity but its
opposite. Digital encoding means you cannot get there 'in time' to
be 'live' – so that the concert goers' open channel, which appears
to be dis-intermediated and 'live', is always – like an arrest these
riotous days – just after the act, and therefore revealed as not 'live'
at all. Once again, consideration of the ways in which technology
organizes us (configures us) through cultural technologies such as
the mobile camera phone – something already very different from
that up-close coupling that was offered in the cinema – suggests
that there remain ways in which bodies continue to intervene,
stalling what might otherwise become technology's determining
trajectory, and producing questions about mediation and its operations. This, finally, invokes the question of what it means not to
be 'live' *at* the event but to be the operator or user of the network.
Adrian Mackenzie, seeking a middle ground between technologies
as 'material orderings of movement' and as 'temporal flows of subjective experience', looks to understand what engagement in media
technologies 'feels like'. His 'machine time', a 'mosaic of relations
and orderings of actions brought into proximity' (Mackenzie),
rewrites the notion of time axis manipulation, but/and also seeks
ways to expose mediation's own actions on the body, notably by
way of an investigation of the (human) experience of *transition*
across networks.

This speculative engagement with Kittler's world-view, which
has taken as its starting point work around *Gramophone, Film,
Typewriter*, and followed Kittler in reading this on beyond these
technologies, thus ends back with a question about experience, a
question he does not countenance. Kittler's demand to follow the
machine does make demands on, and reorganizes the perspectives
of, cultural studies. Without a genuinely media-centric view, the
latter is, if not limited to (here is my disagreement with Kittler),

far less protected from the perspective of the system given to us by what Kittler himself once called, in the heyday of personal computing, 'cyberspace ideology', or the 'foam packing' of the software industry 'turned to the outside' (Kittler, quoted in Johnston 3). Some contemporary 'packaging' that might urgently need unpacking, and that can only be unpacked through consideration of media as a technical system, is the social media rhetoric coming out of the digital cultural industries, which propagates the kinds of readings of media technologies I have discussed – notably those focusing on personalization, intimacy, dis-intermediation. I am thinking in particular of that shibbolethic, *quaint* slogan: 'it's not the technology, it's the people . . .'. This is a slogan chanted in the face of the biggest expansion of networks ever seen – a serpentine system of control, layers deep, ecologically dispersed, only intimate if you also understand it as endlessly entwined, dis-intimate, lethally indifferent, almost as far from 'you' as it is possible to be.

Notes

1 A now 'quaint but no longer very functional discipline' that should become 'part of media theory' (Kittler, 'Thinking Colours' 40).
2 'Artistic praxis in media worlds is a matter of extravagant expenditure. Its privileged locations are not palaces but open laboratories' (Zielinski 276).
3 Mark Hansen's more recent work (notably in this volume) revises his earlier view of Kittler, previously thought to have capitulated more or less entirely to the mechanisms of an inhuman technology. Hansen now discerns a 'subterranean' but none the less real humanism in Kittler's writing, one that is grounded on the centrality of the human body in the latter's work, but that is also characterized by a demand to retain a 'clean separation' between the organic and inorganic. My chapter, exposing a discrepancy between the (proclaimed) intimacy and (real) distance between human and computational operations within networks, but also insisting on the validity of human inputs (the view that selects data) in Kittlerian operations, has a very different emphasis (not least, it seeks to speak to cultural studies and its lacunae). However,

there are resonances here with Hansen's later work. It is striking that, even within an analysis designedly operating in a Kittlerian grain, in which the perspective is switched from the human to the machine, the body demands attention.

Works Cited

Bassett, Caroline. *The Arc and the Machine: Narrative and New Media.* Manchester: Manchester University Press, 2007.

Bassett, Caroline. 'Digital Media.' *Year's Work in Critical and Cultural Theory* 18.1 (2010): 138–54.

Bull, Michael. 'No Dead Air! The iPod and the Culture of Mobile Listening.' *Journal of Leisure Studies* 24.4 (2005): 343–55.

Chion, Michel. 'Projections of Sound on Image.' *Film and Theory: An Anthology.* Eds. Robert Stam and Toby Miller. Oxford: Blackwell, 2000. 111–24.

Cooley, Heidi Rae. 'It's All About the Fit: The Hand, the Mobile Screenic Device and Tactile Vision.' *Journal of Visual Culture* 3.2 (2004): 133–55.

Fuller, Matthew, ed. *Software Studies: A Lexicon.* Boston: MIT Press, 2008.

Hansen, Mark B. N. 'Cinema Beyond Cybernetics, or How to Frame the Digital Image.' *Configurations* 10.1 (2002): 51–90.

Johnston, John. Introduction. *Literature, Media, Information Systems: Essays.* By Friedrich Kittler. Amsterdam: G+B Arts International, 1997. 2–27.

Kittler, Friedrich A. 'Media and Drugs in Pynchon's Second World War.' *Reading Matters: Narratives in the New Media Economy.* Ed. Joseph Tabbi and Michael Wutz. Ithaca, NY, and London: Cornell University Press, 1997. 157–72.

Kittler, Friedrich A. *Gramophone, Film, Typewriter.* Trans. Geofrey Winthrop-Young and Michael Wutz. Stanford: Stanford University Press, 1999.

Kittler, Friedrich A. 'Thinking Colours and/or Machines.' *Theory, Culture & Society* 23.7–8 (2006): 39–50.

Krämer, Sybille. 'The Cultural Techniques of Time Axis Manipulation:

On Friedrich Kittler's Conception of Media.' *Theory, Culture & Society* 23.7–8 (2006): 93–109.

Leirens, Jean. *Le cinéma et le temps*. Paris: Editions du Cerf, 1954.

Mackenzie, Adrian. 'Wirelessness as Experience of Transition.' *Fibreculture* 13 (2008). Web. http://journal.fibreculture.org/issue13/issue13_mac kenzie_print.html

McLuhan, Marshall. *Gutenberg Galaxy*. Toronto: Toronto University Press, 2002.

Massumi, Brian. 'The Autonomy of Affect.' *Cultural Critique*, 31 (1995): 83–109.

Metz, Christian. *Film Language: A Semiotics of Cinema*. Trans. Michael Taylor. New York: Oxford University Press, 1974.

Pynchon, Thomas. *Gravity's Rainbow*. London: Vintage, 2000.

Winthrop-Young, Geoffrey, and Nicholas Gane. 'Friedrich Kittler: An Introduction.' *Theory, Culture & Society* 23.7–8 (2006): 5–16.

Zielinski, Siegfried. *Deep Time of the Media*. Boston: MIT Press, 2006.

11

Symbolizing Time:
Kittler and Twenty-First-Century Media

Mark B. N. Hansen

Returning to the work of German media scientist Friedrich Kittler in 2012, in the midst of minor revolutions in ubiquitous computing and social media, and a full eight years after having denounced what I took to be his unmistakable capitulation to an inhuman machinism,[1] I can now see – or indeed, cannot cease to see – signs of a distinct, if subterranean, 'humanism' everywhere at work in Kittler's method. Certainly the most consequential of such signs – and one I shall focus much attention upon here – is the fundamental role Kittler accords the body in his conception of literature's technical *a priori*, and specifically of the physiological poetics of modernism he develops in the second half of *Discourse Networks*. There explicitly, and elsewhere (at least) by implication, the body designates a locus for an excess of inscription over meaning – and for a veritable post-hermeneutic criticism – that comprises the accomplishment *as much* of nineteenth-century psychophysics as of late nineteenth- and early twentieth-century poetic production. In this configuration, the body grounds what is outside meaning or sense, and thus hosts the massive proliferation of a-signifying energies that characterize the epoch of media differentiation.

What I failed to see in 2004, and what our current media situation renders downright conspicuous, is the extent to which Kittler's work on technical media, including the famous 'Introduction' to *Gramophone, Film, Typewriter* that had left such a deep impression on an earlier me, in fact grows out of his turn to the body, or what we might better describe as his expanded conceptualization of the complex circuits imbricating embodied human sensation with worldly material fluxes. Without further ado, let me simply cite two passages – taken from two central essays in *Draculas Vermächtnis*, Kittler's collection of 'Technical Writings' – that display, at least covertly or backhandedly, this subterranean 'humanism'.

The first passage, which comes towards the beginning of Kittler's essay on Lacan's seminar on the ego (Seminar II), relates Kittler's understanding of Lacan's striking counterfactual experiment designed to explore whether mirror images of mountains in a world without living beings still exist:

> Lacan returns to humanity at the end of the test in order to verify [the function of] the storage of data. This is to say that any representation of the mountain 'exists', according to Lacan, 'for one very simple reason – at the high point of civilization we have attained, which far surpasses our illusions about consciousness, we have manufactured instruments which, without in any way being audacious, we can imagine to be sufficiently complicated to develop films themselves, put them away into little boxes, and store them in the fridge'. A photo-electric cell registers the flash of lightning and triggers the camera which records its reflection in the lake, until a humanity returning at time t_2 can witness the short-lived phenomenon of time t_1. ('The World of the Symbolic' 132)

This return to humanity via data storage has the effect of transforming what, for Lacan, remains a fable of the inherent inhumanity of the symbolic into an allegory of contemporary humanity's complex imbrication with computational machines. Whereas Lacan sees the experiment as proof of the autonomy of the symbolic, a proof merely 'verified' by the return to humanity, Kittler chooses to focus on this return. For him, the key element of the experiment is the way in which the machinic element, which does possess a sensory domain of its own (as pioneering chronophotographer

Étienne-Jules Marey might put it),[2] conjoins with the human: the technical inscription of the image, though autonomous in its genesis from any human activity, nonetheless functions to expand an experience that, at the least, *implicates* the human. This expansion of the role of data storage to address the human informs Kittler's critique of software, for what software does, following this critique, is to obfuscate the capacity of technical media to intensify human experience precisely by expanding its domain beyond what can be directly perceived. That is why Kittler's critique of software is able to expose how the symbolic mandate of computer technology represses our robust contact with the real at the very same time as it manages – precisely on account of the temporal 'feedforward' it thematizes – to present a model for human–machine co-functioning capable of avoiding the very reductions that, on Kittler's view, software is compelled to impose.

The second passage, which concludes Kittler's 'There Is No Software', bears the fruit of this denunciation to the extent that it inaugurates what appears to be a distinctive approach to the human–computer interface:

> Confronted as they are with a continuous environment of weather, waves, and wars, digital computers can cope with this real number avalanche only by adding element to element [. . .] [T]he very isolation between digital or discrete elements accounts for a drawback in connectivity that otherwise, 'according to current force laws' as well as to the basics of combinatorial logics, would be bounded only by a maximum equalling the square number of all elements involved. Precisely this maximal connectivity, on the other, physical side, defines nonprogrammable systems, be they waves or beings. That is why these systems show polynomial growth rates in complexity and, consequently, why only computations done on nonprogrammable machines could keep up with them. In all evidence, this hypothetical, but all too necessary, type of machine would constitute sheer hardware, a physical device working amidst physical devices and subject to the same bounded resources. (154)

After noting the obvious resemblance between these 'badly needed machines' and 'the familiar face of man', Kittler does something that I find truly striking. Rather than rejecting any hint of a lingering 'humanism', as one might expect, he brings home with emphatic force *the similarity of carbon and silicon hardware*:

> our equally familiar silicon hardware obeys many of the requisites for such highly connected, nonprogrammable systems. Between its million transistor cells, some million to the power of two interactions always already take place. There is electron diffusion; there is quantum-mechanical tunneling all over the chip. Technically, however, these interactions are still treated in terms of system limitations, physical side effects, and so on. To minimise all the noise that it would be impossible to eliminate is the price we pay for structurally programmable machines. The inverse strategy of maximizing noise would not only find the way back from IBM to Shannon, it may well be the only way to enter that body of real numbers originally known as chaos. (Kittler, 'There Is No Software' 155)

With this call for a plunge into the body of real numbers, Kittler opens a trajectory of human–computer cooperation that further expands his transformative appropriation of Lacan's generalization of the symbolic. Even more prominently than was the case with his redirection of Lacan's fable to stress the 'return to humanity', Kittler's critique of software is motivated by a fundamental insistence on the homology between human and machine understood as two materially distinct non-programmable systems.

This situation has important implications for how Kittler treats – and indeed transforms fundamentally – the notion of the symbolic. For if the full autonomy of the symbolic inaugurates a *new* discourse network in the aftermath of the Second World War, as John Johnston suggests (82), it is one that we in the twenty-first century can best inherit not by accepting its reduction of the flux of real numbers (and of time and experience) to programmable numbers, but rather by repudiating the very terms of this reduction. That, at any rate, is how I read Kittler's proto-political injunction in favour of non-programmable machines, and it is also, as we shall see, how I understand his work on sound analysis and its key contribution to thinking twenty-first-century media. What Kittler's politically tinged critique of software and his turn to sound analysis have in common is a return to the body, though not necessarily, or at least not exclusively, to the human body. In this sense, far from marking a replacement of 'psychophysics' by 'the computational paradigm', as Johnston would have it, what this turn in Kittler's trajectory performs is a generalization of the body to designate singular materializations of programmable processes and an expansion of psychophysical methods to encompass the operation of both human *and* machinic computations. We must accordingly speak *not* in terms of psychophysics *or* computation, but in a vein that welcomes them both. We must speak of psychophysics in an expanded frame: as a method for exploring non-programmable computing.

Fuelled by his political critique of software, Kittler's injunction in favour of non-programmable machines thus sidesteps – well in advance of their very genesis – recent arguments that software has replaced ideology to the extent that it has rendered its operation machinic. In his book *The Interface Effect*, Alexander Galloway expands Wendy Chun's claim that 'software is a functional analog to ideology' (43) into a full-blown allegory: 'The point', Galloway specifies,

> is not simply that software is functional, but that software's mock resolution of the tension between the machinic and the narrative, the functional and the disciplinary, the fluid and the fixed, the digital and the analog, is an allegorical figure for the way in which these same political and social realities are 'resolved' today: not through oppression of false consciousness, as in the orthodox ideological critique, but through the ruthless rule of code, which proposes that the analog should live on to the end, only to show that the analog never existed in the first place. (76)

Part of what Galloway is here gesturing towards – the fact that software obfuscates its own operation – seems essentially correct, even while the conclusions he elicits – most notably, that the 'virtual (or the new, the *next*) is no longer the site of emancipation' (138) – appear overly pessimistic. Against Galloway's conviction that capital has fully co-opted the new and that, consequently, we can only take stock of what we 'already know to be true', we can thus pit Kittler's eccentric activism on behalf of the non-programmable. For what Kittler's position preserves, even in the face of a becoming-machinic of ideology, is the *sensory* basis of technical mediation. Kittler reminds us that, underneath the layers of software that obfuscate the materiality of the computer at the very moment they afford us functionality, there lies an irreducible sensory reality. His embrace of non-programmable machines serves to affirm that all computational processes (including parallel ones) are temporal processes: insofar as they enframe time, computational processes generate sensibility, and they do so, importantly, before any meaningful distinction between human and non-human systems enters the scene.

In this respect, we can understand Kittler's claim that 'there is no software' as a two-pronged political claim. On one hand, it states that, viewed from the standpoint of their irreducible temporality, all computational processes are fundamentally material and non-abstractable. And on the other, it urges us *not* to make concessions to software qua ideology rendered machinic, but instead to focus on the material, micro-physical effects of computing. Kittler's claim thus draws attention not simply to the fuzziness of the software/hardware divide, but to a certain *impossibility of software* and, with it, to the simple irrelevance of machinic ideology:

> Software in the usual sense of an ever-feasible abstraction would not exist any longer. The procedures of these [non-programmable] machines, though still open to an algorithmic notation, should have to work essentially on a material substrate whose very connectivity would allow for cellular reconfigurations [. . .] [P]rogramming [these machines] will have little to do any longer with approximated Turing machines. ('There Is No Software' 154–5)

Only apparently a paradox, programming non-programmable machines simply requires a revision of what we understand by programming: no longer the fruit of an instrumental reduction, programming must come to designate operations performed on a material substrate in real, which is to say experiential, time. That is why Kittler's approach here can be distinguished by his focus on the irreducible sensory reality of temporal events: eschewing abstraction, Kittler reaffirms the sensory basis of all events, both machinic and human. In what follows, I shall try to justify my conviction that this focus on the sensory basis of programming singularly characterizes Kittler's contribution to media theory. More than any other aspect of his work, this focus should shape Kittler's legacy for those of us currently at work trying to theorize twenty-first-century media.

From Discourse Networks to Real Numbers

In his 'Foreword' to *Discourse Networks*, David Wellbery identifies the body as the site for the operation of media, and specifically for the operation of noise beyond meaning that comprises the focus of 'non-hermeneutic criticism':

> The reason that the concept of corporeality defines the point of reference for post-hermeneutic criticism is clear. The body is the site upon which the various technologies of our culture inscribe themselves, the connecting link to which and from which our medial means of processing, storage, and transmission run. Indeed, in its nervous system, the body itself is a medial apparatus and an elaborate technology. But it is also radically historical in the sense that it is shaped and reshaped by the networks to which it is conjoined [. . .] [T]he point at which discourse networks reveal most sharply their specific impress is in the pathologies they produce [. . .] Whoever would look for the bonds of solidarity that orient Kittler's investigation will find them here: in its unmistakable compassion for the pathos of the body in pain. Hermeneutics would appropriate this corporeal singularity in the construction of a meaning. Post-hermeneutic criticism, however, draws its responsibility precisely from the unassimilable otherness of the singular and mortal body. This is the ethical reason it stops making sense. (xiv–vi)

I want to follow up on Wellbery's remarks by exploring how the focus on the body reflects the literary origin of Kittler's media theory. In particular, I want to suggest that this genealogy serves both to distinguish Kittler from other prominent media theorists and to elucidate his embrace of media effects below the threshold of perception.

Kittler's typology of media stems from a literary source. Indeed, his famous thesis concerning media differentiation in the nineteenth century actually repeats – on a technical platform – an earlier, narrowly literary differentiation: 'Around 1800 the book became both film and record simultaneously – not, however, as a media technical reality, but only in the imaginary of readers' souls' (Kittler, 'Introduction' 39). This initial, literary differentiation prepares for the proper technical differentiation; it foregrounds distinct forms of encoding specific to distinct sensory registers: 'What was new about the storage capacity of the phonograph and the cinematograph [. . .] was their ability to store time; as a mixture of audio frequencies in the acoustic realm, as a movement of single picture sequences in the optic realm' (Kittler, 'Introduction' 34). The 'writing of movement' that captures the temporal flux of the visible domain is as different from the 'writing of the voice' that captures the temporal flux of the sonic domain as both are from the typewriting that captures the temporal flux of the alphabet itself. To the extent that each form of inscription registers and stores experiences particular to certain sensory domains, each possesses a distinct bodily basis and a certain autonomy. Themselves the fruit of Kittler's literary origins, this bodily specificity and quasi-autonomy of media are what render his theory singular.

Just as there is no concept of the medium prior to media differentiation, there can be no understanding of the alphabet as an inscriptional technology without a plurality of inscription systems. That is why, even as it comprises a 'grammatology', the alphabet cannot provide a general model for technical inscription. There simply is no single grammatology that would inform and explicate all cultural inscription, or rather, if there ever was one, it is not because a single theoretical model informs all media inscription, but rather because, for a finite, though certainly quite long historical period, one such technology exercised a monopoly over inscription. And even this historical dominance is mitigated by the existence of graphic and visual arts; as Kittler makes clear in *Optical Media*, images operate alongside script as media for storage and transmission of information. To the extent that such operation anticipates the technical differentiation to come in the nineteenth century, it reiterates the contingency of the alphabetic monopoly, which, it would seem to suggest, is a monopoly only at a sufficient distance. In sum, whether its legacy only becomes recognizable in retrospect or is already legible from its negotiations with the graphic and visual arts, grammatology reigned supreme for the better part of five millennia. Yet what Kittler's developments in *Optical Media* help to make clear is that, far from comprising the general science of mark-making (as it does for Derrida and, following him, Bernard Stiegler), grammatology designates an historically produced contingency that was to see its end, and simultaneously acquire its full specificity, following the invention of new, technically autonomous forms of inscription:

> Texts and scores were Europe's only means to store time. Both are based on writing; the time of this writing is symbolic (in Lacan's terms). This time memorises itself in terms of projections and retrievals – like a chain of chains. Nevertheless, whatever runs as time on a physical or (again in Lacan's terms) real level, blindly and unpredictably, could by no means be encoded. Therefore all data flows, if they were real streams of data, had to pass through the defile of the signifier. Alphabetic monopoly, grammatology. (Kittler, 'Introduction' 35)

Grammatology functions as a general symbolic only so long as it, and it alone, is capable of encoding flows of physical time; once phonography and cinematography allow for alternative techniques of encoding physical time, this general symbolic function comes to an end, or put another way, the symbolic itself becomes differentiated.

That is why, notwithstanding his well-known mapping of gramophone, film and typewriter onto Lacan's triad of real, imaginary and symbolic, Kittler effectively treats film and gramophone as distinct symbolic systems for capturing real streams of data. Crucial in each case is how the symbolic system is understood in relation to the encoding of the temporal flux and in particular how it both implicates a certain sensory domain – hearing or seeing – and addresses bodily materiality specifically in order to 'capture' what

can be sensed. It is equally crucial, however, that these two operations (enframing worldly sensibility and addressing the body) do
not fully overlap, that the sensory affordances of worldly sensibility
exceed the grasp of particular embodied modes of sensing. This
excess is precisely the space in which the machinic can expand the
operation of sensibility through its own proper operation, which is
to say without functioning as a surrogate or substitute for human
sense organs.

More than any other element of his media theory, it is Kittler's
effort to correlate media differentiation with specific sensory and
bodily capacities that most distinguishes his project. To see why,
we need only contrast Kittler's account of media differentiation
with Bernard Stiegler's at first glance quite similar account. Both
Kittler and Stiegler place much importance on the development of
technical inscription media in the nineteenth century: both focus
on the gramophone and the cinematograph as inventions that
provide a certain autonomization of sensory circuits. Yet where
Kittler's interest centres on the liberation of auditory and visual
fluxes from their subordination to the alphabetic signifier, and thus
on a certain expansion in the inscription, storage and transmission
of worldly sensibility, Stiegler positions these inventions in relation
to a unitary model of temporality. As he argues in his work on time
and cinema, both the phonograph and the cinematograph furnish,
for the first time in the history of humanity, the opportunity for
a human consciousness to experience *exactly the same* temporal
object more than once. For this reason, these nineteenth-century
technical inventions carry out the 'phonographic [or equally:
the cinematographic] revelation of the structure of all temporal
objects' (Stiegler, 'The Time of Cinema' 76). That Stiegler goes
on to clarify the grammatological basis of technical recording,
and that his project takes shape as a technical specification of
Derridian grammatology,[3] let us discern the operation of a univo-
cal concept of grammatization at the heart of his exploration of
technical recording. If Stiegler's work thus develops a homology
between language, as the grammatization of speech, and cinema, as
the grammatization of life, the way grammatization works in both
cases is the same: linear fluxes are discretized through the deploy-
ment of grammar.

Kittler's media differentiation arrives at a precisely opposite conclusion: for Kittler, gramophone and film liberate distinct temporal fluxes – auditory and visual respectively – from their subordination to chains of grammar known as alphabetic writing. We might even say that the category of the 'symbolic' plays a similar role for Kittler as does 'grammatization' for Stiegler: in both cases, what is at stake is a certain discretization – and necessary reduction – of a temporal flux. Yet the thrust of Kittler's analysis, as we have seen, is not towards standardization across the board, but towards media differentiation, where differentiation entails distinct technical inscription methods – different symbolics – correlated to distinct sensory registers. For Kittler, therefore, the symbolic that dictates the encoding of the auditory flux is distinct from the symbolic that encodes the visual flux, just as both are distinct from the symbolic that encodes the alphabet. As we shall see, this divergence in the symbolic will allow Kittler to privilege sound recording as an inscription and manipulation not of a symbolic encoding of the real, but of the real – the physical flow of time – itself.

Yet another point of divergence between Stiegler and Kittler not only merits discussion but will provide an opportunity for us to come back to the literary origin of Kittler's project. Whereas Stiegler remains focused on the operation of time-consciousness, and invokes recording technologies insofar as they bear directly on this operation, Kittler not only has no interest in bolstering the functioning of consciousness, but views recording technologies as opportunities for expanding sensory experience to include what, on any phenomenology of consciousness, can only remain its 'outside'. This is why he insists that recording technologies directly sample the real, independently of any human symbolic mediation. The origin of this claim is the direct address to the body at work in literature circa 1900: 'The victory of psychophysics is a paradigm shift. Instead of the classical question of what people would be capable of if they were adequately and affectionately "cultivated," one asks what people have always been capable of when autonomic functions are singly and thoroughly tested' (Kittler, *Discourse Networks* 214). What results is a resolutely materialist account of language: 'What we ordinarily call language is thus a complex linkage of brain centers through no less numerous direct and indirect nerve connections. As Nietzsche had prophesied and, as a paralytic, demonstrated to his psychiatrist Theodor Ziehen, language breaks down into individual elements: into optical, acoustical, sensory, and motoric nervous impulses and only then into signifier/signified/referent' (Kittler, *Discourse Networks* 216). In a circuit that will be technically supplemented by the recording media of 1900, which take the place (and expand the scope) of the body, language is and must be felt by the body before (and as a condition for) being heard by the ear or seen by the eye.

One crucial consequence of this direct address to the decomposed body is a suspension of the evaluative category called 'meaning', and with it, of the possibility to distinguish and to hierarchize sounds according to their sources: 'Psychophysics advances, beyond all attribution of meaning and its transparent arbitrariness, to the meaningless body, which is a machine among machines. A roaring in the ears and the roaring of trains are equally capable of providing disordered brains with assonances, alliterations, and rhymes' (Kittler, *Discourse Networks* 219). Though Kittler never says as much, the resulting expansion in what can be felt by the body yields a massive expansion in the sensibility of the world, though only when coupled to the great analogue recording media:

> In the discourse network of 1900, psychophysical experiments were incorporated as so many random generators that produce discourses without sense or thought. The ordinary, purposeful use of language – so-called communication with others – is excluded. Syllabic hodgepodge and automatic writing, the language of children and the insane – none of it is meant for understanding ears or eyes; all of it takes the quickest path from experimental conditions to data storage [. . .] [D]eposition into writing is impossible, because the random generators produce effects only at extremely high speeds. Automatic writing and reading already exhibit a tendency toward increasing speed: the tempo of dictation races ahead of the hands, that of reading exceeds the articulating organs. Thus, in order to retain anything at all, psychophysics had to join with the new media that revolutionised optics and acoustics circa 1900. (Kittler, *Discourse Networks* 229)

This coupling of psychophysics and technical media installs, at the very heart of Kittler's media theory, an internal correlation between mediatic inscriptions and bodily effects. If the resulting expansion of sensibility adds something to the properly literary origin scene of Kittler's theory – the fragmented body feeling the noise of Morgenstern's 'The Great Lalula' – it in no way alters the bodily destination of sense. For what it adds is a technical mediation of the circuit linking sense and body, a capacity for inscription, storage and manipulation of diverse sensory fluxes of the real that, despite their bodily destination, need no longer be 'generated' and/or 'hosted' by and within the body. In marked contrast to Stiegler's focus on time-consciousness, the point for Kittler is that recording media directly register fluxes of the real independently of any operation of consciousness and any bodily capture or incorporation.

Nowhere is the correlation of mediatic inscription and bodily effect more strikingly manifested than in Kittler's account of sound, and particularly in his conception of 'time axis manipulation'. Time axis manipulation designates the decoupling of playback speed from recording speed, and in this sense stands at the opposite pole from Stiegler's insistence that the coincidence of record-ing time with reception time forms the very basis of media's support of time-consciousness. Indeed, it is precisely because we are dealing with the recording of the real that recorded temporal fluxes – which is to say sense – can be played back faster than they were recorded: 'If the phonographic playback speed differs from its recording speed, there is a shift not only in clear sounds but in entire noise spectra. What is manipulated is the real rather than the symbolic' (Kittler, *Gramophone* 35). Though for me what is manipulated is still the symbolic (albeit a different one from the Lacanian, grammatological symbolic), the key point, to emphasize it once more, is that recording technologies directly inscribe tem-poral fluxes without routing them through time-consciousnesses or subjects: 'Neither gramophone needles nor brain neurons need any self-consciousness to retrace a groove faster than it was engraved' (Kittler, *Gramophone* 34). As directly recorded fluxes, technical recordings capture far more than what can be heard or seen. In this sense, Kittler's emphasis on manipulation stands opposed to Stiegler's reductive identification of recording with a 'tertiary' form of memory that grounds the experience of time-consciousness in media. Freed from this constricting conjunction with consciousness, technical recording directly expands the sensibility of the world well beyond what is accessible through the human senses, and in this way creates opportunities for manipulating the 'unheard-of' so it can be experienced by human ears.

From the 'Symbolic of the Symbolic' to the 'Symbolic of the Real'

Having now clarified the singularity of Kittler's conception of media differentiation, let me turn to a more focused discussion of time axis manipulation in order to lay bare what it tells us about the status of the symbolic in the context of sound recording. In their introduction to a special Kittler issue of *Theory, Culture & Society*, Geoffrey Winthrop-Young and Nicholas Gane divide Kittler's career into three stages, all along reminding us that it is 'not that simple': on their perfectly plausible account, a first literary stage leads into a second media stage which is then broadened into a final stage centred on 'cultural technologies' (8). More aptly conceptualized as a 'deepening, [. . .] widening spiral' than a linear progression, this division furnishes a convenient backdrop against which I can situate the claim I want to make concerning the symbolic: namely, that media for Kittler never get out of the symbolic, or more pointedly, that what is involved in the shift from the alphabetic monopoly to media differentiation and ultimately to the computer is not a move from the symbolic to the real, but a move from one symbolic to another, or if you will, from a symbolic of the Symbolic to a symbolic *of the Real*.

What is crucial, from this perspective, is the fact of *encoding* rather than the specific encoding system; accordingly, the symbolic need not be restricted to that which passes through the 'narrow chasm of the chain of signification' (Krämer 98), which, as we all know, is how it is theorized – and theorized precisely *as directly correlated with human experience* – by Lacan.[4] On the contrary, in the context of analogue technical media and of the digital computer, the symbolic sheds its human clothing in order to assume a generic status as a system for encoding real-time fluxes by discretizing the continuous, or perhaps more precisely, by periodizing the non-periodic. What hangs in the balance – at the very farthest extreme from anxieties, like those of Sybille Krämer (103–4), that Kittler ends by abandoning the sensory altogether – is the possibility of conceptualizing a non-human or machinic symbolic that, even if it doesn't *instantiate* the real-time fluxes of the material real, captures a vast amount of what lies outside human perceptibility and, via time axis manipulation, makes it (at least potentially) experientiable. Far from jettisoning the tie between media and sensation that has marked Kittler's theory from the very beginning, such a machinic symbolic vastly expands the domain of the sensible both for itself and, via technical mediation that makes it accessible, for embodied human beings.

To appreciate this strange correlation between machines and humans fully, we need to bear in mind Kittler's ethical commitment to keeping humans and machines apart: 'I am', Kittler declares in a 1992 interview, 'adamantly in favor of the clean separation of the inorganic from the organic' (Rickels 67). Whatever conjuncture there is between humans and machines will have to respect their distinct forms of autonomy: machines and humans come together not as surrogates or substitutes for one another, but as co-functioning elements in larger sensory systems. In this sense, Kittler's ethical imperative for separation aligns less with a post-humanist vision (whether utopian or dystopian) than with a desire to intensify human sensory experience precisely by expanding it beyond the temporal bottleneck imposed by human perception.

My effort to theorize the generic machinic symbolic in Kittler will return us to the tight imbrication of the symbolic with time, and thereby to the ongoing centrality of sensory experience across the various stages of Kittler's career trajectory. By exploring the paradoxical correlation between time and symbolization that comes to the fore in Kittler's recent work, I shall try to make clear why I now feel that his project can help us theorize twenty-first-century media, by which I mean media that predominantly if not generically evade human perceptibility. Kittler's ethical commitment to separating technical evolution from human evolution forms the basis for an approach to technical media that does not begin by making it a function of human perceptual experience. His project furnishes a theoretical anchoring for a vision that conceptualizes human–machine co-functioning as an *indirect* co-functioning. As we shall see, this becomes particularly clear in Kittler's work on sound frequency analysis, where numerical processing operates to 'symbolize' physical fluxes that are imperceptible to human hearing. The key point in such a vision is that human operations and machinic operations are mutually opaque to one another: machines do their bit, humans theirs, and the resulting expansion in sensory experience can only be registered from a higher-order perspective that is not co-substantial with, and not reducible to, either machinic or human perspectives.

Let us return now to the issue of the symbolic and specifically to its constitutive conjuncture with time. In the computational domain, what I am tempted to call the law of temporal finitude – which stipulates that time is always temporalized in material processes – ensures that computational operations, despite their taking place on timescales well beneath human perceptual thresholds, are forms of symbolization. Indeed, they are forms of symbolization that are precisely *not* coupled directly to human cognition. As such, rather than characterizing the shift from writing to computation (via the analogue technological media of gramophone, film and typewriter) as a shift from the symbolic to the real, we must think it as the shift from one symbolic to another: from a human-centred symbolic to a properly machinic symbolic, from a symbolic correlated with natural language to one correlated with (computable or finite) number. As I shall try to show, this difference in how we characterize Kittler's project is crucial because it closes the door on a certain line of interpretation that seeks to align his media science with a virulently anti-humanist posthumanism, with the final disappearance of so-called Man, whose phenomenological responsibilities will have been rendered superfluous in the wake of those endless and hence timeless machinic loopings of absolute knowledge that Kittler (in)famously invokes in the Introduction to *Gramophone, Film, Typewriter*.

The logic here is as simple as it is sublime: to the extent that computational processes temporalize – that is, both take up time and take place within temporal limitations – they are, in some minimal sense, homologous with the temporalizations that characterize human experience, and indeed that characterize experience as such. In machinic as in human systems, what is at issue is processes that materialize time, that bring time into concrete, finite being, and the underlying commonality thereby instituted ensures that these distinct temporalization processes, their massive scale differential notwithstanding, can never be simply disjoined: both computational temporalization and human temporalization belong to a larger worldly or cosmological process, which means effectively that the distinct symbolic registers they each demarcate do not and cannot relate to one another on a model of simple exclusivity.

Indeed, I want to suggest that it is precisely this homology *at the level of temporalization* that allows for the operation of time axis manipulation. According to Kittler, 'writing is the first technique for manipulating time'. The reason for this – which is also the reason that Kittler *does not* consider speech to be a technique for manipulating time – concerns the spatialization to which writing submits the temporal flow. Alphabetic writing, Kittler claims, operates by 'assigning a space to each element in the temporal series of the chain of speech' (Kittler, 'Real Time Analysis' 183). This spatialization of the irreversible temporal flow is part and parcel of the operation of symbolization as Kittler, following Lacan, understands it. Rooted in the capacity for substitution, the symbolic is produced through the discretization of the continuous flow of time; symbolic substitution, in short, requires the distinction between filled and empty spaces. And because 'filled and empty spaces' cannot be simultaneously 'co-present' in the flow of time, the symbolic is intimately correlated with time: it is a spatialization, and a delinearization, of the linear flux. Writing, then, is unlike speech insofar as speech is strictly bound to the continuous, irreversible flow of time (to the chains of filled and empty spaces that it generates). Writing, that is, is capable of storing time as spatialized patterns of filled and empty spaces. That is why writing allows for the manipulation of time.

Kittler's conceptualization of the symbolic as bound to the discretization of the temporal flux functions both to define it, generically, as a *technical* compression of the real and also to correlate it, in every case – though to be sure, differently in every case – to a specification of the continuous, analogue temporal flux on a certain material domain, a specification which serves beautifully as a technical concretization of my understanding of 'temporaliza-tion'. Kittler makes as much clear when he states that 'every coding [*Jede Codierung*], from the alphabet up to digital signal manipulation [*Signalverarbeitung*], must be able to contain nonperiodic functions within periodic ones' ('Real Time Analysis' 198). I want to suggest that this generic and temporally rooted conception of the symbolic not only replaces the human-centred symbolic order but, in so doing, displaces the pathos so often associated with Kittler's media science. Far from rendering human experience superfluous, the autonomy Kittler attributes to the digital explains how technical media expand symbolic access to the real of sensibility. If human perception becomes an 'optional variable' in today's digital net-works, it is precisely because these networks open non-perceptual modes of access to worldly sensibility that simply have no direct correlation with human perceptual experience. This is why, if we want to follow through on the 'information-theoretical material-ism' Kittler proposes in his work on time axis manipulation, we cannot identify the shift to analogue technological media and sub-sequently to digital computation as a simple movement from the symbolic to the real. To do so would be to impose the human as the sole correlate of the symbolic, and thus to remain blind to the operation of processes of symbolization, of symbolic orderings, on temporal scales beneath those characteristic of human perception.

Turning to Kittler's work on time axis manipulation, we find an altogether different differentiation between alphabetic writing and the technological media. What is at stake here is not whether a symbolic order of time axis manipulation is involved or not, but whether the frequency domain to be compressed coincides or doesn't coincide with that of our properly human optical and acoustical perception: 'Technical media', Kittler claims, 'are defined through nothing other than their strategy of, in principle, going under the lower frequency domain [*Niederfrequenzbereich*] precisely in order to simulate it' ('Real Time Analysis' 191). The word 'simulate' here should remind us of the central role Turing – and specifically his crucial differentiation between computable and non-computable numbers – plays in Kittler's work. Indeed, when Kittler turns to high-frequency analysis in order to describe the symbolization operated by technical media, he broaches the affinity that binds time and number, not simply in the technical epoch, but in our culture as such. If, that is, high-frequency analysis – 'above all in its discrete form as digital signal processing' – is the *'Beinahegabe von Zeit'* (the lateral giving of time), the reason is first and foremost because it transforms what in nature (in the real) is an infinite process into measurable, finite magnitudes: 'Uncountable infinities shrivel, at least on paper, into countable, finite quantities [or numbers, *Mengen*]. Metaphysics was always only the substitution of such data compressions with a so-called essence, always only the presupposition that contingency was removed in writing, noise in music, and entropy in order' (Kittler, 'Real Time Analysis' 195). In contrast to metaphysics, technical media operate in the space of the excluded middle: they are bound by the imperative to quantify contingencies, according to a 'fuzzy logic', as 'an uncountable scale of inbetween-states' (Kittler, 'Real Time Analysis' 195).

In deploying the technique of Fourier analysis, Kittler's aim is to reverse the reduction that inaugurates metaphysics, which is to say to find order in entropy, symbol in contingency. A transformation process that involves transposing time into frequency, linearity into periodicity, Fourier analysis allows for a symbolization of the temporal flow on a far finer scale, and consequently with a greater inclusiveness, than alphabetic writing: 'Thanks to Fourier analysis, everything that is going on can be transferred into the frequency domain and back into irreversible hard time' (Kittler, 'Lightning and Series' 69). As an example, Kittler describes the recording of an unrepeatable soprano vocal, as it is initially brought under a periodicity and subsequently rendered visible as a sum of many different periodicities. Yet when it comes to the striking of a clock or the noise of a consonant, Kittler argues, a Fourier series is no longer sufficient; because such sounds cannot be constructed as the sum of a myriad of overtone fluctuations, which is equally to say because they fall through the cracks of music theory and writing analysis, they require a Fourier *integral*, which is to say the symbolization of the non-periodic *as periodic*.

While the Fourier series can handle beautiful harmonics such as those emitted by a violin string, complex sounds like gongs or chimes, which in Christian times marked time itself, demand Fourier integrals in order to write down their sound events in the shape of innumerable frequencies. Analysis and synthesis in the frequency domain therefore are windows that depict the changing world in standing waves. When it comes to living and dying, we are still left with their opposite, the domain of time, but, when it comes to measuring and calculating, anything that displays some kind of recurrence or periodicity moves into the frequency domain. (Kittler, 'Lightning and Series' 69)

The hard time introduced by Fourier integrals inscribes time as periodicity and thereby introduces irreversibility through a 'physical' or 'material' symbolization that has no need for any human contribution.

What allows the operation of the Fourier integral to periodize the non-periodizable is the recourse to real number analysis that it makes necessary. 'The infinite sums of Fourier series are thus overcome [*überboten*] through an integral, whose argument famously proceeds not only through whole numbers, but also through real ones' (Kittler, 'Real Time Analysis' 199). Because it operates on the continuum of real numbers, the Fourier integral comprises a general example of digital signal processing, and hence a functional example of the computer as such. Put another way, the Fourier integral furnishes a technique for inscribing the flux of real numbers independently of any human-oriented symbolic. This is the reason, announces Kittler in a typical if misleading provocation, why cybernetics and computers are 'becoming ever more necessary', while 'people [. . .] are becoming ever more contingent':

> For computers, in contrast to mathematicians, do not at all concern themselves with the attempt to give the Fourier integral a noise-encompassing and non-periodic, which is to say an information-grasping function, in a closed form. In the place of an elegant comparison, that is either given or not given as a solution, the machines in their blindness instate, over against structures, pure numeric procedures that can be just as automatic as they are exact. ('Real Time Analysis' 199)

It is this physical or material symbolization, generated through the processing of the real as number – of a nature which 'in all likelihood is analog rather than digital' – that differentiates Kittler's account of technics from other contemporary accounts like that by Bernard Stiegler. In this sense, I must insist on the continuity from Kittler's body-centred account of media differentiation, which correlated the symbolization involved in distinct media with distinct fluxes of time (and sensation), to his more recent work on frequency analysis and the even more recent work on music and mathematics that grows out of it. For what the shift from inscription to measurement, from natural language to numerals, accomplishes (whether written by David Hilbert or computed by Turing's famous machine) is nothing less than the giving of a common terrain, indeed a 'well-nigh physical medium' (to cite Kittler's felicitous phrasing) that encompasses, in contradistinction to Aristotle (who could only maintain that there is 'nothing between the units'), all of the measurable, which is to say computable, intervals within such units.

Indeed, this common terrain is precisely the motivating promise of Kittler's more recent return to Greek culture and to the originary conjunction of music and mathematics, in which he proposes to find a language that joins together letters and numbers, an all-encompassing symbolic order, thoroughly indifferent to the phenomenological/cosmological divide. Fundamental to this inaugurally forgotten origin of the West is a de-anthropomorphizing of measure that appears properly, which is to say in a manner that cannot be ignored, only in its second coming as the universal digital computer:

> Evidently numbers had to leave humans behind and become part of machines that run on their own in order for technology to appear as the frame that conjoins being and thought [not to mention being and time] [. . .] Turing's epoch does not implement [Simon] Stevin's twelfth root of two [the value of the tempered semitone] in ironware such as the valve horn or the guitar string that operates at the human level; it buries the half-step much deeper, it miniaturises it into a programmed algebra that may be software or (under its proper name, real time) silicon hardware. Though most end users are unaware of it,

harmonics, even the most unexpected, are at work: Simon Stevin's early modern age lives on in the chords or the keyboards of digital synthesizers, and in their harmonics and Fourier series the sayings of Philolaus [who defines everything that is as number] live on in all eternity, whether we hear them or not. (Kittler, 'Number and Numeral' 58–9)

Ultimately, then, the exhilarating promise of Kittler's project, as inflected by his turn to Greek culture and return to Heidegger, is to furnish a non-anthropocentric basis for theorizing our contemporary coupling with computational processes that operate beneath our perceptual and sensory thresholds.

Unlike Stiegler, whose appropriation of Foucault's analysis of Greek *hyponemata* invests in the possibility for a resymbolization of our culture-defining technics, Kittler adamantly refuses to conceptualize technologies as tools for human ends, and he also refuses to pigeon-hole them as fundamentally or exclusively cultural. On the contrary, for him, technologies – and computers first and foremost – are at once the infrastructure of culture and the agents of a well-nigh Heideggerian gift of Being:

Because cultures, the business of the Humanities, do not depend on individual intentions but on all the media that become possible on the basis of natural languages, their limits do not become visible until viewed in the alphanumerical light of modern machines [. . .] These days, media technologies constructed on the basis of formal languages move the boundary between the possible and the impossible, the thinkable and the unthinkable [. . .] And because [their] feedback loops tend to lead from the machine to the programmer rather than the other way round, computers cannot be classified as tools, which is why the later Heidegger is more relevant when it comes to understanding universal machines than the Heidegger of *Being and Time*. (Kittler, 'Thinking Colours' 49)

That is why, when Heidegger classifies technology not as a mere means to an end but as 'a mode of revealing', it is, Kittler suggests, as if he had just invented the closed circuit: this classification is tantamount to recognizing that 'unlocking, transforming, storing, distributing, and switching are ways of revealing' (Kittler, 'Thinking Colours' 49).

If Heidegger's ontological clarification of technology's essence is equivalent to saying that technology gives time, that technology brings time to existence precisely by temporalizing, by taking up time, then it cannot be the case that technologies simply serve up Being *for us*. Rather, as the French philosopher of technology Gilbert Simondon has demonstrated, technologies enjoy an evolution of their own, even if they have always been and are ever more complexly coupled with human evolution. To say that they now give time as the distinctive periodicities of Fourier frequency integrals, or as the fine-scaled oscillations of the atomic clock underlying the contemporary global satellite network, is to address temporalization in the cosmological perspective. And yet, as Simondon has also underscored, the cosmological being of time is not indifferent for us: ever increasingly, from at least the Industrial Revolution onwards, we discover our possibility for experience, our own being in time, in conjunction with a–human time inscription technologies. Within this terrain, Kittler is uniquely positioned to teach us something crucial about the future of our 'essentially' technical being: namely, that it centres not on the figure of the cyborg or the tool-user, but rather on a cooperation with computational time inscription. If such cooperation is made possible by the common ground of number, it is made actual by the machines that process numbers. These real-number processors symbolize the current order of temporal finitude, on the basis of which all events, human and non–human alike, arise, as so many temporalizations of an in-all-likelihood analogue time that can never simply appear as such.

Time Axis Manipulation and the Convergence of Data and Experience

[I]t is precisely under mediatic conditions that what cannot be processed, what is impossible, is brought into ever sharper focus, in the same way that digitalization and electronicization first made possible the question: can everything be processed? It wouldn't surprise me at all if the symbolic could be relocated beyond the alphabetical to the numerical; then one could say that the symbolic covers all of the signifying batteries that can process what lies beyond letters or ciphers. And only now after fifty years of computer optimism do we recognise the at once hushed-up but fundamental thesis of Alan Turing and his kind: if I, Turing, can build a Turing machine which can compute, then this machine coincides with its object. That is to say, quite simply, that the object of this machine, that is, to use the old-fashioned term, nature itself, is a Turing machine. This is the Turing post-Alonzo Church hypothesis in its strongest, namely physical form. And just now, in the last five years, the people [. . .] at Livermore have put to themselves the tormenting question: is nature a Turing machine? In other words, is the real what Turing says it is or is it what Lacan says it is? And the physicists at Livermore are tending to side with the Lacanian view of the real as the impossible in relation to our machines and systems. If nature isn't a Turing machine, then the digital computer does not signal the end of all history. (Rickels 68)

The significance of the shift from a human to a machinic symbolic, together with its exemplification in the techniques of sound frequency analysis, centres on this same question: is the real what Turing says it is or what Lacan says it is? With physicists of yesteryear but also with those of today, Kittler has increasingly tended to side with the Lacanian view, and that is why it is crucial to underscore the point I have been trying to make here: media – regardless of whether they are pre-technical, technical or digital – always and necessarily operate as symbolizations that can only get asymptotically closer to the real they symbolize.

In this respect, Kittler's exhortation for us to develop forms of non-programmable computing – together with its foundation in frequency analysis and time axis manipulation – can be understood not as a final farewell to the human, but as an integral component in a vision of human–machinic co-functioning that, as I have briefly introduced it, stresses the *indirect* correlation and mutual opacity of humans and computers. While I cannot develop it fully here, Kittler's expansion of the symbolic furnishes a basis for rethinking the role of media today, and specifically for specifying the tendency of twenty-first-century media not simply to evade direct apprehension by the senses but also, and more consequentially, to impact human experience indirectly, by impacting the worldly sensibility that only subsequently informs such experience in a myriad of ways and on a plethora of timescales.

I would thus be tempted to place in the lineage of time axis manipulation the operation of today's digital biometric and environmental microsensors, which, as I argue at length in a forthcoming manuscript,[5] are capable of feeding psychophysical or environmental data 'forward' into a future moment of conscious attention before it would arrive there, as it were, by 'natural' biological processes of emergence. What is involved in a device like Sandy Pentland's 'sociometer', which captures a plethora of data concerning face-to-face business negotiations, is an opening of hitherto 'unheard-of' dimensions of experience – data concerning everything from fine body movements to the ambient temperature of the room – both for themselves, as elements of worldly sensibility, but also for us, as elements that can, for the first time, be made available, though certainly always with a time delay – which is to say, only for a future moment of awareness – to human experience.

Together with his generalization of the symbolic, what Kittler's work on time axis manipulation helps us to grasp is the extent to which experience and data have become one. Indeed, in a world where, as Alexander Galloway and Eugene Thacker put it, there will be 'a coincidence between happening and storage' (133) and where we can only be 'nostalgic [. . .] for a time *when organisms didn't need to produce quantitative data about themselves*' (124), the very capacity to separate experience from data will have become tenuous. Notwithstanding his deep nostalgia for a Greek origin prior to the separation of letter and number, Kittler, unlike Galloway and Thacker, is resolutely not nostalgic for a time when experience did not automatically generate data; indeed, his work helps us understand both how this convergence of experience with data furnishes the material basis for our contemporary culture and how it can be the ground for an intensification of human experience.

To reclaim Kittler's embrace of human–machine co-functioning as the core of his legacy to us will require more than a simple downplaying of his occasionally insistent posthumanist rhetoric. Let us begin by acknowledging just how machinic today's social media and Internet culture actually are. To the extent that the Internet automates computational networking and, with it, knowledge production and sociality, Kittler is able to position it as, in effect, an updating of the logic of software: like software, the Internet and today's social media platforms involve an ideology of participation that obfuscates the reality of their operationality. 'One thing that I find terrible nowadays', Kittler tells an interviewer in 2003, 'is that people continue to imagine that the Internet is the means by which they themselves are linked to others world-wide. For the fact is that it is their computers that are globally linked to other computers. Hence the real connection is not between people but between machines' (Armitage 35). What Kittler doesn't quite say here, and what we might want to say for him, is that embracing this 'fact' – acknowledging the machinic 'essence' of the Internet – will put us in a position to generalize time axis manipulation. Following such a generalization, time axis manipulation would come to encompass not simply the specific affordances of a given technical medium, be it writing or frequency analysis, cinema or ray-tracing, but the entire human–machinic complex in which computational technologies gather – and indeed produce – 'unheard-of' data about worldly sensibility, including human-implicating elements of such sensibility which can be *fed forward* into the properly sensory and perceptual *near-future* experience of human eyes and ears.

Notes

1 See Hansen, *New Philosophy for New Media* (47–92) and 'Cinema Beyond Cybernetics'.
2 See Hansen, 'Digital Technics'.
3 On this point, see Stiegler, 'Derrida and Technology'; Hansen, 'Realtime Synthesis'.
4 See Lacan.
5 See Hansen, *Feed-Forward*.

Works Cited

Armitage, John. 'From Discourse Networks to Cultural Mathematics: An Interview with Friedrich A. Kittler.' *Theory, Culture & Society* 23.7–8 (2006): 17–38.

Chun, Wendy Hui Kyong. 'On Software, or the Persistence of Visual Knowledge.' *Grey Room* 18 (2005): 26–51.

Galloway, Alexander R. *The Interface Effect*. Cambridge: Polity, 2012.

Galloway, Alexander R., and Eugene Thacker. *The Exploit: A Theory of Networks*. Minneapolis: University of Minnesota Press, 2007.

Hansen, Mark B. N. 'Cinema Beyond Cybernetics, or How to Frame the Digital Image.' *Configurations* 10.1 (2002): 51–90.

Hansen, Mark B. N. *New Philosophy for New Media*. Cambridge, MA: MIT Press, 2004.

Hansen, Mark B. N. '"Realtime Synthesis" and the Différance of the Body: Technocultural Studies in the Wake of Deconstruction.' *Culture Machine* 6 (2004). Web. http://www.culturemachine.net/index.php/cm/article/viewArticle/9/8

Hansen, Mark B. N. 'Digital Technics Beyond the "Last Machine": Thinking Digital Media with Hollis Frampton.' *Between Stillness and Motion: Film, Photography, Algorithms*. Ed. E. Rossaak. Amsterdam: Amsterdam University Press, 2012. 45–74.

Hansen, Mark B. N. *Feed-Forward*. Chicago: University of Chicago Press, forthcoming.

Johnston, John. *The Allure of Machinic Life: Cybernetics, Artificial Life, and the New AI*. Cambridge, MA: MIT Press, 2008.

Kittler, Friedrich A. *Discourse Networks 1800/1900*. Trans. Michael Metteer with Chris Cullens. Stanford: Stanford University Press, 1990.

Kittler, Friedrich A. *Draculas Vermächtnis: Technische Schriften*. Leipzig: Reclam, 1993.

Kittler, Friedrich A. 'Real Time Analysis, Time Axis Manipulation.' *Draculas Vermächtnis: Technische Schriften*. Leipzig: Reclam, 1993. 182–207.

Kittler, Friedrich A. 'Introduction to *Gramophone, Film, Typewriter*.' *Literature, Media, Information Systems: Essays*. Ed. John Johnston. Amsterdam: G+B Arts International, 1997. 28–49.

Kittler, Friedrich A. 'The World of the Symbolic.' *Literature, Media,*

Information Systems: Essays. Ed. John Johnston. Amsterdam: G+B Arts International, 1997. 130–46.

Kittler, Friedrich A. 'There Is No Software.' *Literature, Media, Information Systems: Essays.* Ed. John Johnston. Amsterdam: G+B Arts International, 1997. 147–55.

Kittler, Friedrich A. *Gramophone, Film, Typewriter.* Trans. Geoffrey Winthrop-Young and Michael Wutz. Stanford: Stanford University Press, 1999.

Kittler, Friedrich A. 'Lightning and Series: Event and Thunder.' Trans. Geoffrey Winthrop-Young. *Theory, Culture & Society* 23.7–8 (2006): 63–74.

Kittler, Friedrich A. 'Number and Numeral.' *Theory, Culture & Society* 23.7–8 (2006): 51–61.

Kittler, Friedrich A. 'Thinking Colours and/or Machines.' *Theory, Culture & Society* 23.7–8 (2006): 39–50.

Kittler, Friedrich A. *Optical Media: Berlin Lectures 1999.* Trans. Anthony Enns. Cambridge: Polity, 2010.

Krämer, Sybille. 'The Cultural Techniques of Time Axis Manipulation.' *Theory, Culture & Society* 23.7–8 (2006): 93–109.

Lacan, Jacques. *The Four Fundamental Concepts of Psychoanalysis.* Trans. Alan Sheridan. New York: Norton, 1998.

Rickels, Laurence. 'Spooky Electricity: An Interview with Friedrich Kittler.' *Artforum* December (1992): 66–70.

Stiegler, Bernard. 'The Time of Cinema: On the "New World Order" and "Cultural Exception".' *Tekhnema: Journal of Philosophy and Technology* 4 (1998): 62–120.

Stiegler, Bernard. 'Derrida and Technology: Fidelity at the Limits of Deconstruction and the Prosthesis of Faith.' *Jacques Derrida and the Humanities: A Critical Reader.* Ed. Tom Cohen. Cambridge: Cambridge University Press, 2002.

Wellbery, David E. Foreword. *Discourse Networks 1800/1900.* By Friedrich A. Kittler. Trans. Michael Metteer with Chris Cullens. Stanford: Stanford University Press, 1990. vii–xxxiii.

Winthrop-Young, Geoffrey, and Nicholas Gane. 'Friedrich Kittler: An Introduction.' *Theory, Culture & Society* 23.7–8 (2006): 5–16.

Index